19.95

DISCOVERY
AND EXPLORATION

DISCOVERY
AND EXPLORATION
A Concise History
ALAN REID

GENTRY BOOKS · LONDON

First published 1980
© Alan Reid 1980
ISBN 0 85614 071 6

Published by Gentry Books Ltd,
15 Pont Street, London SW1.
Typeset by Preface Ltd, Salisbury.
Printed and bound in the USA.

Contents

Introduction

An American Indian landed by scheduled jet at Rome airport a few years ago, and on disembarking dramatically announced the discovery of Italy. Why shouldn't he? After all, the North American continent had been the familiar home of his forefathers long before the Vikings, let alone the Spaniards, Portuguese, French and English 'discovered' it.

Throughout the history of Western civilization, in fact, no explorer or traveller ever discovered a substantial area of habitable land that was not already inhabited. Even parts of the world we would not regard as habitable have long been homes to Eskimos, Tuaregs, Watusis, Yanoamas and countless other peoples, for thousands of years.

It is essential, therefore, to remember that in a geographical context 'discovery' is used in this book (and in practically every other book that uses the word) to mean the first sighting of a land or country or geographical feature by a traveller from Europe, who then records the discovery for his country, and for general knowledge. 'Exploration', it follows, is the deliberate attempt to make discoveries – again in the limited context of Western civilization.

With only a few exceptions, early discoverers, charged with that peculiar Western assumption of superiority over other civilizations, rode roughshod over the lands they 'discovered', changing the names of lakes, rivers, mountains and whole countries, disrupting societies, imposing new laws and religions with scarcely a second thought. The discovery of the world by Europe was, in very many cases, synonymous with the conquering of the world by Europe.

But amid the accounts of hundreds of years of Europeans trampling heavy-footed across the unveiling globe, there are refreshing narratives of those who travelled to observe and learn, like ibn-Batuta, Marco Polo,

Humboldt or Burton. This contrast reveals another incongruity; that the driving force behind the major discoveries, especially those of the 15th and 16th centuries, was seldom the 'eternal quest for new knowledge' that fills true explorers with zeal, but the quest for something far more tangible. The long heroic struggle to find a sea route around Africa was dictated by Portugal's desire to establish a trading link with the Orient which would be independent – and so less expensive – than the traditional Moslem-ruled routes. Without the commercial lure of the East, discovery of the world would have taken a slower, more systematic route. As it was, Africa's vast unknown regions were ignored (except by slave traders) until the 18th and 19th centuries, although the continent was more accessible to Europe than any of the other unknown lands. Moslem dominance of trade in the north and east, and the apparent lack of gold and jewels, kept Africa for missionaries and the 'real' explorers.

Even true explorers, however, can never guarantee that their approach (which ideally should leave places and peoples unchanged) will be respected by those who come after them, and it is difficult to think of any place on earth which, having experienced the passage of Western civilization, has not been permanently marked by it – even the moon carries our debris. It is worse when the 'explorers' are fired by avarice, megalomania, or missionary zeal, for then discovery is merely the first step in acquisition, whether of riches, power or people's souls. The savagery of the Conquistadores is an extreme example, but even minor well-meaning missionaries, intolerant and unwilling to learn, changed customs, broke up traditions, inflicted European taboos and habits regardless of their suitability, and hacked away the foundations of hundreds of societies.

Despite the enormous wrongs that accompanied or succeeded much of discovery, however, the story of the exploration and discovery of the world is constantly fascinating. Throughout there run countless tales of tremendous courage, resourcefulness, endurance, and mental and physical hardiness – not only of the leaders who receive all the acknowledgement, but of the many ordinary men and women whose lives were no easier. There is the constant appeal of man against adversity, man against the elements, in danger and triumphing over fear, man surviving through circumstances that should, by rights, be the death of him – ingredients that have held every story-teller's audience since time began.

Very few can now be pioneers and discoverers; exploration as of old, and the discovery of unknown lands, is all but gone. If one can pinpoint any area that has not been penetrated before, anticipation is diluted by the realization that in all probability it has already been minutely photo-graphed by a satellite 200 miles (320 km) above the earth. Opportunities for pioneering firsts grow more and more elusive and bizarre. Continents or oceans have been flown, sailed, driven, rowed or walked in almost every conceivable fashion – it is even too late to be the first to push a handcart across the Sahara desert. At the time of writing, the Transglobe Expedition is attempting the first circumnavigation of the world via the North and South Poles. This is one of the few significant 'firsts' still left to man and will utilize the most modern technology available, including satellites to bring immediate coverage to millions. The two major areas of 'geographic' discovery today – in space and underwater – are well beyond the financial scope of all but a handful. Exploration is now a curiously solitary pursuit, where more backers and helpers are needed than ever before, but where they remain earthbound, or on the deck of a prosaically pitching vessel.

On the smallest and most modest scale, a traveller wishing to search some remote area, or hoping to follow in the footsteps of yesterday's intrepid discoverers, will frequently find that bureaucracy, paranoiac dictators of minor states, resourceful package-tour operators and ubiquitous cold-drink merchants destroy many of the vestiges of excitement and wonder.

The armchair explorer, however, is superbly provided for, and the bibliography at the end of this book only shows the surface of the reading than can be enjoyed, for the cast of the story of exploration and discovery is huge and its exploits are momentous. A guide to the whole saga and its characters enables every facet to be enjoyed more: this book will have served its purpose if it leads the reader to some 'discoveries' of his own.

The book is in four sections, of which the first (an extremely condensed story of discovery and exploration) and the last (an outline of the technological developments that aided this aspect of our history) are written in narative form.

The Chronology (second section) is obviously a source of quick reference and a reminder of the sequence of main events. With the Index, it should be a frequent starting point to information in other parts of the book – particularly to the third section, the Biographies.

These Biographies are more detailed accounts of particular discoveries and explorations, and should not simply be read from A to Z. Rather turn to them when you want a part of the narrative of the first section to be enlarged on, or when a date in the chronology arouses your interest.

Apart from curiosity, YOU DO NEED AN ATLAS to make the best use of this book. (Since practically every home, library, school and office already has an atlas, this should present few problems.) Working out a rough route in an atlas from the information given in the Biographies will be a lot more interesting than simply looking at a pre-drawn arrow, and, with an atlas open in front of you as you read parts of this book, you will be able to see how Europe gradually 'discovered' the world.

No matter how much information is given, and how many books are read from the Bibliography, many fascinating questions remain unanswered. Did the Phoenicians reach North America? What was the origin of the rumours of Saint Brendan's Island? Did Egyptians cross the Atlantic? Could South Sea islanders cross the Pacific with ease? And how did Chinese silks come to be placed in a Celtic prince's burial mound in Germany 2,500 years ago? Our story of discovery is only a small and very recent part of the world's history.

The World Discovered
and Explored

Exploration in Ancient History
4000 BC – AD 400

The formation of the first village with a permanently settled community was a significant stage in man's adaptation to his environment. It was an equally significant event when a small group decided to leave Jarmo, north-west of Baghdad, and sail down the Euphrates to the plains of Mesopotamia, the home of the first of the great civilizations. From the principle town of Eridu, predecessor of Ur, in boats of growing sophistication, Mesopotamians went on longer and longer journeys, venturing further and further south down the Persian Gulf. Coast-hugging Mesopotamian ships eventually reached Egypt well over 3,000 miles (4,800 km) away, and while natural disasters, overpopulation and hunger drove earliest man into unknown areas, a great deal of the simple curiosity that compels exploration must have been present on the first voyages around the Hadramaut coast.

The civilization of Egypt was also becoming established by the time the first foreign ships arrived, and Egyptian boat builders were quick to adapt the far more advanced designs to their own craft. Dominated by the Nile, the Egyptians seldom undertook sea voyages – and then purely for trade, such as their first recorded voyage to Byblos for cedar wood in 2600 BC. Although they rapidly became proficient boat builders, the Egyptians could afford to relegate the risks of long journeys to other peoples anxious to trade with them, though Herkhuf journeyed far up the Nile in 2270 BC in search of ivory and frankincense.

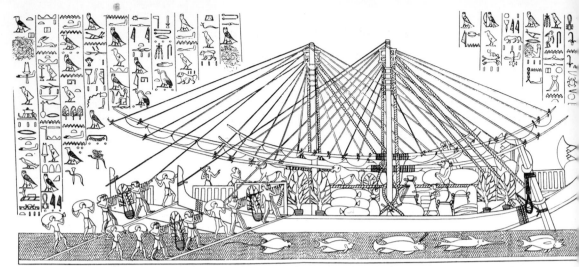

Egyptian boats being loaded for Queen Hatshepsut's expedition of c 1500 BC. (Mary Evans Picture Library)

Among the more adventurous and developed peoples at that time were the Minoans on the island of Crete, and there is little doubt that they obtained grain from Asia Minor's Fertile Crescent well before 5000 BC – which must have involved ships crossing more than 30 miles (48 km) of open sea. The Minoans were the maritime masters of the Mediterranean, exploring its shores extensively, but their civilization began to decline after 2000 BC and 600 years later had collapsed entirely.

The Egyptians, however, were then enjoying one of their great ages, and Queen Hatshepsut instigated Egypt's first long sea voyage when she ordered Nehsi to sail through the Red Sea to Punt, on the Eritrean coast.

It was the Phoenicians, however, who took over from the Minoans as master mariners. Trade was an inevitable and essential way of life in their tiny country. When over-population threatened to overwhelm them, moving to distant lands was the only alternative to war with powerful neighbours; Carthage was to become their most important settlement.

The Phoenicians were far more adventurous sailors than any before them; they frequently sailed through the Strait of Gibraltar, and may even have crossed the Atlantic. They sailed down the Red Sea from the Gulf of Aqaba, and Herodotus wrote of a Phoenician circumnavigation of Africa in c 600 BC, his maps subsequently showing Africa to be almost entirely surrounded by water. It must have been the Phoenicians' last great voyage, however, for they were defeated by the Babylonians and their maritime supremacy passed to their former colony, Carthage.

The Carthaginians easily dominated the Mediterranean and, with an aggression unlike their founders', began to subdue or settle an empire that occupied much of the western Mediterranean and stretched well into the Iberian Peninsula. During numerous Atlantic voyages the Carthaginians discovered Madeira, the Canary Islands and the Azores. Himilco, perhaps searching for Cornish tin (which would have been reaching Carthage via trading posts), sailed to Britain and to Ireland; but it is Hanno who perhaps best deserves to be remembered as the first named 'true' explorer, for he extended a colonizing journey along Africa's north-west coast into a voyage of curiosity and discovery that led him as far as Sierra Leone, and possibly to Cameroon.

Other events in the eastern Mediterranean were to have important repercussions on exploration, though scientific discovery took precedence over heroic voyages. The Greeks were beginning the Golden Age of Athens, and Sophocles, Plato, Socrates, Archimedes, Aristotle and many others were laying down the foundation of our present civilization, while Herodotus took the revolutionary step of declaring the world to be a globe and not a disk. Tremendous physical exploits were undertaken too – in one of the great journeys of history Xenophon led his Greek mercenaries home from the heart of Persia, a distance of over 700 miles (1,130 km). Alexander the Great's conquests became, under his untiring curiosity, exploratory as well as military, and if so many of his army had not been convinced that they were about to reach the end of the world, Alexander would have added a substantial part of India to his empire. Another Greek, Pytheas, went in search of the end of the world in the opposite direction, sailing from Massalia (Marseille) in 325 BC hoping to find Thule, which was considered the last piece of land, and was probably Iceland. Pytheas noted the moon's effects on tides and made other astronomical observations. Many years were to pass before Greece's next

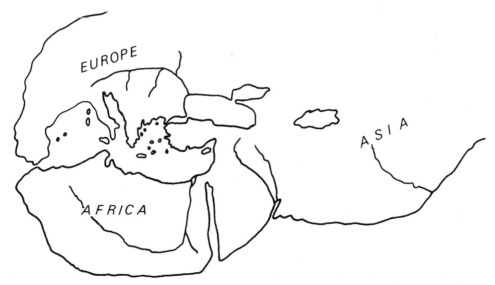

The world as drawn by Herodotus, c 450 BC. The Mediterranean was known in detail while conjecture plotted the Nile. Having recorded a Phoenician voyage around Africa in his writings, Herodotus was able to show the continent surrounded by water.

The writings of the Greek astronomer, geographer and mathematician Ptolemy, who lived in Alexandria (c AD 150), were influential for over a thousand years. (Mary Evans Picture Library)

The World Discovered and Explored

great geographer, Ptolemy, set scientific standards that were to last a thousand years.

Carthaginian supremacy eventually fell before the might of Rome in the Punic Wars, culminating in the destruction of Carthage in 146 BC. But the Romans had none of the Greeks' curiosity or the Carthaginians' adventurousness. Britain was about as far as they ventured across the sea, and few expeditions were undertaken that did not have some military or colonial objective – a voyage down the Red Sea and an expedition into Arabia by Gallus, a purely investigative journey over North Africa's Atlas Mountains by Paulinus in AD 42, and very little else.

Far to the east, the Han Empire had emerged dominant over China at the same time as the Roman Empire grew in the west. An early official expedition was headed by Chang Ch'ien, whose discoveries led to the establishment of the Silk Route in about 105 BC. This tenuously linked the East with the outposts of Hellenistic culture and eventually became the route followed by Arab traders and by European travellers. Mariners too were venturing further and further east, and by c AD 120 the coast of China had been reached.

But the 5th century AD saw the rise of the Barbarians, the fall of Rome, and the beginning of the chaos, terror and prejudice of the Dark Ages. In

The extent of the world familiar to Europeans before the conquests of the Barbarians in the 5th century AD.

China emperors learnt of the instability of Europe, and once again drew back into their separate world.

The Insular Middle Ages
AD 400 – 1400

The literal acceptance by early Christians of the words of the Bible fed on the inward-looking attitudes that a hostile world encouraged, and all the hard-won scientific and intellectual knowledge of the Greeks, Phoenicians and Carthaginians was forgotten. The earth was again declared flat, and the Devil and dire punishment waited 'over the edge' – which put paid to long sea-voyages for many hundreds of years.

Nothing illustrates the backward steps of this period so well as the Beatus maps, named after the 8th-century Benedictine monk and cartographer whose religious maps accompanied his writings. Palestine was given pride of place, and north moved to the left, the continents being rather haphazardly arranged to fit into the circular or rectangular oceans that marked the edge of the world. Such maps – compared to Herodotus' of 1,000 years before – were totally useless geographically, yet were widely

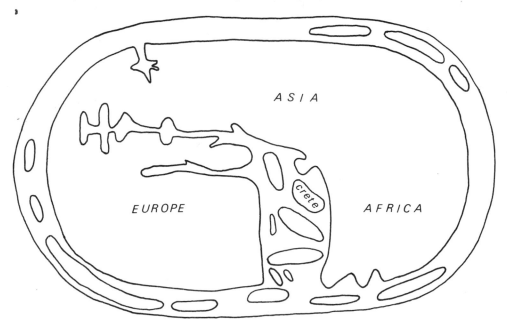

The 'Beatus' maps of the world were prevalent throughout the Dark Ages, but were not much use to geographers or navigators. They make a little more sense if they are turned 90° to the right, restoring the points of the compass to their rightful positions.

reproduced as late as the 13th century.

As Europe cowered in intellectual gloom, the Islam Empire burgeoned from the 7th century, and by 900 extended from Arabia to South-west Asia and to North Africa and Spain. From this solid block between Europe and the East, Moslems dominated world trade until well into the 16th century.

An Egyptian geographer known both as Cosmas and Indicopleustes recorded China as the country of silk in the 6th century, and asserted that it could be reached by sea, though this perception did not extend to his maps – his world map, one of the earliest, was based on the concept of the earth as a rectangular plane on which rested two layers, the sky and heaven. Equally anxious for trade, some Chinese adventurers chose to ignore their emperors' isolationist decrees and Chinese ships called at the mouth of the Euphrates in the 5th century, while in 628 a Buddhist monk, Hsuan-tsang, began a journey of study and discovery in India and Central Europe that was to last 16 years. Various sea routes between Canton and the Euphrates were recorded at this time.

Christianity's religious fervour did result in some exploration and adventure, however. Irish monks set off into the changeable Atlantic in frail, primitive boats during the 5th to 9th centuries, initially to seek converts in Cornwall and Wales, and then France. The Scottish islands were reached and the boats ranged further and further. Legend has obscured history, and if stories are believed then the greatest of these monks, Saint Brendan, was frequently able to be in more than one place at the same time – though it does seem likely that he reached the Shetland Islands and that Saint Columba, a contemporary, established a monastery on Iona (Mull) in 563.

Whether by accident or guidance, Irish monks eventually reached Iceland, but whatever frugal tranquillity they found there was shattered in about 860 when Gardar Svarsson and his boats were swept onto the island's remote shores. The Vikings – then at the height of their aggressive colonizing-cum-plundering campaign – saw no reason to leave Thule, but their presence was too much for the Irish and within ten years they had all gone, settling eventually on Greenland. No sooner had they become established there, however, than Eric the Red was exiled from Iceland and sailed westwards with his followers, meeting, inevitably, Greenland.

The Irish decamped yet again. Perhaps they reached North America first, but it was Eric the Red's son, Leif Ericsson, who, it seems, should be credited with the landing on what the Vikings called Vinland. However the sagas tell of Bjarni Herjulfsson making a voyage south-west from Iceland in 986, and sighting, but not landing on, land which could be that between Long Island and Baffin Island. American Indians were far more intractable than retiring Irish monks, however, and 'Vinland' was not seen by another European until some 500 years later.

17

The Viking Eric the Red, banished from Iceland, makes a dramatic arrival at Greenland in AD 983. (Mary Evans Picture Library)

After their defeat by Genghis Khan, many Chinese were sold into slavery. (Mary Evans Picture Library)

The World Discovered and Explored

The introspection of Europe during the Dark Ages and Middle Ages produced only a few geographical developments. An Arab geographer and scientist at Roger II's royal court in Sicily produced a world map and summarized Greek and Arabic writings on geography, and John Holywood, also called Sacrobosco, wrote *Treatise on the Sphere*, which was to be a navigator's standard work for 300 years. But what activity there was, was mainly in the Far East, with the rapid rise of the Mongols until, at Genghis Khan's death, their empire stretched from the Yellow Sea to the Caspian Sea.

The real or imagined threat from Asia shook Europe out of its insularity, and the first great journey since the Vikings was instigated by Pope Innocent IV who sent Carpini on a peaceful errand to the Mongols in 1245. Carpini got as far as the Gobi desert but the new Khan was not much more amenable than Genghis, and another traveller to the East, William of Rubrouck, brought back warnings a few years later.

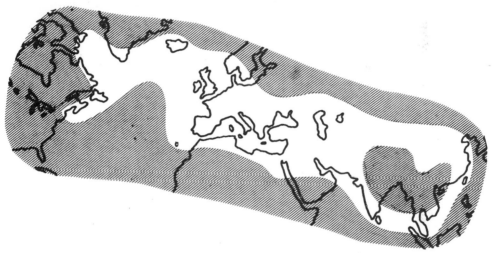

The extent of European discovery at the end of the Dark Ages.

Fortunately domestic problems intervened and when the Empire regained its stability its new ruler was the extremely enlightened Kublai Khan, grandson of Genghis. Under Kublai Khan all China was conquered, and Cathay then stretched from the Black Sea to the Pacific, with a magnificent temple at Cambaluc (Peking). Kublai Khan was far less of an isolationist, and greeted the Venetians Maffeo and Niccolo Polo so warmly that they later returned with Niccolo Polo's son, Marco Polo.

Marco Polo spent 16 years in Kublai Khan's service and travelled extensively in Cathay. His vivid descriptions of his travels, and of the splendour of Cambaluc did a lot to throw aside the last dark drapes of the

19

A Venetian galley of the 14th century. (The National Maritime Museum, London)

Middle Ages. His writings, and those of Odoric 20 years later, strongly influenced Cresques' Catalan Atlas of c 1375. Another remarkable traveller and explorer, as courageous, curious and enterprising as Marco Polo, was ibn-Batuta, who set out from Tangiers in 1325 on travels that were to take him, over some 28 years, to practically every Moslem country. Marco Polo and ibn-Batuta wrote and spoke vividly of the vast world (and riches) beyond Europe, thus setting the scene for the explorers and adventurers who were to proliferate in the extraordinary rebirth of Europe.

Europe Awakes
1400–1600

The brilliant Renaissance was also a great age of exploration and discovery, and though most nations were frequently preoccupied with endless wars, more became known about the world in two hundred years than had been discovered in the previous thousand.

The centres of power and civilization had been moving gradually westward across the Mediterranean, and at the dawn of the 15th century two strong maritime powers, Spain and Portugal, occupied the strategic and symbolic Iberian Peninsula. Between them, and principally because of the activities of Henry, Prince of Portugal – 'the Navigator' – these two countries revealed most of the earth's fabric with surprisingly little conflict of intent, and for 150 years regarded the world as rightfully belonging to no one but themselves (with some concession to the mighty and powerful Moslem empire).

Portugal's small size in relation to other ambitious nations made her vulnerable and subject to many shortages, and so she attempted to gain extra power by strenghening her strategic position at the door to the Mediterranean. The city of Ceuta, on the African coast, was chosen for its location and for being not too formidable an opponent. Henry took part in the battle which captured Ceuta in 1411, was appointed its governor, and became interested in the expanse of Africa to the south. Adding to his curiosity was an attraction for the Moors' gold and a concern for their spiritual well-being – missionary zeal and a desire for gold were to carry Christian Europe to the four corners of the earth.

Henry established a School of Navigation at Sagres, which became the focal point of all knowledge and progress in navigation, seamanship and shipbuilding; the caravel, for instance, was developed there, making possible the African voyages and Columbus' Atlantic crossing. Initially, however, Henry's greatest ambitions were obstructed, for Portuguese sailors, still influenced by Beatus-like concepts, believed that the world ended somewhere near Cape Bojador, and that travellers beyond that point would meet a hideous death or, at best, be turned completely black.

The first Portuguese voyages went only as far as the Canary Islands, Madeira or the Azores, but a faithful admirer of Henry's, Gil Eannes, finally steeled himself and his crew to pass the 'point of no return' in 1434. Then it was as if a door had been opened to a queue of mariners. Eannes found signs of habitation near the mouth of the Rio de Oro and two years later Henry's pilots had reached Cape Blanc and realized one of his ambitions – to send his ships beyond the region of Moslem power and influence.

By 1448 the Portuguese had ventured as far south as the Cape Verde Islands, but then there was a lull until Cadamosto reached the Gambia River seven years later. He explored some of the West African coast and sailed a little way up the river, bringing back the first reliable reports about the area.

The last voyage commissioned by Henry was led by Diogo Gomes in 1458, who reached Cape Palmas at the western extremity of the Gulf of Guinea – a discovery that was put on Behaim's globe of 1490, the oldest surviving terrestrial globe. Responsibility for Portugal's exploration then fell to King Alfonso, who had little of Henry's zeal, and was mainly interested in extracting wealth from the continent. He eventually handed the whole matter over to Prince John, Portuguese mariners by now having reached Point St Catherine.

John 'the Perfect' succeeded to the crown in 1481, and he was determined to derive the maximum benefit from the voyages. His captains erected stone pillars – *padroas* – carrying the Portuguese coat of arms to claim the land they reached (taking it for granted that it did not already belong to someone else). The first voyage sponsored by John was led by Diogo Cam and sailed well past Point St Catherine. Cam put up two *padroas*, and on another voyage three years later he reached 22° 10′ S.

Missionary zeal underwent a revival, fuelled by the desire to link Christian Europe with Prester John's rumoured Christian kingdom, thus forming a vast and superior counter to Islam. With this as much in mind as the wealth of the Orient, John commissioned Bartolomeu Dias to find the end of the African continent (and therefore the sea route to India), and Pedro da Covilhã to find a good overland route to India and locate the land of Prester John.

Dias followed the coast-hugging route of the earlier mariners, but in January 1488 fierce storms forced his three ships to sail southwards, keeping them out of sight of land for two weeks. When the storms abated Dias regained sight of Africa only by heading north. He had found the end of the continent, but within days his crew persuaded him to return to Portugal.

Covilhã, meanwhile, had set off in 1487 down the Red Sea, sending an expedition into Ethiopia to look for Prester John while he continued on to India. Covilhã returned through Persia, and then sailed south along Africa's east coast as far as Sofala before turning back. He sent his report to Portugal from Cairo, then went himself to Ethiopia to continue the search for Prester John.

Portugal was close to the prize of the route to the Orient, but the concentration of all interest and activities in that direction meant that she was to miss any major share in a series of discoveries that were to prove to have the most far-reaching consequences of any geographical discovery.

A Genoan who had renounced his home and his native language was shipwrecked off the Sagres promontory and swam ashore, making an unorthodox arrival at the fount of Portugal's maritime expertise. This was Christopher Columbus who, as Spanish-speaking Cristóbal Colón, soon gained a reputation as a forceful, ambitious mariner. Inspired by the theories of the cosmographer Toscanelli and even more by his own egotistic interpretations of religious study, Columbus argued that the East could be

The Niña, Santa Maria *and* Pinta *approach land on Columbus' first voyage in 1492.*
(Mary Evans Picture Library)

reached by continually sailing west. Portugal had already turned aside the
arrogant Columbus as, at first, did the Spanish court. Only the
intervention of the ship-owner, Martin Pinzón, gained Columbus a second
hearing with King Ferdinand and Queen Isabella. (At the same time as
the ex-Genoan was in search of a sponsor in Iberia, an ex-Venetian, John
Cabot, was putting forward identical proposals in England, but with even
less success.)

Columbus finally got the backing of Spain and left with the Pinzón
brothers and three ships to sail into the unknown. Eventually, 'after sailing
the ocean blue, he sighted land in 1492' – at 2 am on 12 October to be
precise, and the land was the Bahama island of Guanahani, which he
promptly named San Salvador, taking away some of the astounded native
inhabitants for 'study'. A combination of complex mistakes arising from
wrong assumptions – some of which could be attributed to Ptolemy's
writings – had led Columbus to believe that he would find the Orient
where in fact he found the islands that came to be called the West Indies.

The old world meets the new at San Salvador (Watling Island in the Bahamas) and Columbus tries to win over the inhabitants with trinkets. (Mary Evans Picture Library)

Had he read accounts by Marco Polo or Odoric, Columbus might have felt uneasy about his claims. But he firmly believed, indeed insisted, that Hispaniola (Haiti and Dominica) was Japan, and that Cuba was the Chinese mainland.

The discovery of land to the west, whether it was the Orient or a New World, began a hurried period of exploration — and exploitation — across the Atlantic, with the Spanish the undisputed pace-setters. John Cabot finally used Columbus' success to obtain a commission from England's Henry VIII to look for lands and routes in the West. He sailed from Bristol in 1497 and rediscovered Nova Scotia and Newfoundland, the first European since the Vikings to sail that coast. But Cabot compounded Columbus' error by claiming that he had discovered the land of the Great Khan.

Europe's obsession with the East was reflected in Portugal's view of Africa purely as an obstacle that had to be by-passed on the way to India, and in Spain's ready belief that she had found the Orient, even though there was little positive evidence to support her claim. After Dias' discovery of Africa's southern cape, Vasco da Gama set off on a voyage in 1497 to reach India. He became the first to avoid the long, often becalmed route along the Gulf of Guinea, and took a wide sweep out into the Atlantic to reach more favourable winds. The Cape of Good Hope was successfully found and passed, Natal was named on Christmas Day, and eventually the Portuguese reached the East African ports that had been trading with Moslem countries for many years.

Not surprisingly, the Moslems strongly opposed the Christian pioneers. Only at Malindi did da Gama find a pilot willing to guide him to India, and in May 1498 he reached Calicut — and more Moslem opposition, though Goa provided better conditions.

Pedro Cabral led the second expedition in 1500. This started auspiciously when Cabral overdid the da Gama-inspired sweep to miss the Gulf of Guinea and in so doing discovered the coast of Brazil. But the voyage was overtaken by disaster, with four ships lost before Malindi was reached (Bartolomeu Dias perishing in one of them). Cabral's reception in Calicut was hostile and he went on to Cochin, though not before causing considerable slaughter in Calicut. He lost another four ships and their crews on the return journey, but nevertheless was indignant when da Gama was given leadership of the third Portuguese expedition, which sailed in 1502.

Cabral's discovery of the Brazilian coast (at about 18°S) was the cause of the first clash of interests between Spain and Portugal over the west Atlantic territories. It resulted in the Treaty of Tordesillas, which fixed a

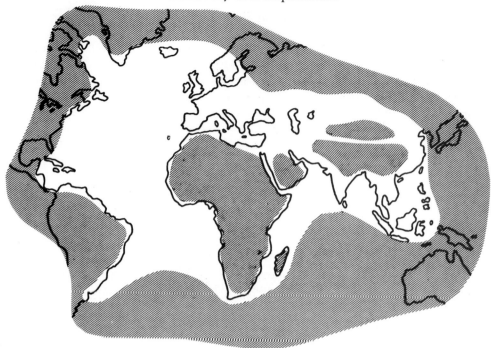

In the 100 years from 1400 to 1500 the world 'expanded' dramatically, but the shape of the American continents was still unknown, Africa was totally unexplored, and the Pacific completely unknown.

line of longitude roughly between Cabral's and Columbus' landing points, granting land to the west to Spain, and that to the east to Portugal. Vicente Pinzón (who had commanded the *Niña* with Colombus) gave a further indication of the extent of land to the south when, in 1500, he landed on the coast at Cabo de Santo Agostinho. Sailing north-west he came to the mouth of the Amazon, and gave the river the name Rio Santa Maria de la Mar Dulce. The land was obviously far more extensive than was first supposed, but seemed suspiciously un-Oriental, and was unlike anything heard of before.

The Spanish court then ordered a Florentine, Amerigo Vespucci, to trace the coast between these new discoveries and the Spanish Caribbean. After he had done this he sailed again, this time for Portugal, to the area of Cabral's southern landing, reached the Rio de la Plata, and claimed to have sailed as far south as 50°. Vespucci was accompanied by the cartographer Juan de la Cosa who drew the first map to show the discoveries of Columbus, da Gama and Cabot. Nothing was known of the interior beyond a few miles, and Cosa showed the new lands fading out to the west – though he did show Cuba as an island, despite Columbus'

26

assertions that it was not, and even though it was not proved to be one until 1508. Vespucci, however, was convinced that South America was a separate, new continent. His arguments convinced the cartographer Waldseemüller, who named the country after Amerigo on his map of 1507.

Portugal also made tentative approaches to the land found by Cabot further north, and in 1501 Gaspar and Miguel Corte-Real reached Labrador, capturing some Indians as proof. A few years later Sebastian Cabot, John Cabot's son, observed the coast from Hudson Strait past Newfoundland and Nova Scotia almost as far south as Chesapeake Bay, before concluding positively that no Oriental route whatsoever was to be found in that part of the world. Vespucci's declaration that these newly found lands constituted a new continent spread rapidly, and it momentarily gave the Americas (the existence of two continents was not yet realized) a status similar to Africa's – a barrier that had to be overcome on the way to the prime target of India and the Far East.

Any image of the Orient that had become dulled through lack of reminding would have been recharged by the colourful accounts of Ludovico di Varthema, who returned to Venice in 1508 after a six-year journey to India and the East Indies, a journey of considerable value to the cartographers of Europe – who were constantly having to revise their presentations of the world.

Portugal never let up in her determination to win control of Eastern trade, and in 1505 Francisco de Almeida was appointed her first representative to India. Over the next four years Almeida broke the Moslem monopoly, mainly through a number of defeats of Arabian and Indian fleets in battles at sea, though he was unable to gain control of the vital and fiercely Moslem port of Malacca before he handed over to Alfonso d'Albuquerque. The Moslems found Albuquerque a more formidable opponent. After capturing Goa in 1510, he was able to rule the whole of the western Indian Ocean and control shipping between Arabia and Persia and the East Indies. A year later, Malacca fell to the Portuguese, and 400 years of European control over southern and eastern Asia had begun.

Soon after the successful annexation of the Indian Ocean came Europe's discovery of the Pacific by Balboa in 1513, as he led Spanish attempts to settle Darien (Panama). The Spanish were on the verge of many discoveries, and Vicente Pinzón was sent by the Spanish crown to find a route to the Spice Islands, for by then it was obvious that they were nowhere near the islands that Columbus had stumbled on. It was probably Pinzón who discovered Honduras and Yucatan, and heard the first rumours of disciplined and very wealthy societies living in that area.

27

Sebastian Cabot leaves the wintry Labrador coast in 1509. (Mary Evans Picture Library)

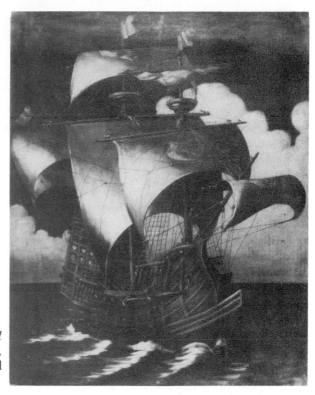

'A Carrack before the wind' – oil painting by Pieter Brueghel, c 1569. (The National Maritime Museum, London)

Once again Portugal's King Manuel lost a major discovery to the Spanish when one of his own subjects, Ferdinand Magellan, received the backing of Spain to attempt to find a westward passage to the Orient. Magellan's plan was simply to sail south along the American coast, beyond the areas already covered, and to keep on going until a passage was found. The huge Rio de la Plata estuary was a time-consuming decoy, and a mutinous crew almost stopped him during the winter of mid-1520, but eventually three ships discovered the tortuous Magellan Strait separating Tierra del Fuego from South America, and on 28 November 1520 Magellan sailed into the Pacific. Although he met his death in the Phillipines, it is Magellan who is recalled as the first circumnavigator – at least his spirit must still have been aboard the *Victoria* as it returned to Spain in September 1522.

Spain then began to derive the first real returns for the effort of discovering and settling the islands between the Americas, though as much shame as wealth was to come her way. In Central and South America, Spain found fortunes of gold and silver, and precious stones in abundance. To get them, a generation of tough, ambitious, devoutly Catholic and highly avaricious conquerors, the Conquistadores, picked the bones of the dying Maya civilization, and obliterated two remarkable societies, the Aztecs and the Incas. Though in many respects highly advanced, the Aztecs and the Incas proved no match for the gunpowder and armour of the Spaniards, although what really defeated them and killed them in their hundreds of thousands were the diseases of Africa and Europe, against which they had no immunity at all.

The early rumours of peoples rich in gold were given more substance after Juan de Grijalva had attempted an expedition into Yucatan, and

The Conquistadores were totally ruthless in their pursuit of conquests and of wealth. Here the last Aztec emperor is tortured by Cortes to reveal the whereabouts of treasure. (Mary Evans Picture Library)

within a year the archetypical Conquistador, Hernando Cortes, had landed on the Central American coast near present-day Veracruz. The arrival of Cortes coincided with Aztec religious predictions, and the welcome from Montezuma at the capital of Tenochtitlan hardly befitted the true nature of the Spanish mission. The uneasy truce broke after a foolish blunder by Pedro de Alvarado, who was temporarily in command. In the climacteric battle of 1520 Montezuma was killed, but Cortes and Alvarado were among those Spaniards who managed to flee the city to the safety of the lake shore. During the following year Cortes became the dominant figure in Central America, but eventually conflict and intrigue back in Spain undermined his standing and, like Columbus, Hernando Cortes died in poverty and humiliation.

Other discoveries rapidly followed the Conquistadores' searches. Juan Ponce de León, reputedly looking for a fountain granting eternal youth instead of searching for the more conventional gold, sailed through the Bahamas and discovered Florida on Easter Sunday 1513, though he would have been better remembered had he not decided that Florida was a large island. However his reports were enough to inspire Panfilo de Narváez to search the 'island' for gold, and in 1527 he landed at Tampa Bay. His expedition was a disaster; he found no riches of any kind, and when he returned to the coast found none of his ships either. Narváez and most of his followers died in storms that wrecked their frail small boats. One survivor was Alvar de Vaca, who became the 'guest' of a nomadic Indian tribe, and only managed to reach Mexico City nine years later.

South America again became the focus of attention in 1526 when Sebastian Cabot reached Cape São Roque on a journey to establish a Spanish route to the East. Unfortunately he was intrigued by the estuary and tributaries of the Rio de la Plata and spent three years there before returning to Spain, where he found himself in disgrace for wasting time and money.

It was on the other side of the continent, however, that the next major drama of Spain's conquests was unfolding. Pascual de Andagoya, venturing southwards on an official survey, had reached Cape Corrientes and picked up rumours about a wealthy, sophisticated empire further south known as Biru. These were the Incas who were to be destroyed by a Conquistador in many ways very similar to Cortes, who destroyed the Aztecs. It took Francisco Pizarro some time to reach the Inca kingdom, but time was on his side. As he ventured further south the Incas were suffering depleting catastrophes of civil war and waves of diseases carried ahead of the invaders by Indian travellers.

Backed by new assistance and power from the Spanish crown, Pizarro eventually confronted the first Inca delegation at Cajamarca in November

1432. Potential deceit on the part of the Incas was beaten by quicker and greater Spanish deceit, and the Inca leader Atahuallpa was garrotted after the Incas had handed over a fortune in gold and jewels to secure his release. Then the Spaniards went on a rampage of pillage, rape and destruction, and sacked the Inca capital of Cusco. Pizarro eventually managed to establish some form of control, and the Incas were, for a while, allowed to govern themselves under Spanish direction.

Further north, at Cusco, an expedition set out in 1540 that was to become one of the most extraordinary ever undertaken. Gonzalo Pizarro and Francisco de Orellana were searching for the source of a supply of cinnamon, and at one stage, east of Quito, Orellana went down the Coca River to look for food. The swift river took him into the Napo, and that flowed into the massive Rio Santa Maria de la Mar Dulce, which took him for thousands of miles to the Atlantic Ocean. Orellana's remarkable journey caused a considerable stir in Europe, and an incident in the record taken down by Gaspar de Carvajal resulted in the river being renamed the Amazon.

The Aztec and Inca riches rapidly flowed to Spain, into Conquistadores' travelling bags, into pirate ships, and, much of it, down to the bottom of the Atlantic Ocean, while those who arrived too late to make a large fortune began to look elsewhere. One of the first to do so was Hernando de Soto, who had been with Pizarro in Peru. He went gold hunting – in vain – in Northern America, making a wide sweep across the southern Mississippi plains. Alvar de Vaca, the sole important survivor of Narváez's Florida expedition, told tales of rich tribes of Indians. A fact-finding expedition sent from Mexico seemed to confirm his account while a story about the fabulous Seven Cities of Cibola, and the vast fortunes to be found there, was rapidly taken to heart.

The Viceroy of Mexico sent Francisco de Coronado on an expedition to find Cibola. It turned out to be a modest Indian village, but the venture resulted in the discovery of the Grand Canyon in the Colorado River, and of the river's mouth in the Gulf of California when the expedition's supply ships called there.

The assessment by then of the rough shape of the world (excluding the vast stretch of the Pacific and the southern polar region) led to allegations that the huge land masses of the northern hemisphere would have to be 'balanced' by a great southern continent. One of the earliest voyages in search of this land – usually known as Terra Australis or Terra Incognita – left Peru in 1567, commanded by Álvaro de Mendaña. He discovered the Solomon Islands and began years of frustration and speculation when he recorded their position so incorrectly that not even he was able to find them again 18 years later.

After Drake's voyages of the 1570s, Spanish supremacy of the seas around the New World was constantly being challenged and weakened. Here a Spanish treasure galleon is captured by three English ships off Peru. (Mary Evans Picture Library)

England, by this stage, had begun to look beyond the horizons of Europe, and the days of Spanish supremacy were numbered. The great fortunes of the Mayas, Aztecs and Incas had already been carried off, and even secondary Indian tribes had been defeated and robbed. Accordingly, when Queen Elizabeth of England commissioned Francis Drake to circumnavigate the world and to search for opportunities for England abroad, it was understood that the best way to win the fortunes of the New World was to wrest them from the Spaniards, who had taken them from the Indians.

Drake discovered the true southernmost point of South America, thus ending speculation that Tierra del Fuego was joined to Terra Incognita. After finding Drake's Passage, Drake and the *Golden Hind* burst upon the unsuspecting Spanish ships and harbours along the coasts of Chile and Peru. With his ships low in the water from bounty, he continued to the East Indies and finally returned to England late in 1580, three years after he had set out – the first ship's captain, and the first Englishman, to circumnavigate the world.

Drake continued to torment Spain. He was enormously successful at pirating and also defeated them in battles in the West Indies, the Cape Verde Islands – and finally and conclusively when he routed the Spanish Armada in 1588. But England failed to capitalize on his successes or to follow them up with further expeditions, instead relying heavily on piracy and, increasingly, on the burgeoning slave trade. Meanwhile, the French moved to begin settlements in the New World, while in the East Indies, England was foiled by the Dutch. With the two prime areas taken, England eventually turned to India and Central Asia as outlets for her policies of expansion.

33

Discovery and Exploration

The East was not being ignored entirely during this period. Fernão Pinto took 15 years to explore the east coast of Asia from Malay to Peking, and was probably the first European to visit Japan, followed by Saint Francis Xavier, greatest of all the modern missionaries.

For the awakening France, however, the attraction was the new lands in the West, and in 1534 a Frenchman, Cartier, discovered the Gulf of St Lawrence. He subsequently ventured further upstream, but some 50 years were to pass before French exploration really got under way under Champlain.

England's attempts to explore and colonize in the New World were rather tentative, and give no indication that there were nevertheless strong movements for settlement. Hakluyt, the wealthy geographer with considerable influence in Parliament and at court, pressed hard for England to colonize the new discoveries, but it was Humphrey Gilbert's conviction that a sea route existed round the north of North America that

Anchoring in the mouth of the St Charles River, Cartier explores Canada on behalf of France. (Mary Evans Picture Library)

The World Discovered and Explored

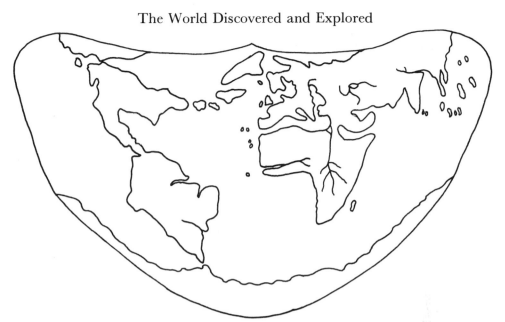

Map of the world – after Sir Humphrey Gilbert's map published in 1576. Drake's Passage had been discovered by then, but it took some time before discoveries were included on maps.

led Martin Frobisher to make two voyages between 1576 and 1578 to look for the passage. His attempts were somewhat haphazard, and an unsuccessful attempt was also made at beginning a settlement. Frobisher found two passages which he thought were the entrances to the North-west Passage, but in fact neither of them were. Gilbert himself attempted to establish a colony on Newfoundland, but he was drowned in a storm at sea and his colony did not last long either.

Walter Raleigh, Gilbert's half-brother, attempted more colonization in 1584, and Queen Elizabeth named one of the fledgling settlements Virginia. All three proved unsuccessful, however, and Raleigh tried to regain Elizabeth's favour by going in search of the kingdom of El Dorado, desperately, but vainly, covering the lower regions of the Orinoco River in South America.

The rapid accumulation of discoveries was making new demands on cartographers, and in 1570 Ortelius set definitive standards with his Atlas, which contained 70 maps specially drawn for the publication. The need to show an increasingly large part of the world with accuracy and detail proved too much for various methods of projecting the globe onto a flat surface, until Gerardus Mercator devised the Mercator projection and published his world map in 1569. And dominating all the maps of the time was the huge, variously shaped, vaguely outlined Terra Australis.

South Pacific voyages were still some way in the future, however, and even Frobisher's search for the North-west Passage had been preceded by attempts to reach the Orient by sailing north of Asia. Hugh Willoughby's 1553 expedition ran into storms beyond Novaya Zemlya and he was drowned before he reached the rendezvous point with Richard Chancellor – who survived the storms and found himself at what is now Archangel. Chancellor took the opportunity to travel to Moscow instead of continuing the north-east voyage; there he met Czar Ivan and opened up Anglo-Russian trade. His successor, Anthony Jenkinson, explored as far as Astrakan and the Caspian Sea, and later initiated European trade with Persia; so began England's belated efforts to establish overseas markets and colonies.

Central Asia was also coming under new scrutiny, with the first revelations coming from Cossack bands that pushed east into the lands of the marauding Mongols, and re-opened trade east of the Urals.

The 16th century closed with Portugal in decline, unable to maintain the extensive defences on which trading supremacy depended. But as Portugal

Members of one of Barents' expeditions are kept fully occupied in the Arctic regions. (Mary Evans Picture Library)

slithered towards bankruptcy, another sea-faring country, Holland, was getting ready to take her place.

The first major voyages commissioned by the Dutch were undertaken by Willem Barents, who tried to find Asia's North-east Passage to China. He discovered Spitzbergen and Bear Island, and in 1596 managed to pass Novaya Zemlya before encountering impassable ice. With his ship caught in the ice floes, Barents and his crew began a heroic struggle for survival, one of the great dramas of exploration. Accompanying Barents on two of his earlier expeditions was Jan van Linschoten. He did more to establish Holland in the East than any other man, for it was his writings and maps, compiled after years as the book-keeper to Portugal's Archbishop of Goa, that aroused Dutch interest in that part of the world. The first Dutch expedition was not greatly successful, but in 1598 Oliver van Noort led two Dutch fleets along Magellan's route to circumnavigate the world, and the Dutch could then consolidate their hold.

Building on the Great Age
1600–1750

Both England and Holland were poised to fill the gap in the Far East trade caused by Portugal's inability to maintain and protect its fleets. England's interest in the East Indies had increased sharply after Drake's visit to the islands during his circumnavigation, and both countries were stimulated by Linschoten's *Itinerario*.

The first English fleet sent to trade in the East sailed in 1591, and within four years the Dutch were also active. Initially, there was a great lack of co-operation among the Dutch fleets, and England gained an advantage, forming an organization formally known as 'The Governor and Company of Merchants of London Trading into the East Indies'. Fortunately it was almost immediately known as the East India Company.

The merchants and captains of Holland, however, discovered some of the problems that had defeated Portugal, and realized that with so many sources, outlets, and middlemen, only a monopoly would guarantee the necessary profits. With far greater alacrity than the English, the Dutch began to colonize the islands and as a final counter formed, in 1602, the Dutch East India Company. This enabled them to establish their supremacy, forcing England to turn to India as an alternative.

James Lancaster led the first English expedition to establish a trading post, though his approach to trade owed a lot to Drake, for he found that it was more profitable to lie in wait at Penang Island and plunder the richly laden ships using the busy Malacca Strait. In a more orthodox manner, Lancaster led the first East India Company fleet of 1601, and returned two years later with a substantial cargo of pepper. The Company's second fleet went out in 1604, led by Henry Middleton; but by then the Dutch were consolidated, and Middleton found it difficult to put together a worthwhile cargo.

The English were finding things slightly easier in the seemingly ideal climate and terrain of North America's north-eastern territory. In 1605 George Waymouth, on a colonizing expedition, discovered the Kennebec River and Penobscot Bay, and a year later James I gave patents to two companies for the colonization of North America. The plainly named John Smith was far from ordinary, and did as much as anyone to establish the English in North America. Serving with the London Company, he founded Jamestown while consolidating colonization efforts in the Chesapeake Bay area. He surveyed the coastal strip north from Cape Cod in 1614, and it was Smith who named that area 'New England'. 'El Dorado fever' also infected King James who released Raleigh from the Tower of London under orders to make another attempt to find the fortune in South America. The voyage was disastrous on almost every front, and Raleigh was executed on his return.

The Dutch were not so busy in the East that they ignored the New World, but at first they were mainly interested in finding quicker routes to the Indies. The Dutch East India Company commissioned the English navigator Henry Hudson to find a North-east Passage round Asia, but ice in the Barents Sea prevented much progress in attempts made in 1607 and 1608. Hudson began another voyage round the North Cape a year later, but then turned about, sailed south-west across the Atlantic, and explored the American coast from Newfoundland to Chesapeake Bay. Sailing inland of Long Island he discovered and named the Hudson River, venturing far enough to make certain that it was not a route to the East. The area made a favourable impression on Hudson, and his reports brought the first Dutch to the continent, where they began to trade for furs.

Hudson's next voyage, in 1610, was for his fellow Englishmen. Although the Orient was again the objective, his immediate purpose was to find an American North-west Passage. He found instead Hudson Strait, and sailed into Hudson Bay, whose vast size led many to believe that it was the hoped-for route. Although Hudson's trip ended in tragedy, the Dutch followed up his favourable impressions of the Hudson River. Their colonists chose Manhattan Island instead, and called it New Amsterdam, until the English renamed it New York. Lancaster Sound, the approach everyone was looking for, was discovered by William Baffin in 1616, but he never went far enough to realize its importance.

After their unfortunate start with Cartier, the French really came on to the map when Champlain arrived at the Gulf of St Lawrence in 1603, and sailed as far as present-day Montreal; later he founded the first French colony on Nova Scotia and established a fur-trading base at what is now Quebec. Champlain learnt much about the inner areas from Etienne Brulé, the discoverer of four of the five Great Lakes (Ontario, Huron, Erie and Superior) between 1610 and 1622. The discoverer of Lake Michigan, Jean Nicolet, was a Champlain protégé: his principal discovery was the watershed between the Fox and Mississippi Rivers, and he went some distance down the Wisconsin River towards the Mississippi.

Although cartographers' maps were becoming more accurate, it was still all too easy for navigators to be confused by the various interpretations, and there was always a considerable time-lag between any new discovery being made and becoming widely known. At the turn of the century, for example, it was not entirely certain whether the China whose coast Portugal had reached by sea was the same as Marco Polo's Cathay. To try to solve this uncertainty, Bento de Goes left Agra in 1603, dressed as a Moslem merchant, and travelled through the Hindu Kush and the Pamirs to

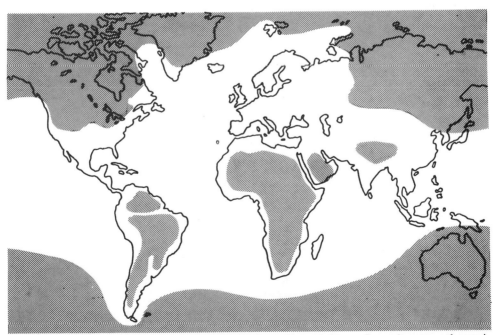

At the beginning of the 17th century, Terra Australis and Terra Incognita were the main mysteries awaiting discovery – apart from the unexplored interiors and the northern routes to the East.

Yarkand, eventually reaching Suchow. This was the first overland journey to China made by a European for some 300 years, and it established that Cathay and China were one and the same.

It was proving considerably more difficult to establish the truth about Terra Australis, however. Pedro de Quiros had been on Mendaña's expedition, and remained fascinated by the thought of a huge southern continent. A rather disastrous expedition under Pedro de Quiros left Peru in 1605, eventually breaking up in the New Hebrides. The pilot of one of the ships, Luis Vaez de Torres, decided to continue westwards on a bearing which took him south of New Guinea, and so discovered the Torres Strait between New Guinea and Australia's Cape York. Torres was nearly beaten to the Strait's discovery by Willem Janz, one of the most important of the Dutch mariners, who, after sailing east past New Guinea's southern shore, drifted further south and met the Cape York coast. In fact, Torres' discovery did not become widely known for some 200 years. Understandably, many deduced that Cape York was just another part of the New Guinea coast, and so believed that New Guinea was joined to Terra Australis. Nevertheless some cartographers, Mercator among them, showed New Guinea as a separate island many years before Torres' discovery was made, let alone recognized.

In Africa, the Nile was already attracting explorers, while the Coptic Christian church in Ethiopia – quite likely the source of the rumours about Prester John – attracted missionaries. One of the earliest was Pedro Paez, a Jesuit who travelled from Massawa to Gondar on Lake Tana, and also visited the Springs of Geesh in 1613. The springs feed Lake Tana, and the outflow of the lake is the beginning of the Blue Nile. Another missionary, Jerônimo Lobo, later visited Lake Tana as well, and followed the river well beyond the Tisisat Falls.

Rapidly escalating trade and better ships produced a constant stream of new discoveries. Holland's successes in the East Indies encouraged more and more merchants and more and more ships and mariners. Willem Schouten and Jakob le Maire rounded Tierra del Fuego in 1615, discovered the useful Le Maire Strait and named Cape Horn. Crossing the Pacific, the mariners also discovered the Tuamotu Islands, the Tonga Islands and the Horn islands.

The Dutch made what can best be called 'half a discovery' in 1616. Dirk Hartog, after rounding the Cape of Good Hope on a journey to the East, eventually sighted the west coast of Australia, at Dirk Hartog's Island off Shark Bay. This was the first of a whole series of usually accidental landfalls made by the Dutch on Australia's west coast. In 1618 Jacobszoon landed on the North-West Cape; Houtman arrived off Perth a year later, and Leeuwin on the south-west Cape Leeuwin in 1622. One of the most important sightings was Francois Thyssen's in 1627. He sailed further south than Leeuwin, and turned back only when he had reached the Great Australian Bight. Over the years there were more and more landings, the rather barren country was named New Holland, and in 1629 the first Dutch settlers arrived at present-day Northampton.

Another Dutchman, Willem Blaeu, made a significant improvement to cartography at that time. He was a notable geographer and his world map of 1630 included most of the later discoveries. But it was not long before even Blaeu's maps were outdated by some puzzling discoveries in the southern Pacific. These were made by Abel Tasman, who landed on Tasmania's west coast in 1642. He named it van Diemen's Land but did not investigate it thoroughly enough to discover that it was an island, and not part of any vast continent. He sailed on and discovered New Zealand, which he named Staaten Land; but once again Tasman's surveys were less than exhaustive. He missed the strait between the two islands, and so considered it the west coast of another land mass. Remarkably, Tasman

Abel Tasman discovers Fiji, in 1643 – a moment in history recorded in a picture with some very unusual proportions. (Mary Evans Picture Library)

made a third near miss when he reached New Britain's east coast and sailed north, instead of south, round the Bismarck Archipelago. This made him miss the strait later discovered by Dampier, and gave a false picture of the northern outline of New Guinea. In 1644 Tasman was instructed to map New Guinea's southern coast but, true to form (and not knowing about Torres' voyage), he turned slightly south just in time to miss the Torres Strait and charted York Peninsula as part of southern New Guinea.

Missionaries always played an important, if intermittent role in exploration, though some were naturally more interested in what they could change than in what they could discover. It certainly was missionary zeal that took the first Europeans into the heart of Tibet. A Jesuit, Antonio de Andrade, travelled from Agra and Delhi into the Himalayas – prudently dressed as a Hindu on a pilgrimage – and received a generous welcome from the Buddhist ruler of Tsaparang. A mission that he set up was eventually demolished by the Buddhists and though it was later

The Taj Mahal, Agra – the beautiful marble mausoleum built by the Mogul Emperor Shah-Jahan in 1631–45. (Mary Evans Picture Library)

re-established, local antagonism triumphed, and the Christian effort was abandoned. Another mission was established in another part of the mountains altogether, while a very different manifestation of Europe's concern with central Asia came in the form of England's first ambassador to India's Mogul court, sent by James I in 1615 as one of England's early attempts to compensate for the lost monopoly of the East Indies.

Further north, the Russians methodically conquered and explored Siberia. Stadukhin reached the Kolyma River in 1641, and Vasily Poyarkov discovered the Amur River and followed it to its mouth at the southern end of the Sea of Okhotsk. This part of the world also had a 'Torres-like' discovery which did not become known for quite some time. Semen Ivanov Deshnef discovered the gap between Siberia and Alaska and sailed on to the Kamchatka peninsula, but the existence of this very important strait was not properly acknowledged until Bering's voyage.

On the North American continent two French brothers-in-law, Groseilliers and Radisson, made observations which helped surveyors to fix the position of the Great Lakes more exactly, and Nicolet's reports of a huge river were justified in 1673 when Louis Jolliet travelled via the Fox and Wisconsin Rivers to the Mississippi. Another Mississippi explorer was Robert Cavelier, Sieur de La Salle, who on reaching the great Mississippi valley area claimed it for France, naming it Louisiana. La Salle was later unable to find the mouth of the river on a voyage to the Gulf of Mexico, and was one of those who still felt that some route to the Pacific would be found from the vast water system of eastern America. Further north, Canada's enormous central plains were seen for the first time by a European when Henry Kelsey, an employee of the Hudson's Bay Company, travelled west from York Factory to drum up more business for the Company. This was to be the last expedition into the north-west for some 60 years.

A great contribution to the knowledge of the vast, complex interior of Asia came from a long journey across the continent by Johann Grueber and Albert d'Orville. They left Peking in 1661, and eventually came to the awesome capital city of Lhasa, becoming the first Europeans to enter the city for 300 years. From there they went to Shigatse, and through Nepal to India. D'Orville died in Agra, but Grueber continued to the Indus, travelled into Persia and eventually reached the Mediterranean and Rome. The next Europeans in Lhasa were Desideri and Freyre, who arrived in 1716 – after an extensive expedition in the Himalayas. Desideri remained there until 1721, but the city and its environs then stayed hidden from

European eyes for another 200 years.

India was far more receptive to European overtures, and the English steadily built up their hold. Francis Day founded St George (later named Madras) in 1639, and English rule was established in Bombay in 1660. Calcutta was founded 30 years later, and since Mogul power had declined by then, England decided to establish direct influence over the whole country. The French had much the same idea, leading to the Anglo-French conflict which began in 1746.

In the Pacific it was a buccaneer, following in the footsteps of Drake by plundering whenever he could, who made the next significant discoveries.

Dampier's ship under attack from islanders off New Ireland, near New Guinea, in 1700. (Mary Evans Picture Library)

William Dampier took Drake's route into the Pacific in 1683, and after profitable piracy – especially in the rich seas of the Moluccas – took temporary refuge on the north-west coast of Australia (then still New Holland). He was commissioned to lead an expedition back to New Holland some years later and more or less accidentally discovered Salat Dampier and Dampier Strait, so reducing New Guinea to its proper size.

Dutch interest in New Holland had begun to dwindle by 1700, but this made little difference to England because Dampier's report on the country was unenthusiastic; it was quite some time before the incentive was found to settle that part of Australia.

Scientists were beginning to take a greater part in exploration, just as they were becoming more important in other fields. In Russia the Prussian naturalist Messerschmidt took advantage of Czar Peter I's more enlightened outlook and carried out very extensive expeditions in Siberia – although his findings gained little attention. The Czar's map did show the Siberian-Alaska gap discovered by Deshnef in 1644, but since no-one could swear to its existence, he commissioned Vitus Jonassen Bering to investigate the area. Bering built his ships on the eastern seaboard, and in 1728 sailed through the strait which now bears his name.

Another important scientific expedition was led by la Condamine, who completed a series of geographical measurements in Peru and Quito, and in 1743 started the first voyage by an eminent scientist down the length of the Amazon River, an area that was to provide botanists with innumerable specimens and curiosities. These first methodical steps in new worlds taken by scientists who were not primarily geographers marked the beginning of a significantly new and different era in exploration.

Speculations Resolved
1750–1850

Once the two southern routes to the East had been found, the next prize in the southern hemisphere was the 'Southern Continent'. In the North the possibility of an ice-ridden North-west Passage beckoned, while the hopes of thousands were focused upon the expanse of North America. And perpetually attractive were Tibet and central Asia, and the brooding interior of Africa.

In the middle of the 18th century, however, nothing captured the minds

The meticulous accuracy of Cook's surveys dispelled the last myths about Australia and New Zealand and, soon after, about Antarctica as well. This map shows how Tasman missed Torres Strait, Bass Strait and Cook Strait, and so formed a wrong impression of Australia and New Zealand.

of mariners, cartographers, geographers, or empire builders as much as the thought of some great voyage in which another vast new continent would be found. The English believed in Terra Australis, or Terra Incognita, as firmly as anyone else and in 1764 John Byron sailed on a voyage to find the lost land. He found nothing in the South Atlantic, however, and nothing in the Pacific either, apart from a few small and already known islands. Two years later, however, another expedition by Samuel Wallis and Philip Carteret discovered Tahiti, the Wallis Islands, and the Pitcairn and Admiralty Islands – but not Terra Australis.

A Frenchman next joined the growing ranks of circumnavigators. Louis-Antoine de Bougainville reached the Pacific via the Straits of Magellan, and continuing westwards after Tahiti was finally forced to head north by Australia's Great Barrier Reef, though he never caught sight of the continent just over the horizon. Bougainville's was yet another voyage

The Queen of Otaheite (Tahiti) reluctantly bids farewell to Captain Wallis, in 1767. (Mary Evans Picture Library)

which found no evidence for or against the existence of Terra Australis, for he had followed the same prevailing winds that had taken all other ships across the Pacific. Beyond about 80° W, no ship had yet sailed south of the 40th parallel, and that meant that there was still an unexplored portion of the southern hemisphere that was large enough to hold a continent.

Eventually the Pacific Ocean gave up her secrets, thanks to one of the greatest navigators, captains and explorers of all time – James Cook. He was a natural choice to take a group of scientists to the Pacific in 1768 and his course from Tahiti took him almost at once into uncharted seas. Sailing west on 40° S he came to the east coast of New Zealand, discovered Cook Strait, and sailed round South Island, which ruled out Tasman's Staaten Land as the coast of a southern continent.

Cook continued westwards until he sighted Australia's south-east coast, discovered Botany Bay, and claimed the land for England, naming it New South Wales. The following year Cook became the first to cross the Antarctic Circle and accurately charted a large number of Pacific islands. A second crossing of the circle was achieved before he went on to discover the South Georgia and South Sandwich islands. This epic voyage showed conclusively that the great 'Southern Continent' did not exist, and was of immense value to geography and cartography.

Cook sailed again for the Pacific, on his third great voyage, in 1776, one of his aims being to find a North-west Passage from the Pacific end. Sailing with Cook was William Bligh, future captain of the *Bounty*, and the expedition discovered Christmas Island and the Sandwich Islands (Hawaiian Islands), and surveyed the coasts of north-west America and Alaska and the Bering Strait, before Cook was killed in the Sandwich Islands.

The long-ignored African continent was also being explored at its southern and northern extremities. By 1752 the Dutch colony at the Cape of Good Hope, founded as a permanent staging post on the way to the East Indies, was 100 years old, and groups and individuals soon started venturing inland or along the coast, away from the increasingly ordered and crowded life of the colony. Beutler led a group along the southern coast, past Algoa Bay and across the Great Kei River, and in 1777 Robert Gordon and William Paterson went on an inland expedition up on to the highveld plateau, discovering part of the Orange River's course.

In the north, James Bruce led the first scientific expedition to find the source of the Blue Nile, confirming that it was Lake Tana and the Springs of Geesh. But he claimed this was the source of the whole Nile, for he

On Shakespeare Head, in New Zealand's Mercury Bay, Cook erected a temporary observatory.
(Mary Evans Picture Library)

thought that the White Nile, joining at Khartoum, was merely a tributary.

With so much at stake in India, England soon became interested in Tibet, with hopes of establishing firm commercial links that would also allow a military alliance, for the country had a strategic position between India and China and Russia. The first mission, led by George Bogle, established good relations with the Tashi Lama, but not good enough to overcome official opposition to England. The second mission was just as unsuccessful, in spite of Samuel Turner's auspicious arrival at the time of the reincarnation of the soul of the Tashi Lama in the body of his successor, then only 18 months old. The Ghurkas invaded Tibet five years later in 1788, but were themselves driven out by the Chinese – who stayed for good.

Commerce rather than curiosity dictated most of the exploratory moves in North America as well as in Asia. Anthony Henday combined looking for new sources of furs with exploring the North and South Saskatchewan rivers, while Samuel Hearne tried to find a waterway from Hudson Bay to the Pacific Ocean by exploring overland, at the same time searching for a river reputedly rich in copper. On his second expedition, in 1770, Hearne discovered the Coppermine River north of the Great Slave Lake, but this led into the Arctic and not the Pacific Ocean, and there was little copper to be found.

The monopolistic methods of the Hudson's Bay Company were used without compunction against those who preferred to work alone as independent traders, but the independents made a significant contribution to the exploration of North America. One of them, Peter Pond, was also convinced that a waterway to the Pacific would be found and his convictions led to his fellow trader, Alexander Mackenzie, becoming one of the greatest explorers of North America. In 1789, he discovered the river that bears his name and followed it to its mouth. Four years later he headed west into the Rockies and ended up at the mouth of the Dean River on the Pacific Coast, at the end of a journey that had made him the first European to cross the North American continent north of Mexico.

Another important explorer of that time was David Thompson, who between 1790 and 1811 covered a wide band of country from Lake Superior to the Pacific in the west, and from Lake Athabasca south to the sources of the Columbia, Mississippi and Missouri rivers. One of Thompson's journeys, begun in 1807, took him the full length of the Columbia River to the Pacific Ocean, demonstrating that there was no navigable water route to the Pacific, but that a continental crossing which involved only a number of fairly short overland stretches was possible.

One of the few mysteries of the Pacific that Cook left unsolved was the whereabouts of the Solomon Islands, which had not been identified since Mendaña had incorrectly plotted their position in 1567. Finding and identifying the Solomons was one of the missions on the voyage of Jean de la Pérouse, whose journey took in much of Asia's east coast as far north as Kamchatka, and many Pacific islands. Whether he found the Solomon

Islands, however, is not known, for his ship was never seen again after he called at New South Wales. But they were identified by Bruni d'Entrecasteaux three years later, when he led an expedition to try to find out what had happened to Pérouse.

More uncertainties were resolved by one of Cook's midshipmen, George Vancouver, who spent three years carrying out a meticulously detailed survey of the North American coast from San Francisco Bay to Cook Inlet, including precise mapping of the fragmented Canadian and Alaskan areas. By the time he headed back to England round Cape Horn from his base in the Sandwich Islands, he had proved beyond doubt that there was no access to the Pacific between the Bering Strait in the north and the Magellan Strait in the south. Those straits, and Drake Passage, remained the sole westbound routes until the Panama Canal was opened 120 years later, in 1914.

With no further need to speculate about undiscovered sea routes to the Pacific, attention was turned to the countries that existed in place of the mythical southern continent – Australia and New Zealand. At first Australia's distance from Europe made it seem a forbidding continent, and reports about the country itself scarcely compensated for that disadvantage. As a place of banishment, however, it possessed indisputable advantages, and in 1780 twelve ships sailed from Britain with the appropriate passengers to found the first penal colony. It was decided that the huge inlet just north of Botany Bay would be the most suitable location. This was Port Jackson, which eventually became Sydney. The coastal mountain range behind Botany Bay and Port Jackson formed a barrier isolating the interior, but in 1795 George Bass and Matthew Flinders explored a river course into the Blue Mountains, the first Europeans to venture inland. Bass and Flinders later discovered the Bass Strait, and proved that Van Diemen's Land (Tasmania) was an island.

At that stage the map of Australia's outline was far from complete, but in 1800 a Frenchman, Nicolas Baudin, began a survey of the coast south and then west from Port Jackson to Encounter Bay. It was Matthew Flinders, however, who deserved most of the credit for discovering the continent's true shape, for between 1801 and 1803 he mapped practically the entire coast, missing out only that part guarded by the Great Barrier Reef, and the section already mapped by Baudin. Credit was a long time coming, however, for Flinders called at Mauritius on his way back to England, unaware that France and England were at war. While Flinders languished in the French garrison's prison, Baudin tried, unsuccessfully, to pass off the Englishman's work as his own.

In contrast, much of the exploration of southern Africa was undertaken by missionaries, such as John Campbell, who discovered the source of the Limpopo River. To cross Africa from one ocean's coast to the other was a natural ambition and in 1798 Francisco de Lacerda travelled from the Indian Ocean up the Zambezi River, but died near Lake Mweru, only halfway towards reaching his goal. The crossing was eventually achieved from the Atlantic side, when Pedra Baptista and Amaro José crossed from Luanda to the Zambezi.

The central and southern areas were not the focus of attention, however. Of far greater interest were the northern regions, the huge Sahara desert and the unknown Moslem lands. West Africa and the Gambia River had been known to Europe since the middle of the 15th century, when Henry the Navigator's captains brought back precise information but also confusing rumours about a large river well inland. Cartographers' varying interpretations added to the confusion. Some drew a big river flowing across West Africa and becoming the Gambia, while at least one had a branch of the Nile stretching right across the widest part of Africa. The big river was actually the Niger, whose crescent course is confusing, and which can easily be thought to be flowing the wrong way. On top of that, its source is only a few miles from those of the Gambia and the Senegal, yet it reaches the Atlantic thousands of miles away from them.

Africa held many mysteries and many dangers. Daniel Houghton, on an expedition to reach Timbuktu, was decoyed by local tribesmen, attacked and robbed, and left to die. Next in that region was the great Scottish surgeon and explorer, Mungo Park, on an expedition to trace the Niger in 1795. After locating where Houghton had died, Park himself was captured, but he escaped and reached the river, and established that it flowed from west to east. Some years later he was commissioned to lead another expedition, but on this trip he and his companions were drowned in the Niger. Many more were to die in attempts to unravel the mysteries of this river.

In South America, la Condamine's pioneering scientific expedition was followed some 60 years later by the Orinoco River expedition led by the famous botanist Alexander von Humboldt. After he had confirmed la Condamine's report on the extraordinary Casiquiare River, which links the Orinoco and Amazon river systems, Humboldt collected and catalogued the vast number of unique specimens he found in that region. Later he moved to the Colombian and Ecuador Andes, and his findings were to prompt visits by many other scientists, the continent providing limitless opportunities for naturalists.

A view that so many European travellers tried to see, but that was seen by so few — the forbidden Tibetan capital city of Lhasa. (Mary Evans Picture Library)

The first accurate, dependable information was also coming from another remote romantic region, as a result of Hyder Hearsey's expedition into the Western Himalayas. Growing Russian influence in Central Asia prompted Britain to send a roving diplomatic mission in 1807, led by Harford Brydges, which travelled from Bombay into the Persian Gulf at Bushire, and then to Isfahan, Teheran and Qazvin. Brydges gathered much new knowledge about Persia and the coastal Baluchistan region, and about parts of Afghanistan, as did Charles Christie and Henry Pottinger, and other Englishmen visiting this vast area. One of these was Thomas Manning, who became the first Englishman to enter Lhasa and see the Dalai Lama, while William Moorcroft explored the mountainous country between Lahore and Leh, and the Hindu Kush, before he was killed by tribesmen in Afghanistan.

As fast as some mysteries in the old world were being explained, new ones

53

were arising in Australia. The first explorers to go west of the Great Dividing Range were puzzled by the apparent courses of the westward-flowing rivers – and they were also about to discover the hardships of the continent's vast, barren interior. First across the Blue Mountains behind Sydney was Gregory Blaxland, and in his trail came a dozen others. Hamilton Hume followed part of the Murrumbidgee, crossed the Murray River, and concluded that there must be a huge inland lake into which all these rivers flowed.

New South Wales began to fill rapidly as ship after ship arrived from England and Europe. For some, however, the arrival of reports and rumours about New Zealand hinted that a better future awaited them even further away. One of the first to go was the chaplain to the New South Wales colony, Samuel Marsden, who founded the first mission in New Zealand in 1814, and made three extensive explorations of North Island.

No country was growing quite as fast as North America, however, with pioneers from all over Europe and the British Isles arriving in the path of the *Mayflower* Pilgrims. Land claims spread rapidly westwards, and the escalating population became increasingly ordered and formalized. The United States were formed and President Jefferson wasted little time before sending Meriweather Lewis and William Clark from St Louis on another search for a water route to the western areas of the continent. Lewis and Clark's journey turned out to be one of the longest single journeys undertaken on land, and was also the first-ever crossing of the central region of North America. The information they recorded played a major role in opening vast areas of North America.

It was obviously vital that reports about unknown territory should be accurate. Zebulon Pike demonstrated this all too clearly in 1806, when he reported unfavourably on the upper regions of the Arkansas and Red rivers. The impression subsequently held was of a semi-arid country unsuited to cultivation, and the fertile, rich plains lay unsettled for over 30 years.

First to travel from north to south along the length of the west country was Peter Skene Ogden, a fur trader, who discovered a number of significant rivers and lakes, and was the first to explore the eastern face of the Sierra. The area covered by Jedediah Smith during and after 1826 was even more extensive – he was the first to reach California overland, travelling via Great Salt Lake to San Gabriel (Los Angeles).

The meticulously accurate surveys made over some 20 years by John Frémont encouraged huge numbers of settlers to go to California, and he also discovered the reality of the rich plains that Zebulon Pike had discounted. By the time Frémont had added his findings, little of significance in North America remained to be discovered, and detailed exploration and mapping became an off-shoot of settlement.

For over 200 years Britain had shown little interest in the earth's higher latitudes, but a mild winter in 1818, which reduced the amount of Arctic ice, led to an expedition under David Buchan in an attempt to get close to the North Pole. Expectations were far too high, however, and Buchan's journey was halted by impassable ice a short distance beyond Spitzbergen. More practically conceived was the despatch of John Ross on another attempt to find a North-west Passage, accompanied by William Parry and James Clark Ross. Over a number of years these three, together or independently, were to make significant finds. Lancaster Sound was established as the beginning of the North-west Passage, but the maze of islands and inlets made progress slow. Parry managed to pass Barrow Strait to Melville Island and Viscount Melville Sound before being turned back by ice, and later made an attempt on the North Pole. Although the expedition was forced to turn back a long way short of its goal, Parry did set a new 'furthest north' mark.

The determined search for the North-west Passage became the setting for another great drama of courage, endurance, and sacrifice, in which the search for a sea-route and the search for the lost members of an expedition became interwoven. John Franklin had been on Buchan's unsuccessful Arctic/polar voyage, and led a three-year expedition to Canada in 1819. He made another journey to Canada a few years later, again accompanied by George Back and John Richardson. Richardson surveyed 900 miles (1,500 km) of coastline between the Mackenzie and Coppermine rivers, while Franklin surveyed the coast westwards to Point Barrow.

In 1845 Franklin was chosen to lead a major expedition to search for the North-west Passage. His ships were seen entering Lancaster Sound, but when nothing further had been heard by the spring of 1847 anxiety grew in Britain and search parties were mounted. The first expeditions were in vain, but in 1850 Robert McClure tried to find the Passage from the other end, sailing through the Bering Strait and heading eastwards. He discovered Prince of Wales Strait and the routes past Banks Island, and proved that a North-west Passage did exist, ice permitting.

The 30 years after 1820 saw the discovery of nearly all the major features of northern North America, and the mapping of huge areas of coastline – John Rae, for instance, travelled over 5,000 miles (8,000 km) searching for Franklin, and while doing so managed to map some 1,400 miles (2,250 km) of the northern coastline.

Discovery and Exploration

The search for the North-west Passage had detracted attention almost entirely from the far south. In 1820 Gottlieb von Bellingshausen became the first to sight and circumnavigate Antarctica whilst on a Russian expedition. Sealing in the southern Atlantic was becoming a wealthy industry and on his fourth sealing trip, James Weddell crossed the Antarctic circle and reached 74° 15'. Weddell had a sea named after him, and it was this sea that Jules D'Urville attempted to penetrate in 1839, only to be foiled by thick ice. He sighted part of Graham Land, and the following year discovered Adélie Land.

The most valuable exploration of Antarctica was carried out by James Clark Ross and F R M Crozier (who later died on Franklin's expedition). Ross discovered the permanently frozen bay, the Ross Ice Shelf, and witnessed the incongruity of an active volcano in a frozen land. Two years later he reached 78° 10'. But Franklin's disappearance drew the attention of the world's leading polar explorers away from Antarctica and it was 60 years before real interest returned to the frozen continent.

Of the three major 'forbidden cities' – Lhasa, Mecca, and Timbuktu – Timbuktu was the last to be seen by a European. Although its importance had begun to decline after the 16th century, it was still a very important Moslem city, 'untainted' by outsiders for centuries.

The first European to visit Timbuktu – and to live to tell about it – was René-Auguste Caillié, who in 1828 took a year to travel from the west coast. The distinction of having lived to speak about Timbuktu is important, for the first European known to have reached and seen Timbuktu – Alexander Laing in 1826 – was killed by Tuaregs two days after leaving the city.

Timbuktu was not all that attracted explorers to West Africa; equally demanding were the Niger River and, further inland, Lake Chad. Lake Chad was first seen by Europeans in 1822, but journeys to it and along the mysterious, baffling Niger took a high toll of explorers' lives – Oudney, Clapperton, Lander were three leaders who died in this region.

It was not until the middle of the century that a true picture of central West Africa and much of the Sahara emerged. Heinrich Barth showed Africa as far more than a huge space that needed to be crossed, and gave innumerable details about vast areas from Tripoli to Lake Chad and around Timbuktu. He was also the first to define the middle regions of the Niger.

Arabia was still as mysterious a land as that surrounding Timbuktu, with the added attraction of close links with some of the oldest civilizations.

The World Discovered and Explored

One of these links, the remains of the ancient city of Petra, was discovered by Johann Burckhardt, who explored much of the land bordering the Red Sea and parts of the Nile, disguising himself as a Moslem in order to enter Mecca and Medina. The first accurate details of the Hejaz region, and of the holy cities, were supplied by Burckhardt. The southern coast of Arabia, the Hadramout, was still quite unknown to Europeans until 1834 when a naval officer, James Wellsted, made a number of trips inland, and was the first to see the eastern edge of perhaps the most formidable desert – the Empty Quarter of Arabia, an area avoided even by the Bedouin.

For the first time since Desideri some 200 years before, Tibet was again visited by a Jesuit missionary, when, in 1844, Evariste Huc and Joseph Gabet travelled along the 17th century missionary route from Peking to Lhasa. The intervening years and Chinese dominance had made it no friendlier, and they were eventually escorted out of the holy city.

Only 70 years after Cook's discoveries, the coasts and waters of Australia and New Zealand were becoming familiar to many, and the interiors were fast giving up their secrets. William Colenso arrived in New Zealand's North Island in 1838 and over the next six years extensively explored the island, providing information to the settlers who arrived to establish the first colony, which was named Wellington.

Across the Tasman Sea, Edward Eyre was the first to discover the huge salt lakes in the interior of Australia, but he believed that there was an arc of them above Spencer Gulf that would make it impossible to reach the centre of the continent

This Maori leader of the early 19th century had become used to various European accessories. (Mary Evans Picture Library)

from that point. The questions that had bothered so many about the westward-flowing rivers were largely answered when Charles Sturt made a hazardous and exhausting journey down the Murrumbidgee and Murray Rivers to Murray's lagoon. The hardship of the expedition and the struggle back up the river courses all but caused Sturt's death, but he went on to become one of the greatest explorers of Australia's interior.

That harsh interior took a tragic toll of lives. Ludwig Leichhardt disappeared in 1848 while attempting to walk across the continent. In the same year Edmund Kennedy, leading an expedition to explore the Queensland territory, was murdered by Aborigines, and few of the other members of the expedition survived. Some successful expeditions were completed, however, among them those led by two brothers, Augustus and Frank Gregory, the latter discovering numerous places in Western Australia that were suitable for settlement.

If Australia was initially turning out to be something of an anti-climax, with little of interest apart from its highly unusual fauna and flora, the world's attention was shortly to be centred on the excitement and mystery of Africa's dark interior. David Livingstone's inauspicious arrival in 1841 at Robert Moffat's Kuruman mission hardly hinted at his later actions or subsequent fame, but since Moffat had explored into Matebeleland (Zimbabwe), it was natural that Livingstone should soon explore part of the Transvaal highveld. After that taste of venturing into virgin Africa, he became as dedicated an explorer as he was missionary.

Further north Johannes Rebmann discovered Mount Kilimanjaro, and Johann Krapf was the first European to see Mount Kenya. More important, though, were the rumours they heard of a huge inland sea and of a towering range of mountains. For hundreds of years, fanciful maps of Africa had shown the Nile flowing from a great lake, set amongst the 'Mountains of the Moon'.

Completion, and New Horizons
1850 onwards

In matters of exploration and discovery, spectators long for drama. Nothing satisfies this better than a discovery of immense proportions or repercussions, unless it is the drama of an explorer gone missing – and the second half of the 19th century supplied an abundance of drama to an

Richard Burton disguised himself as a Moslem pilgrim and managed to draw and measure forbidden Moslem areas in great detail. On the pilgrimage to Mecca and Medina, he drew this picture of Mount Arafat. (Mary Evans Picture Library)

eager world in which communications were rapidly improving. In 1850 most eyes were still on northern Canada with the search for Franklin and the North-west Passage, but minds were not left to dwell on iced-in ships and frozen straits for long.

Africa began to claim attention with the search for the Nile, one of the greatest adventures in exploration. The drama of the search was due in no small measure to the colourful and controversial nature of the first expedition's leader, Richard Burton – a linguist, scholar, poet, ethnologist, translator and writer. Burton made his first major mark in exploration in 1853 with a visit to Mecca under the disguise of a Moslem, sketching and measuring and so providing the first really detailed and accurate information about the city. Two years later he led his first expedition to the Nile with John Hanning Speke, but the attempt was abandoned near Berbera, after the party was attacked by tribesmen.

The Nile was temporarily forgotten during the Crimean War, but once Krapf and Rebmann had heard about East Africa's inland 'sea', enthusiasm returned and the Royal Geographical Society commissioned Burton and Speke to make a second attempt. They discovered Lake Ujiji (Lake Tanganyika), and Speke then went on to discover Lake Victoria, Burton being too ill to accompany him. Burton never shared Speke's hasty

59

Travelworn and weary, Speke and Grant enjoy hospitality and refreshment with Samuel Baker and Mrs Baker on the White Nile in 1863. (Mary Evans Picture Library)

assertion that Lake Victoria was the Nile's source, and his envy and Speke's aggravating boasts kept the controversy in the public eye, Burton's arguments being accepted by a sufficient number for the source of the Nile to be regarded as unproved.

These disagreements and doubts prompted the Royal Geographical Society to ask Livingstone to prove the Nile's source, but for all his abilities, he too was unable to settle the dispute.

Livingstone's first epic journey began in 1854, and resulted in the discovery of the Victoria Falls. Thereafter, he was never short of willing assistants, and led numerous explorations into inland Africa from the east coast. Lakes Shirwa (Chilwa) and Nyasa (Malawi) were discovered, and the Rovuma and Shire rivers extensively explored. Further inland Livingstone discovered Lake Mweru and Lake Bangweulu, and the Lualaba River whose northerly course caused him to wonder whether it was the headwaters of the Nile. Stanley was to prove it was the start of the Congo, but the distinction between the watersheds of these huge rivers was at that time being established further north, where Schweinfurt explored west of the Nile and became the first to see the Uele River and to explore that catchment area.

The Victoria Falls discovery caused a degree of interest only surpassed by the news that their discoverer was missing – or at least had not been heard of for a disturbingly long time. While Livingstone's disappearance lacked the elements of catastrophe that marked the loss of the whole Franklin expedition, it was dramatic enough, and the editor of *The New York Herald* saw in it an ideal opportunity to increase his paper's circulation. He announced that his correspondent, Henry Morton Stanley, was going into Africa to find and rescue the missionary.

When Stanley did reach Livingstone he found a great deal to admire and respect in the ageing Scot. Although Livingstone's health was worsening rapidly, Stanley was unable to persuade him to leave Africa, and together they explored a good deal of Lake Tanganyika.

Another invaluable service performed by Stanley was to establish that the Nile, as Speke asserted, was the only outlet from Lake Victoria, and that no stream of special significance flowed into the Lake. From then on it was accepted that the source of the Nile River was Lake Victoria – though some, including Stanley, waited until the Lualaba's course was established.

Stanley crosses Makata Swamp on the way to his historic meeting with Livingstone. (Mary Evans Picture Library)

The first east-to-west crossing of equatorial Africa was also achieved at about this time, by Verney Cameron.

Stanley was now intrigued by Africa and he became one of the greatest of the continent's explorers, driven to complete Livingstone's planned explorations. His most successful expedition was his crossing of Africa from east to west, during which he finalized all Nile speculation by following the Lualaba into the Congo River.

Livingstone and others had spent considerable time trying to find easy routes from the coast to Lake Nyasa, and this was the aim of the Royal Geographical Society's expedition of 1878 led by Joseph Thomson, who did much of the important work in determining East Africa's geological make-up. Although he never found an easy route to Lake Nyasa, Thomson went further inland and established that Lake Tanganyika's outlet was into the Lualaba-Congo system. The Royal Geographical Society mounted another expedition in 1882, this time to find a good route to Lake Victoria from the coast. Thomson explored new areas and discovered Lake Baringo, but the eastern seaboard offers no easy access to the interior higlands – Lake Victoria itself chooses to empty into the distant Mediterranean, rather than the nearby Indian Ocean.

Stanley was called on to make yet another 'rescue' in Africa. This was his last major expedition and undoubtedly his worst too, in practically every respect. The person to be rescued this time was a brilliant but eccentric German named Eduard Schnitzer, or Emin Pasha. The last official to hold out against the Mahdi and the Moslem rebels of Egypt, he had taken refuge at a base on Lake Albert. Considerable speculation and controversy was caused by Stanley's methods on the 'rescue', while many wondered whether it was necessary at all. The relationship between Stanley and Emin Pasha was acrimonious, with Stanley only too keen to get to Bagamoyo, and Emin thinking mainly of launching a gloriously successful attack on the rebels. Although the two men duly reached Bagamoyo, Emin Pasha soon headed back into the continent bound on an east-west crossing, and was murdered south-west of Lake Albert.

Although Europe was aware of Africa many hundreds of years before Australia was discovered, their interiors were explored more or less simultaneously. The early theory of a horseshoe of lakes in central Australia was disproved by Peter Warburton in 1858 when he travelled between Lake Torrens and Lake Eyre, and two years later John Stuart began his attempts to traverse the continent from south to north. West of Lake Eyre he discovered The Neales River and in 1861 he reached the 'centre', now known as Alice Springs. On his third attempt Stuart got to the site of present-day Darwin, and within ten years the Central Telegraph

The beginning of the ill-fated attempt by the Burke and Wills expedition of 1860 to try to cross Australia. (Mary Evans Picture Library)

Line followed his route across Australia.

The first west to east crossing of Australia was made some years later by John Forrest, who had previously explored parts of the west and south-west, and had travelled from Perth to Yorke Peninsula. The harsh desert conditions of the interior claimed many lives – Gray, Burke and Wills died on a foolhardy expedition in 1861, and another death is commemorated in the name of the Gibson Desert in Western Australia. Alfred Gibson accompanied Ernest Giles on an expedition in 1873, got lost and was never seen again, though Giles spent a considerable time looking for him. Two years later Giles crossed from Spencer Gulf to Perth via the Great Victorian Desert. William Gosse's vain attempt to cross the continent had the compensation of the discovery of Ayers Rock, and some years later Lawrence Wells and David Carnegie made independent south-to-north crossings of Western Australia, traversing both the Gibson and Great Sandy Deserts.

Discovery and Exploration

The huge expanse of Africa between the equator and the Mediterranean continued to attract explorers, anthropologists and travellers. Henri Duveyrier spent some years living and travelling with Tuaregs in the northern Sahara, while one of the most experienced land travellers of the 19th century was Friedrich Gerhard Rohlfs, who was the first to cross Africa from the Mediterranean to the Gulf of Guinea. European countries were then at the height of colonial fever, and the King of Prussia sent Gustav Nachtigal to Africa in 1868 to bring back first-hand information on the continent. After travelling from Tripoli to Chad, Nachtigal became the first European to cross the south-east desert between Lake Chad and the White Nile, and finally established the geographical relationship of North Africa's dominant features. Timbuktu was a safer, if less interesting place when Oskar Lenz spent three weeks there before exploring part of the Niger. Six years later, he travelled up the Congo, reaching Lake Tanganyika by way of the Lualaba River.

France's interest in North Africa was also increasing, and two expeditions, led by Paul-Xavier Flatters and, a number of years later, by Fernand Foureau, went in search for a rail route, both of them ending in disaster at the hands of hostile warriors.

In East Africa, the last major features were discovered by Samuel Teleki, who found Lake Naivasha, the intriguing Lake Rudolf and the Omo River, and the marshy Lake Stefanie.

Although a circumnavigation of the earth had ceased to make news many years before, the three-year voyage of HMS *Challenger* was a major achievement – a 69,000 mile (111,000 km) voyage that produced a report 50 volumes long, and included the discovery of the then deepest undersea chasm near Guam. The hundreds of measurements taken of the sea and the ocean floor during the *Challenger*'s voyage focused attention on the fact that two-thirds of the earth's surface was scarcely known at all, and gave the first major impetus to the science of oceanography.

Scientists were quick to visit newly found areas that gave them the opportunity to study anything fundamentally different. Fridtjof Nansen, the Norwegian scientist, led an expedition to Spitzbergen to collect zoological specimens, and in 1888 he and Otto Sverdrup made important discoveries about the enormous volume of Greenland's ice-cap. Robert Peary had been in Greenland before Nansen, and he carried on the Norwegian's studies in a number of further expeditions.

Huge expanses of Asia were unmapped after even the remotest parts of Greenland's coasts were defined. Knowledge of the geography and geology of eastern Asia was greatly aided – and revised – by the detailed work carried out in the 1860s by Peter Kropotkin, who later became better known as the foremost theorist and idealist of the anarchist movement.

With China still barring all foreigners from Tibet, the mountain kingdom seemed as mysterious and intriguing as ever. For the British who were so eager to know exactly what lay beyond India's northern borders, necessity brought the invention of 'pundit-explorers'. These were Indians (and any others who could pass untroubled in Tibet) who were specially trained to take surreptitious measurements that would give British surveyors enough data to draw passable maps. The 'pundit explorers', taking measurements by counting their paces, brought back invaluable information about the Himalayas and the courses of rivers, and other features of Central Asia. Foremost of them all was Nain Singh. Kishen Singh made a major contribution by going as far afield as the edge of the Gobi Desert, while Kintup established that the Tsangpo River was the upper part of the Brahmaputra River.

Rivalry between Russia and Britain for influence in Central Asia – the 'Great Game' as it came to be known – resulted in a surprising amount of knowledge being shared.

Much of it came from Nikolay Mikhaylovich Przhevalsky, who got nearer to Lhasa than any European for many years, though even that was all of 170 miles (275 km) distant.

Tibet's reputation for inhospitality was almost matched by that of Arabia, which consequently attracted some of the most colourful explorers and travellers. One who fitted this category well was Charles Doughty, who not only did not bother to conceal his nationality and Christian background, but actually boasted of his 'difference'. Somehow he survived his travels, although he was occasionally robbed and once almost killed. Wilfrid and Anne Blunt, a few years later, were protected by travelling in an Arab sheik's company, and perhaps by their expressed anti-colonial views.

Far to the north attempts were still being made to negotiate a North-east Passage. Nils Nordenskjöld made two futile attempts in 1875 and 1876, but two years later he sailed from Tromsø, and after being stuck in ice for some 10 months, reached the Bering Strait in 1879. An attempt to negotiate the route from east to west led to tragedy, though also to a major discovery about the Arctic ice cap. Washington de Long's ship was caught in ice not long after passing through the Bering Strait, and he found himself being carried steadily north and west. But the pressure of the ice eventually broke up the ship and only one of the three groups that set out for safety survived. Three years later, however, some of the expedition's wreckage was found on the Greenland coast and this led to Nansen's bid to reach the North Pole by drifting towards it.

A slackening of Chinese intractability enabled a Swedish diplomat and explorer, Sven Hedin, to make a number of extensive journeys in Central Asia, during which he found valuable remains of cities in the Taklamakan, and visited Koko Nor, the Gobi Desert, Peking, Mongolia and Lop Nor. However much the Chinese had relented, they still maintained a strict control over inner Tibet, and although Hedin tried to disguise himself as a Mongolian, he was turned back when he was still some 150 miles (240 km) from Lhasa. Science broke some diplomatic barriers, however, and a Swedish/Chinese scientific mission led by Hedin located 327 archaeological sites and made many important finds in Central Asia.

An Englishman also became well known through his association with this disputed part of Asia. Francis Younghusband had spent many years exploring numerous parts of Asia, and after being arrested by Russians in the Pamirs, was given an opportunity for indirect revenge when Lord Curzon, Viceroy of India, decided to counter Russian influence with a display of military power. Younghusband led a large force into Tibet, easily beat off the Tibetan soldiers, and became the first European since Huc and Gabet to enter Lhasa – though he found that the Dalai Lama had fled to China. Britain soon realized that keeping close contact with all Tibet was next to impossible, and two years later China was recognized as the custodian of the country.

While most of the world had become reasonably familiar by the end of the 19th century, some important goals still attracted and eluded explorers and adventurers. The North-west Passage had taunted men for some 400 years. Although the route could be plotted on a map, no ship had yet completed the voyage – the fact that the North-east Passage had already been travelled only made matters worse. The pressure to prove the route mounted, and eventually the first passage was made by the tough and ambitious Norwegian Roald Amundsen.

Another longed-for distinction was to be the first at the North Pole. On Greenland Nansen and Sverdrup heard about the ice-bound 'voyage' of de Long's wrecked ship, and decided to try to reach the Pole by deliberately getting caught in the ice. In 1893 Nansen sailed into the ice north of the New Siberia Islands, and hoped for the best. The northerly drift was not sufficiently pronounced, however, and even an attempt by dog-sledge took Nansen to only 86° 14′.

Next to try for the North Pole was Peary, already well experienced in

Nansen's Fram *at the start of his expedition to try to reach the North Pole largely by drifting in the ice to an accessible point.* (Mary Evans Picture Library)

Greenland. On his second attempt, his expedition stood at the Pole, the first men at the 'very top of the world'. Some of their thunder was stolen by the claim of a Dr Cook to have reached the Pole in 1908, although he found few believers in his story. At the time that Peary reached the Pole, Amundsen had been about to make an attempt for the same prize. Indebted to his financiers for some noteworthy achievement, he turned his attention to the South Pole instead.

The Antarctic had been largely ignored by all except sealers and whalers since the time of Ross, but in 1900 Robert Scott led a Royal Geographical Society Antarctic expedition, whose members included Shackleton, Wilson, and Wild. They were the first to gather accurate information about the continent's great plateau, Scott leading a team that reached 83° 17'. Four years later Shackleton and Wild managed to get a tantalizing 97 miles (156 km) from the South Pole before the weather turned for the worse and drove them back.

Amundsen, beaten to the North Pole and startled by Shackleton's near success, headed south with all speed, notifying Scott – already committed to a polar attempt – that he too was making a bid. Amundsen was a hard taskmaster at the best of times, and he rushed to the South Pole with a desperation that gave him his goal, but little acclaim. Unhindered by attempts to make the expedition double as a scientific one, and having sensibly chosen dog sledges, he reached the Pole in December 1912. Scott, Wilson, Bowers, Oates and Evans arrived a month later, and perished before they reached their base camp.

The history of South America was as full of contrasts as its geography. Extravagant, bountiful riches of gold and jewellery had been found in cities of sophisticated engineering, inhabited by peoples with complex religious and social orders – yet on the eastern side of the Andes were some of the most primitive savages, ferociously hostile and frequently cannabalistic. The hot, steaming jungle of the Amazon basin was an almost impenetrable vastness harbouring people, reptiles, fish and insects of a deadliness unimagined by European travellers. For all this, or because of all this, South America continued to attract scientists, adventurers, fortune hunters, travellers and explorers.

Border disputes sprang up here as they did in most expanding countries, and in 1906 a survey was begun of the remote Bolivia/Peru/Brazil boundaries. The expedition was led by Percy Fawcett, who grew deeply absorbed with the continent – so much so that he was to play the leading role in another drama of a lost explorer in 1925. Before that, however, South America was the destination of a very distinguished 'amateur' explorer – Theodore Roosevelt. He and his son Kermit joined forces with a Brazilian explorer to trace the unknown course of a river discovered in 1909. They had a hazardous journey, twice speeding into larger rivers until they reached the Amazon. The former Rio Duvido was then renamed after Roosevelt.

When Percy Fawcett returned to South America in 1920 rumours of 'lost cities' and of El Dorados were not hard to come by. He discovered apparent documentary evidence of the existence of one of these, located somewhere between the Tocantins and São Francisco rivers. Five years later he led an expedition back to Mato Grosso, but somewhere west of the Xingu River, Fawcett and the entire expedition vanished without trace.

The whole world changed after the shock of the Great War. To Western eyes, romantic Arabia shrank to become a backdrop to the legend of Lawrence of Arabia. Exploration had frequently been a matter of military necessity, and even the pre-war details noted by Gertrude Bell on her journey from Damascus to the centre of Arabia and then to Baghdad had aided militarists as much as they enlightened geographers. The country still held one major challenge, but that fell in 1931 when Bertram Thomas became the first European to cross the Rub 'al Khālī, the notorious desert of the Empty Quarter of southern Arabia. Thomas travelled extensively in

Arabia while employed by the Sultan of Muscat, but even more widely travelled was the English Arabist Harold St John Philby, who made the second crossing of the Empty Quarter, a year after Thomas. Motor transport and the changes brought by the thirst for oil soon changed desert areas irrevocably, and Wilfred Thesiger was perhaps the last to know untainted Arabia.

In Arabia, Africa, Australia and every newly opened country, a crossing was the first goal to follow discovery. After the South Pole was reached by Amundsen and by Scott, a crossing of the frozen continent became Shackleton's ambition. Although his attempt was unsuccessful, the expedition turned into a remarkable exploit of survival from which the leader emerged as a man of heroic courage and endurance.

The aeroplane achieved sufficient sophistication by 1925 for more daring or desperate men to use it in polar regions, and in that year Roald Amundsen, who had hoped to be the first at the North Pole, tried instead to be the first to fly over it. He and Lincoln Ellsworth got within 170 miles (274 km) on their first attempt, but the following year, with Umberto Nobile, they succeeded, crossing the Arctic in Nobile's giant airship, the *Norge*, a flight that has never been repeated. Byrd claimed to have flown over the North Pole before Amundsen, although this was never proved. However, he was certainly the first to fly over the South Pole, and was the first American in the area since Wilkes.

Another pioneer in this form of transport in polar regions – not always regarded as 'true exploring' – was Hubert Wilkins, who had already been on many more conventional polar expeditions with Stefannson and with Shackleton. He discovered several islands from the air, and in 1931 became the first to use a submarine below Arctic waters, reaching 82° 15′ N. The controversial Byrd then caused a considerable stir by spending five months of the Antarctic winter of 1934 alone in a small base 123 miles (198 km) south of the Bay of Whales – an ordeal which he barely survived.

World War II brought with premature and unseemly haste the arrival of the technological revolution, and the advances made in every branch of science and technology had far-reaching repercussions. It was only natural that technological developments should be used to help men achieve objectives that had always eluded their forerunners, but what gave the illusion of 'unfairness' was that technology was advancing in leaps and bounds, instead of at a steady, gradual pace. No one would have suggested that Henry the Navigator's sailors should have used primitive Mediterranean boats instead of caravels, that Cook should not have conquered scurvy, or that Antarctic ice floes should be penetrated under sailpower alone. But suddenly, in the space of one generation, months of travel could be accomplished in days; equipment of every sort became stronger yet lighter, more reliable yet smaller. Even so, Nature remained formidable, and Mount Everest's peak remained untouched until 1953.

In the Antarctic, aircraft and versatile motor sledges frequently had to give way to more traditional human strength and determination in the 1957–8 Trans-Antarctic Expedition, when Fuchs led the first-ever crossing of the continent. Remarkably, the Arctic ice-cap was traversed by air and below the ice long before man crossed its surface. In 1959 an American nuclear submarine completed a voyage beneath the ice-cap, but it was ten years before Wally Herbert's expedition of men and dogs – indispensibly aided by aircraft drops – completed an arduous and hazardous crossing of the Arctic ice. One of the last great expeditions left to man, the Transglobe longitudinal circumnavigation of the globe via both polar ice-caps, is now under way, and scheduled to return to Greenwich in 1982.

The Space Age and a whole new era of discovery and exploration began in 1957 when Russia launched into earth's orbit a simple artificial satellite. Less than 12 years later – the time-span taken by Henry's Portuguese mariners to push their horizons from Cape Blanc to Cape Verde – Neil Armstrong became the first man to stand on the surface of the moon. In space exploration, practically everything has become possible, and with each remarkable step forward, man's capacity for bewilderment has been blunted. For earth-bound, airbreathing mankind, reality is on earth, and distant space and the black ocean depths are worlds of fantasy.

The exploration of space is perhaps our future; but the discovery and exploration of this world is our history, the story of mankind, and can be remembered, retold and relived countless times.

The Chronology
of Exploration

The Western Atlantic, the West Indies and Central America, and North America

The Middle Ages

c AD 860 Irish monks, disturbed from Iceland by arrival of Vikings, reached southern Greenland.

AD 982 Viking Eric the Red, exiled from Iceland, reached and named Greenland; in 985 colonized the west coast.

AD 986 Bjarni Herjulfsson sailed

Vikings discover Greenland – and once again drive away the Irish monks, who had already fled from the Viking arrival on Iceland. (Mary Evans Picture Library)

south-west from Iceland; passed, but did not land on, Nova Scotia, Newfoundland, Labrador.

c 1000 Leif Ericsson discovered, named Vinland (roughly Cape Cod to Nova Scotia), after sailing past Helluland (probably Baffin Island) and Markland (Labrador and Newfound-land).

1002 Thorwald retraced Ericsson's voyage, settled in Vinland, but was killed by Indians.

1006 Thorfinn Karlsefni abandoned Viking attempt to settle Vinland, owing to Indian hostility.

1400–1600

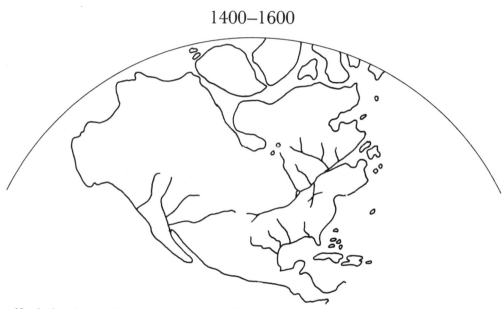

North America – after a map drawn in 1587 by Rumold Mercator based on his father's 1569 world map. A North-west Passage was shown, though it was not be navigated for another 300 years.

1492 Columbus crossed Atlantic, reached Bahamas (San Salvador) and made base on Hispaniola (Haiti and Dominica). Believed Cuba was Chinese coast.

1493 Second voyage by Columbus; discovered part of Lesser Antilles, Puerto Rico and Jamaica. Founded first 'New World' settlement, Isabella, on Dominica.

1497 John Cabot became first European since Vikings to sight Nova Scotia and Newfoundland.

1498 Columbus on third voyage discovered Trinidad.

1498 Cabot sailed along North American coast to Cape Hatteras.

1501 Gaspar and Miguel Corte-Real reached Labrador; captured Indians on Newfoundland. Both eventually disappeared on American coastal voyages.

1502 Columbus discovered Martinique in Lesser Antilles; reached Honduras.

1509 John Cabot reached Hudson Strait; sailed south along American coast to Chesapeake Bay.

Christopher Columbus in a very stylized drawing, holding an early astrolabe to represent his navigational skills. (Mary Evans Picture Library)

1513 On Darien expedition to found colonies, Vasco de Balboa was first to see Pacific Ocean.

1513 Juan Ponce de León sighted, named Florida; believed it an island after voyage from off Okefenokee Swamp to Tampa Bay.

1518 Juan de Grijalva explored Yucatan coast, Bay of Campeche. Attempted inland expedition brought evidence of wealthy civilizations of Mayas and Aztecs.

1519 Hernando Cortes landed near present-day Veracruz with 500 soldiers; burnt his ships and began march into interior.

1520 Aztecs drove Cortes and Spanish from Tenochtitlan, but Montezuma was killed.

1521 Cortes returned to besiege and eventually occupy Tenochtitlan. Aztec numbers rapidly diminishing due to imported disease and Spanish slaughter. Colony of New Spain founded; Tenochtitlan became Mexico City.

1527 Panfilo de Narváez briefly explored inland from Florida's Tampa Bay. 1528 most of expedition perished in Gulf of Mexico storm.

1528 After expedition with Narváez, Alvar de Vaca escaped storm to land near present-day Galveston and spent six years travelling south-west of continent with Indians.

The Indian village of Secotan in North America, as found in 1585. (Mary Evans Picture Library)

1534 Gulf of St Lawrence and Gaspé Peninsula discovered by Jacques Cartier in search for North-west Passage to the Orient.

1535 Cartier explored St Lawrence to Lachine Rapids and site of present-day Montreal.

1539 Hernando de Soto, governor of Cuba, landed at Tampa Bay, Florida; explored in wide arc north and westwards to Arkansas and Mississippi rivers.

1540 Large area south of Arkansas River explored by Francisco de Coronado in vain search for the gold of Cibola.

1541 Grand Canyon of Colorado River discovered by Cárdenas on Coronado's expedition.

1541 Mouth of Colorado River in Gulf of California discovered by Alarcón, as part of Coronado's expedition.

1542 Cartier abandoned Quebec base.

1576 Greenland and Baffin Bay rediscovered (after Vikings) by Martin Frobisher.

1577 Frobisher sailed into Hudson Strait; believed he had found North-west Passage.

1583 Unsuccessful attempt to colonize Newfoundland by Humphrey Gilbert.

1584 Walter Raleigh began first of three vain attempts to establish colonies in North America. Virginia named by Queen Elizabeth.

1600–1750

1602 Cape Cod named and explored by Bartholomew Gosnold.

1603 Champlain made first voyage to North America; sailed up St Lawrence to Montreal.

1605 George Waymouth attempted to found colony, and explored Kennebec River and Penobscot Bay.

1607 John Smith founded English settlement of Jamestown for the London Company.

1607 Champlain founded first French colony in New World, at Port Royal on Nova Scotia.

1608 Quebec founded by Champlain, who formed association with Huron Indians.

1609 Henry Hudson, for Dutch East India Company, sailed south past Newfoundland to Delaware Bay and Chesapeake Bay. On return northwards, discovered Hudson River.

1610–11 Hudson, for England, discovered Hudson Bay, but was abandoned there after mutiny by his crew.

1612 Etienne Brulé discovered Lake Huron while living with Indians at Georgia Bay.

1614 Following explorations by Adriaen Block, Dutch established colony at mouth of Hudson River.

1615 Brulé joined up with Champlain, and discovered Lakes Ontario and Erie. Champlain discovered Lake Champlain.

1616 Baffin and Bylot on second voyage discovered Lancaster Sound (200 years later shown to be entrance to North-west Passage).

1619 First American Parliament met at Jamestown, Virginia.

1620 Pilgrim Fathers landed from *Mayflower*; founded New Plymouth. First negro slaves brought to North America.

1620 Lake Superior discovered by Brulé.

75

1621 Scots abandoned Nova Scotia settlement.

1623 English and French settlements established on St Kitts, Leeward Islands.

1624 Barbados occupied by England. Dutch founded New Amsterdam (New York). Virginia became Crown Colony.

1627 English occupied Nova Scotia; eastern seaboard of North America settled rapidly from this time.

1626–35 Rapid colonization and settlement of West Indies by English and French.

1634 Lake Michigan discovered by Jean Nicolet, who also found watershed between Fox and Mississippi rivers and heard Indians' accounts of the river.

1654–63 Groseilliers and Radisson explored area of Great Lakes, especially Lake Superior, and country between the Lakes and James Bay.

1667 After English annexation of New Netherland, New Amsterdam renamed New York.

1668–71 Radisson and Groseilliers worked for English, exploring Hudson Bay area and Great Lakes, and founded Moose Factory.

1669 La Salle explored Ohio region, discovered Ohio River and followed it to present-day Louisville.

1670 Hudson's Bay Company formed by England.

1673 Louis Jolliet followed Nicolet's route to Fox and Wisconsin rivers; went on to the Mississippi, and was first to travel down river to its junction with the Arkansas.

1678–80 La Salle explored south of Lake Michigan and founded three 'Fort' settlements.

1680–2 La Salle sailed down Mississippi to Gulf of Mexico; claimed Louisiana for France, giving France a colonial empire stretching from Gulf of Mexico to Quebec.

1690–2 Henry Kelsey travelled west from York Factory on trading expedition – first European in Canada's central plains (and last for over 60 years).

1709 First mass emigration of Germans to America arrived at Pennsylvania.

1739 War between England and Spain in the West Indies.

1750–1850

1754 Anglo-French war broke out in North America.

1754–5 Anthony Henday went from Hudson Bay to upper waters of North Saskatchewan River; returned via South Saskatchewan.

1759–63 English defeated French at battle of Quebec – further victories in Canada and in West Indies.

1770 Samuel Hearne, on second expedition from Hudson Bay, explored unknown land north of Great Slave Lake, and in search for copper followed Coppermine River to its mouth.

1776 American Declaration of Independence.

1778 Peter Pond travelled from Lake Winnepegosis to Lake Athabasca and established trading post.

1783 England recognized USA.

1789 Hoping to find water route to Pacific, Alexander Mackenzie travelled from Lake Athabasca to Great Slave Lake; then followed Mackenzie River to its mouth.

1790 David Thompson surveyed Saskatchewan River for Hudson's Bay Company.

1792 Mackenzie became first to cross North America (north of Mexico) after taking Peace River west from Lake Athabasca to Finlay Forks, exploring upper part of Fraser River and then following Dean River to Canada's west coast.

1792–1802 Thompson surveyed Nelson River and Lake Athabasca, Lake Winnipeg and Lake Superior, Peace River, and South Saskatchewan and Bow rivers.

1803 United States bought Louisiana from France.

1804 Meriweather Lewis and William Clark left St Louis to try to find water route to Pacific; travelled up Missouri, crossed Bitterroot Range in spring 1805, and joined Snake River to reach Columbia River and Pacific Ocean. Arrived back September 1806 after one of most successful journeys of exploration in North America.

1805–8 Simon Fraser crossed Rockies on fur-trading mission and established post at Trout Lake. Later followed Mackenzie's route in Rockies and traced full course of Fraser River to Pacific – initially believing it was the Columbia.

1806 Zebulon Pike explored upper regions of Arkansas and Red Rivers (after expedition to find source of Mississippi) but erroneously concluded the area to be barren. Explored Rio Grande instead of Red River.

1807–11 Thompson completed surveys with one of full course of Columbia River.

1811–12 Wilson Hunt and Robert Stuart led expedition from St Louis to mouth of Columbia. On return, Stuart discovered South Pass, which greatly cut journey time from St Louis.

1818 John Ross, James Clark Ross and William Parry explored Baffin Bay in search for North-west Passage, but Parry was unable to convince Ross to explore Lancaster Sound.

1819–25 Parry made three voyages in search of North-west Passage (close to success on first voyage, when he reached Viscount Melville Sound), making great contribution to knowledge of the area.

1819–22 John Franklin made first expedition to Canada, west of Hudson Bay, and then north to Arctic coast at Coronation Gulf. From there he mapped coast to Bathurst Inlet and Kent Peninsula.

1825–7 Franklin followed Mackenzie River to mouth; mapped Beaufort Sea coast to Point Barrow, while John Richardson mapped eastwards from Mackenzie Bay to Coppermine River.

1824–30 Extensive journeys by Peter Skene Ogden, one of most widely travelled people in North America's West Country. Discovered Klamath River and river now known as Humboldt. Having started at Vancouver, gradually went south to the Colorado, and discovered Carson and Owens Lakes.

1826–7 California reached overland for first time when John Smith went via Great Salt Lake to Los Angeles, and later sailed to San Francisco Bay. Smith travelled overland to Vancouver, and his explorations opened up large areas of West Country to settlers.

1829–33 John and James Clark Ross made expedition to Lancaster Sound and Boothia Peninsula, during which John Ross determined position of Magnetic North Pole.

1833 George Back explored Great Fish River, south of King William Island, after which it was named Back River. Joseph Walker explored area of Great Salt Lake, named river and lake east of Sierra Nevada, and discovered Walker Pass in southern Sierras.

Discovery and Exploration

1838—44 Frémont made meticulously accurate surveys of Mississippi–Missouri area and of Des Moines River. In 1842 began settlement of great plains after discounting Pike's conclusions; then undertook two-year exploration and survey of western belt from Columbia River south almost to Los Angeles – after this California settlers arrived in great numbers.

1845 Franklin and Crozier sailed to look for North-west Passage, but in mid-1846 their two ships became ice-bound north of King William Island. Franklin died 1847, and in spring 1848 Crozier led survivors away from the doomed ships, intending to reach Back River.

1847 John Richardson and John Rae on expedition from Mackenzie Bay eastwards in combined survey and search for Franklin; forced by ice to abandon journey at Coronation Gulf.

1848–9 James C Ross, Leopold McClintock and Robert McClure sailed in attempt to trace Franklin by following his intended route, but only reached Somerset Island.

1850 Onwards

1850 McClure and Richard Collinson began search for North-west Passage and Franklin by approaching eastwards from Bering Strait. McClure discovered

Seamen prepare a large ship for the long cold winter at Quebec. (Mary Evans Picture Library)

openings from Beaufort Sea which would provide a passage, ice-permitting.

1850 John Ross and McClintock searched fruitlessly on Prince Wales and Melville islands for Franklin.

1851 John Rae mapped 700 miles (1,125 km) of Victoria Island, while searching for lost expedition.

1853 Rae met Eskimo north of Repulse Bay who provided account and evidence of deaths of all (nearly 140) in Franklin's expedition.

1857 McClintock found notes, relics, etc, of Franklin expedition.

1861 American Civil War broke out.

1865 Confederates capitulated at Appomattox. Lincoln assassinated.

1888 Fridtjof Nansen and Otto Sverdrup on expedition to interior of Greenland established vast thickness of ice-cap.

1891–5 Two expeditions by Peary to northern Greenland. On second, crossed from Hayes Peninsula to Independence Fjord on east coast.

1895–1902 Peary explored Ellesmere Island and rounded Greenland's northernmost point from west to Peary Land.

1903–6 Roald Amundsen, in the *Gjöa*, became first to navigate North-west Passage, via Lancaster Sound, Peel Sound and Franklin Strait, James Ross Strait, Queen Maud Gulf, Dease Strait to Amundsen Gulf and Beaufort Sea, eventually arriving at Nome, Alaska.

1906–12 Stefansson, living with various Eskimo tribes, made extensive scientific study of Canada's far northern territory.

South America

1400–1600

South America – after a map by Sebastian Münster in 1540. The Magellan Strait separates the continent from the unknown southern continent (actually Tierra del Fuego), and a gruesome picture of an Amazonian shelter warns that the area is frequented by cannibals.

1498 Columbus, on third voyage to New World, sailed through Gulf of Paria after discovering Trinidad. Landed on mainland but did not realize it was a large landmass, and attributed the sea's low salinity (diluted by the Orinoco) to one of the 'Rivers of Paradise'.

1499 Amerigo Vespucci discovered more of northern coast, but was also unaware of extent of landmass.

1500 Cabral, attempting to miss unfavourable Gulf of Guinea winds on way to Cape of Good Hope, sailed too far east, and discovered Brazilian coast north of present-day Caravelas, claiming land for Portugal. First indication that extensive landmass lay south of West Indies.

1500 Vicente Pinzón landed on Brazilian coast at about present-day Recife, and sailing north-west along coast discovered mouth of Amazon, which he named Rio Santa Maria de la Mar Dulce.

1501–2 Vespucci led Portuguese expedition to discover extent of Brazilian coast. Although his claim to have reached 50°S was probably false, he established that South America was a continent and helped dispel the belief that the 'New World' had anything to do with Asia.

1507 The geographer Waldseemüller named the continent America after Amerigo Vespucci.

1520 Magellan's expedition wintered at Port St Julian after exploring Rio de la Plata. Resumed voyage south in October and entered Magellan Strait with three ships. South-west route to Pacific discovered when ocean was entered in November.

1522 Pascual de Andagoya brought back first report indicating existence of Inca civilization in Peru, after leading coastal survey south of Panama almost to Cabo Corrientes.

Pizarro, for once not victorious, is forced to retreat by Inca warriors. (Mary Evans Picture Library)

A Portuguese ship of 1569 sails out of harbour. The great voyages of discovery were undertaken in ships that were surprisingly small, and the proportions in this painting by Brueghel are fairly accurate. (The National Maritime Museum, London)

1524 Francisco Pizarro and Diego de Almagro made first, but abortive voyage in search of Peru, turning back shortly after Cabo Corrientes.

1526 Pizarro and Almagro made second voyage and at Tumbes received confirmation of wealthy Inca civilization. Continued south to Chimbote, while Almagro went back to Panama for more men and money.

1526 Sebastian Cabot reached Cabo São Roque, bound for the Orient, but spent nearly three years searching Rio de la Plata for possible route to Pacific.

1530 Portuguese began colonization of Brazil.

1531 Pizarro, four half brothers and Almagro sailed again for Peru, where internal conflict and diseases brought

by invaders had rocked and weakened the Inca kingdom.

1532 Pizarro landed on Peru coast and reached Cajamarca.

1533 Atahuallpa and many Incas murdered by Pizarro's Conquistadores after bulk of Inca gold obtained by deception.

1533 Almagro stopped de Alvarado's attempt to conquer and destroy kingdom of Quito (present-day Ecuador).

1534 Conquistadores sacked Inca capital of Cusco and completed defeat of Incas.

1536 Quesada entered Magdalena River estuary on Colombia's Caribbean coast and defeated last wealthy Indians, the Chibcha, on plains of Bogotá.

1536 Almagro, given governorship of

land south of Peru, toured area but was angered by lack of riches in Chile compared to Peru.

1537 Incas rose against Pizarro and besieged Cusco, isolating it from Lima. Almagro returned to Peru and drove back Incas, but then usurped control and occupied Cusco.

1538 Pizarro defeated Almagro and had him executed.

1540 Colony in northern Chile founded by Pedro de Valdivia.

1540–2 Francisco de Orellana and Gonzalo Pizarro travelled from Cusco to Quito, and to east slope of Andes. Orellana went down Coca and Napo Rivers, then to the Marañon and down Amazon, becoming first to discover extent of river, and to cross continent.

1541–6 Valdivia founded Santiago and pushed south to Bío Bío River.

1550 Southern part of Chile conquered by Spanish expeditions; Concepción founded by Valdivia.

1569–71 Quesada travelled east from Bogotá plains to Venezuela and explored upper area of Orinoco River.

1577 Francis Drake negotiated Magellan Strait and was blown southeast in storm, so discovering Drake Passage. Sailed north up coasts of Chile, Peru and Ecuador, plundering Spanish shipping; attacked Valparaiso and Callao.

1595–6 Walter Raleigh ventured up Orinoco and Caroní rivers in search of 'El Dorado'; explored Lake Parime and other rivers on Guiana coast.

1600–1750

1617 Raleigh, with son and Lawrence Keymis, returned to Guiana. Raleigh remained at Trinidad ill with fever while Keymis explored Orinoco and then attacked Spanish. Raleigh's son killed; Keymis committed suicide.

1644 Dutch conquests of Portuguese in Indian Ocean also gave them governorship of Brazil.

1645 Portuguese in Brazil rebelled against Dutch rule.

1654 Dutch lost Brazil to Portugal.

1674 French Guiana established.

1713 Peace of Utrecht: Spain ceded San Sacramento north of Rio de la Plata to Portugal.

1735 La Condamine began eight-year scientific expedition to area between Quito and Cuenca – largely concerned with determining shape and dimensions of earth, but making many other observations.

1743 La Condamine made first scientific voyage down full length of Amazon River to Atlantic Ocean, opening much of central South America to further study.

1750–1850

1766 England took possession of Falkland Islands – ceded by Spain in 1771 but not settled until 1833.

1776 Spanish Viceroyalty of River Plate established (comprising Argentine, Bolivia, Paraguay, Uruguay).

1799 With protection of Spanish king, Alexander von Humboldt began expedition to establish link between Orinoco and Amazon systems (joined by Casiquiare). Made great number of botanical and other scientific observations while tracing Orinoco river, part of Negro, and Casiquiare.

1801–3 Humboldt's second expedition to South America landed at Cartagena on Colombia's Caribbean coast; followed Magdalena River and travelled south along Andes to Cotopaxi, Cajamarca and Lima.

1801 Portugal ceded part of Guiana to Spain.

1803 British captured Dutch Guiana.

1811 Paraguay declared independence from Spain and Argentine.

1813–16 Colombia, Uruguay and Chile declared independence from Spain.

1815 Brazil became Empire under Prince John of Portugal.

1821–5 Brazil declared independence from Portugal, Peru from Spain. Bolivia declared independence.

1830 Colombia divided into Venezuela, Colombia and Ecuador.

1832–5 Charles Darwin carried out exploration and scientific observations on east and west coasts of Patagonia and traversed southern region, on first stage of HMS *Beagle* circumnavigation.

1848–61 Large scale scientific expedition to Amazon mouth and Tocantins River by Alfred Wallace and Henry Bates. Joined 1849 by Richard Spruce and Herbert Wallace. Explored Amazon basin from Santarém base, later from Manaus. 1851 Herbert Wallace died. 1852 Alfred Wallace left Brazil after collecting specimens from Orinoco and Uaupés Rivers. Bates also explored Tapajós River and returned to England 1855 with nearly 15,000 specimens. Spruce left in 1861, after travelling into western foothills and up to Andes.

1850 Onwards

1865–70 Paraguay at war with Argentina, Brazil and Uruguay.

1906–10 Fawcett made three expeditions to survey Peru/Bolivia/Brazil border areas; another expedition 1913–14.

1913 Theodore and Kermit Roosevelt, with Candido Rondon, explored course of Rio Duvido to Amazon, and followed Amazon to Atlantic.

1925 On exploration of Mato Grosso area, travelling eastwards in search of a 'lost city', Fawcett disappeared with all members of his expedition.

Africa

Ancient History

c 2270 BC Herkhuf, governor of Egypt's southern province, made expedition up Nile into Central Africa – mainly for ivory, frankincense and ebony, but also brought back a pygmy.

c 1490 BC Nehsi commissioned by Queen Hatshepsut to make Egypt's first major journey by sea, to Punt near Gulf of Aden.

c 600 BC According to later writings of Herodotus, Phoenicians, led by Nechos, circumnavigated Africa.

c 500 BC Carthaginia became dominant sea power and its colonies occupied much of North African coast.

c 450 BC Herodotus drew world map, showing Africa surrounded by sea.

c 450 BC Carthaginians discovered Madeira, Canaries, Azores. Hanno became first true explorer – after founding six cities in region of present-day Moroccan Atlantic coast, sailed south and founded Cerne, probably at mouth of Senegal River; went on to Sierra Leone and possibly into Gulf of Guinea.

AD 42 Paulinus crossed mountain range between Grand Atlas and Sahara Atlas and ventured short distance into Sahara, on one of very few Roman journeys of non-military exploration.

The Middle Ages

1325 Ibn-Batuta left Tangier for Cairo, beginning years of travel in Arabia and the East.

1349–53 Ibn-Batuta travelled south from Tangier across Grand Atlas and Sahara to discover Niger near Djeuné; visited Timbuktu and Kabara, and returned via Tamanrassct.

1400–1600

1415 Portuguese established foothold in North Africa with capture of Ceuta; Prince Henry ('the Navigator') became governor of Ceuta.

1432 Cabral rediscovered Azores, claiming the islands for Portugal.

1433 Gil Eannes sailed to Tenerife in Canaries, but Portuguese superstition that the world ended beyond Cape Bojador forced him to turn back.

1434 Eannes first to sail beyond Cape Bojador.

1435 Eannes and Baldaya landed at Bay of Rio de Oro, near Tropic of Cancer, and noticed human and camel tracks.

1436 Baldaya reached southern extremity of Moslem territory in Africa, but was unable to contact inhabitants in vicinity of Cape Blanc.

1445 Dinis Dias reached mouth of Senegal, and possibly Cape Verde.

1455 Cadamosto reached Gambia River; explored short way up river but was driven away by natives. Possibly discovered Cape Verde Islands.

Discovery and Exploration

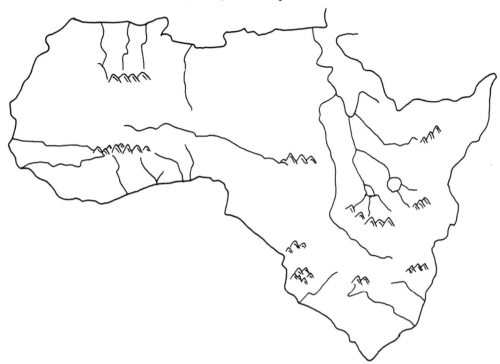

Africa – after a woodcut of 1508 used in a book about Portuguese travels to India. It can already be seen that explorers were going to have difficulty in discovering the facts about the Nile, the Niger, Lake Chad and the lakes of Central Africa.

1458–60 Diogo Gomes, the last to lead Portuguese fleet for Prince Henry, reached Cape Palmas and, with Cadamosto, supplied valuable accounts of Gambia and Senegal rivers. Could also have been discoverer of Cape Verde Islands.

1469–74 Contract given to Fernão Gomes by King Alfonso to explore 100 leagues of Africa's Guinea coast per year in exchange for trading rights; Gomes reached Point St Catherine.

1482 Diogo Cam led first voyage for King John II; discovered mouth of Congo River and went on south to Cabo Santa Maria (13° 26′).

1485 Cam's second voyage; erected *padroa* at Cape Cross, north of Walvis Bay, and sailed as far south as 22° 10′.

1486–90 Pedro da Covilhã commissioned to find overland route to India and to link up with Prester John. De Paiva undertook search for Prester John in Ethiopia, and da Covilhã went to India and Persian Gulf, before also travelling to Ethiopia.

1487 Bartolomeu Dias led three ships on expedition to find southern end of African continent.

1488 Storms in early January blew Dias beyond Cape Point; after briefly sailing west, Dias realized he had passed south of Africa; then he turned north and sighted land on 3 February. Continued east to Algoa Bay but turned back off the Great Fish River.

1491 Portugal sent major expedition to Angola.

1497–9 Vasco da Gama sailed south to find route to India, rounded Cape of Good Hope in November, and on Christmas Day sailed past and named Natal. Moslem opposition at East African ports caused delays until a pilot was taken on at Malindi for voyage to India.

1500 Four ships on Portugal's second mission to India sank in storm off Cape of Good Hope; Bartolomeu Dias one of those drowned.

1505–7 Portugal established factories in East African ports to increase facilities in opposition to Moslem dominance.

1562 Slave trade between West Africa and America started; first expeditions to African coast led by John Hawkins.

1574 Portugal began to colonize Angola.

1600–1750

1613 Source of Blue Nile at Lake Tana first seen by Pedro Paez, Jesuit missionary at Ethiopian court.

c 1628 Jerônimo Lobo made two expeditions to Gondar and Lake Tana, and followed Blue Nile downstream past Tisisat Falls.

1652 Cape Town founded by Dutch as staging post en route to the East.

1660 Royal African Company founded for trading in West Africa (mainly slaves).

1672 English Guinea Company merged with Royal African Company to secure slave trade monopoly.

1682 Danes settled colony on Gold Coast.

1687–9 Brandenburgian (later Prussian) colony established at Arguin, Guinea. French Huguenots settled at Cape of Good Hope. Dutch founded settlement on Gold Coast. Natal became Dutch Colony.

1721 Last Prussian factories and colonies sold to Dutch by this date.

1750–1850

1752 August Beutler led a group along Africa's southern coast past Algoa Bay to Great Kei River.

1768–73 James Bruce carried out first scientific expedition to Lake Tana and source of Blue Nile, and followed river all the way to Cairo. Despite seeing entrance of White Nile at Khartoum, he assumed that Lake Tana was main source.

1777–9 Robert Gordon and William Paterson among first to explore southern coast of Africa and penetrate into South African highveld. Orange River discovered.

1787 Sierra Leone became settlement for freed negro slaves and homeless children.

1788 Association for Promoting the Discovery of the Interior Parts of Africa founded – generally known as the African Association.

1790 In bid to discover course of Niger River, Daniel Houghton explored inland from mouth of Gambia, but was led into desert and abandoned to die.

1795 Mungo Park, on expedition from mouth of Gambia, reached Niger at Ségou, and returned to Gambia via Bamako.

1798 On one of the longest single expeditions of that time, Friedrich Hornemann travelled from Cairo past Siwah Oasis to Marzūq and then south across Sahara to Lake Chad. From there he tried to reach the Niger, but died after travelling to Kano and Katsina.

1798 Francisco de Lacerda explored Zambezi River from mouth to Quebrabasa Rapids; turned north to Luangwe River but in effort to reach west coast, died near Lake Mweru.

1804 First crossing of Africa from Luanda, via Cuanza River, Lake Mweru, Luangwe and Zambezi Rivers, by Pedra Baptista and Amaro José.

1805 Mungo Park's second expedition to the Niger ended when Park and others drowned in Bussa rapids, after travelling along the river from Sansanding, near Ségou.

1806 Britain occupied Cape of Good Hope.

1812–14 John Campbell one of first British missionaries to venture from Cape Town east along coast to Algoa Bay, and inland to present-day Transvaal and Botswana. In 1820 Campbell discovered source of Limpopo River.

1816 From Dakar, René-Auguste Caillé explored towards Senegal River, then to the Gambia.

1817–20 Robert Moffat became one of the most widely travelled missionaries in South Africa on journeys between Cape Town and his Botswana and Kuruman missions.

1818 Expedition organized by British Government to cross Sahara ended a short distance into the Fezzan after the leader, Joseph Ritchie, died at Marzūq.

1822 Alexander Gordon Laing made short expedition north-east from Freetown towards the Niger's source.

1822–5 Major expedition led by Hugh Clapperton, with Dixon Denham and Walter Oudney, left Tripoli and crossed Sahara Desert to Lake Chad. Oudney later died at Kano, but Clapperton continued to Sokoto and returned via Kano and Katsina to Marzūq and Tripoli.

1825 Clapperton's second expedition, with Richard Lander, approached from Gulf of Guinea, crossed the Niger and went on to Kano and Sokoto. Clapperton died at Sokoto, but Lander returned to coast.

1825–6 Alexander Laing became the first European known to have reached Timbuktu, having crossed Sahara from Tripoli, via Grand Erg Oriental to In Salah. Murdered not long after leaving the city.

1827–8 René Caillié arrived in Timbuktu one year after leaving west coast, and reached Tangier after crossing Sahara to Fez and Rabat; thus became the first European to live to describe the Moslem centre.

1830–2 Richard and John Lander successfully located final course and mouth of the Niger by sailing downstream from Bussa. Captured by Ibos, but eventually freed for ransom.

1830–5 Moffat made two expeditions from Kuruman into present-day central Transvaal, almost to source of Olifants River.

1834 Richard Lander travelled up Niger River on trading expedition, but was attacked and died of his wounds.

1838 Battle of Blood River, Natal, between Boers and Zulus.

1841 David Livingstone joined Moffat at his Kuruman mission.

1843 Natal proclaimed British colony.

1848 Sir Harry Smith annexed country between Orange and Vaal Rivers for Britain.

1848 Johannes Rebmann made first journey into East Africa and discovered

Richard and John Lander, explorers of the Niger River, parley with a tribal chief in West Africa. (Mary Evans Picture Library)

Mount Kilimanjaro. In 1849 joined by Johann Krapf, who discovered Mount Kenya. Tales heard by Krapf about high mountain ranges and a vast inland sea in East Africa, led to the Royal Geographical Society commissioning the search for the Nile.

1849–51 Livingstone made first major expeditions from new mission at Kolobeng, first to Lake Ngami in northern Kalahari, and later north to the Zambezi, returning via Linyanti.

1850 Onwards

1850–5 First really sound scientific exploration of Central and West Africa and Sahara carried out by Heinrich Barth, sole survivor of the Richardson/Overweg/Barth expedition that set out from Tripoli. Richardson died before Lake Chad, and Overweg died after exploring the lake's northern area. Barth continued alone via Kano and Katsina to Sokoto and to Timbuktu, then returned to Tripoli at end of 10,000 mile (16,000 km) expedition.

1852 South African Republic established.

1852–6 Livingstone left Cape Town to explore Zambezi, and followed its course upstream from north of Linyanti, then ventured into southern watershed of Congo. Reached Cuanza River and Luanda on Atlantic coast before returning to Zambezi. In November 1855 discovered Victoria Falls, and arrived at Quelimane in 1856.

1855 Richard Burton and John Speke

began first Nile River expedition, but abandoned it near Berbera after being attacked.

1857 On second expedition Burton and Speke travelled west from Bagamoyo to Tabora and continued west to discover Lake Tanganyika (then called the Sea of Ujiji). After hearing of another lake they returned to Tabora, and Speke went north to discover Lake Victoria.

1857–61 Moffat made long expeditions into present-day Zimbabwe as far as Matabeleland and Que Que and the Sabi River.

1858–63 Livingstone made numerous journeys inland from Quelimane and up Rovuma River; discovered Lake Shirwa and Lake Nyasa (Lake Malawi).

1859–61 Henri Duveyrier travelled extensively with the feared but little-known Tuaregs in northern Sahara.

1860–3 Speke and James Grant explored west and north of Lake Victoria, discovered Ripon Falls, followed this river (the early White Nile) intermittently and rejoined it downstream from Lake Albert; thus discovered, though did not prove, the Nile's source.

1862 Samuel Baker began attempt to trace source of Nile by following the river upstream. After meeting Speke and Grant at Gondokoro, Baker went on to discover Lake Albert and Murchison Falls.

1865 Friedrich Gerhard Rohlfs, who had been travelling in North Africa since 1862, became first to cross North Africa from Mediterranean to Gulf of Guinea (Tripoli – Lake Chad – Niger – Lagos). Rohlfs also explored Abyssinian highlands, Libyan Desert and other parts of Africa until 1881.

1866 Livingstone commissioned by Royal Geographical Society to determine relationship of Nile and East African lakes. On way to Ujiji discovered Lake Bangweulu. Explored west from Lake Tanganyika and Ujiji to Nyangwe on the Lualaba, which he speculated could be part of Nile.

1868–74 Gustav Nachtigal made significant journey from Tripoli to Lake Chad and then became first to cross south-eastern desert from Kousseri on Lake Chad to Nile river south of Khartoum.

1869–71 Bahr-el Ghazal watershed west of the Nile (at about 9°N) explored by Georg Schweinfurt, who also discovered Uele River and northern Nile-Congo watershed.

1871 Britain annexed Kimberley diamond fields.

1871 H M Stanley, on 'rescue' expedition for *The New York Herald*, found Livingstone at Ujiji on Lake Tanganyika and explored northern parts of lake with the missionary. Later unable to persuade Livingstone to leave the interior.

1872 Second 'rescue Livingstone' expedition led by Cameron who only arrived in Africa after the missionary's death. After travelling to the Lualaba – and correctly concluding it was part of the Congo – Cameron continued to Benguela, so becoming first to cross equatorial Africa.

1874 Stanley began greatest of his expeditions, first travelling from Zanzibar to Lake Victoria where he proved that the only outlet was the Nile. Then explored entire shoreline of Lake Tanganyika, continued to the Lualaba, and followed it to the Congo and eventually the Atlantic, reaching Boma 999 days after leaving Zanzibar. By then, his hair had turned grey and only a third of the expedition was alive.

1878 Lukuga River established as the only outlet from Lake Tanganyika by Joseph Thomson, who also discovered

Stanley made use of various collapsible boats in Africa; some were made of steel and some, as here, of wood. (Mary Evans Picture Library)

Lake Rukwa. He later led expedition from Mombasa to find new route to Lake Victoria and discovered Lake Baringo.

1880 French military expedition led by Flatters attempted to survey railway route across Sahara, from Algiers and Ouargla through Ahaggar Mountains – where Flatters and most of the expedition were killed by Tuaregs.

1883 Stanley, on Congo expedition for King of Belgium, discovered Lake Tumba and Lake Leopold.

1885 Gold discovered in Transvaal.

1888 Stanley travelled up Congo River and across Africa to Lake Albert to bring out the beleaguered Emin Pasha. On way to Bagamoyo with Emin, discovered Semliki River linking Lake Edward to Lake Albert, and Ruwenzori Mountain range, thus finalizing details of lakes and rivers in that area.

1888 Samuel Teleki discovered Lake Rudolf, Omo River and Lake Stefanie.

1898 Second French attempt to forge railway link across Sahara led by Fernand Foureau escorted by Major Lamy; successfully reached Kousseri, but an attack there cost Lamy his life. Foureau continued south down the Chari and then the Ubangi to the Congo and the Atlantic.

1898 Kitchener defeated Khalifa's Dervishes at Omdurman.

1899 Boer War broke out.

1902 Cecil Rhodes died. Boer War ended by Peace of Vereeniging.

Asia and Indonesia

Ancient History

327–323 BC After conquest of Persia, Alexander the Great continued towards India, explored Sogdiana, Bactria and Punjab, sailed down Indus, travelled overland along Makran coast back to Persia. Alexander sent expeditions to explore shores of Caspian Sea, and Arabian coast of Persian Gulf.

138 BC Chang Ch'ien travelled from China to Central Asia in search of allies against the Huns. Information brought back helped establish Silk Route. Later travelled to Tarim Basin, Sinkiang Province, Afghanistan and west Turkistan, and made contact with outposts of Greek influence.

25 BC Early knowledge of part of Arabia gained from expedition led by Aelius Gallus to Marib.

The Middle Ages

c 535 AD China described as accessible by sea in writings of Indicopleustes, with observation that it was shorter to go overland via Persia.

629 AD Hsuan-tsang began 16-year journey of religious exploration from China to Bactria, Kashmir and India.

630 AD Mohammed conquered Mecca, marking beginning of expansion of Islam to become dominant African and Asian trading empire.

1227 Genghis Khan died after expanding Mongol empire to cover vast area of Central and Eastern Asia. In 1234 it spread from Caspian Sea to Yellow Sea.

1245 Carpini, on Papal peace mission, travelled from Rome to Syra Orda, near Karakoram, in Mongolia.

1253–5 William of Rubrouck left Constantinople and travelled north of Caspian and Aral Seas to meet Mongol ruler of upper Volga River; then journeyed to central court of Great Khan at Karakoram, becoming first European in the city.

1255–69 Maffeo and Niccolo Polo became the first Europeans to reach China (which they called Cathay) and to enter Kublai Khan's capital of Cambaluc (now Peking), after following Silk Trade route.

1271–95 Marco Polo left Venice with his father and uncle (Niccolo and Maffeo Polo) and travelled to Cambaluc in Cathay via Jerusalem, Persia, the Pamirs, the Taklamakan and Gobi Deserts. Remained in service of Kublai Khan and travelled all over Far East before beginning return journey via South China Sea, Malaya and Strait of Malacca, Sumatra, Ceylon and Persian Gulf to Constantinople.

1318 Odoric of Pordenone began 12-year mission to the East; travelled to Canton by sea from Persian Gulf and Strait of Malacca; from Canton went overland to Peking, and eventually returned through Tibet and Hindu Kush.

1400–1600

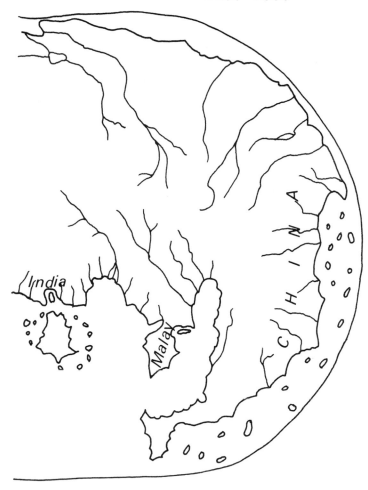

East Asia – after a world map drawn by Henricus Martellus in c 1490.

1444 Niccolo dei Conti returned to Venice after travels lasting 25 years through many parts of India, Indonesia and South-east Asia, bringing back information of enormous benefit to geographers and map makers.

1488 Pedro da Covilhã arrived in India on commission from Portugal's Henry the Navigator to find suitable overland route to the East. Returned to Africa via north-west coast of India, across Arabian Sea to Gulf of Oman, and then to Aden.

1498 In May Vasco da Gama's voyage to chart sea route round Cape of Good Hope ended at anchor off Calicut, but hostile reception from Moslems drove da Gama to Goa.

1500 Cabral arrived at Goa on second Portuguese expedition via newly found Cape, but also met considerable opposition at Calicut.

1502 Da Gama sailed with 30 ships on third major expedition from

Vasco da Gama, the first to arrive at India by sea, pays his respects to an Eastern potentate in 1498. (Mary Evans Picture Library)

Portugal to the East. In a show of force da Gama set fire to a laden passenger ship off Cannanore, bombarded Calicut, and murdered many Hindu fishermen. Made trading alliance at Cochin in opposition to Arabs and Moslem supremacy.

1502 Ludovico di Varthema began voyage from Venice on which he discovered Spice Islands (Moluccas). In 1503 he became first European Christian known to have visited Mecca. He travelled to west and east coasts of India as well as Siam and Bay of Bengal, before sailing through Strait of Malacca to Spice Islands.

1503 Portugal built first fortress in Asia, at Cochin on south-west Indian coast.

1505 Francisco de Almeida, appointed as first Portuguese representative in the East, arrived at Cochin with task of overcoming Moslem trade supremacy.

1509 After destruction of Mombasa, Portuguese defeated combined Arab/Indian fleet in battle off Diu, and set up trading post at Pedir, in Sumatra.

1510 Alfonso d'Albuquerque succeeded Almeida in the East, and took Goa.

Portugal then had control of Western Indian Ocean (Hormuz and Socotra had already been taken).

1511 Portuguese established final dominance of trade in the East with capture of Malacca.

1513 First Portuguese ships reached China taking Cape of Good Hope sea route.

1521 After Magellan's death in Philippines during his circumnavigation, del Cano sailed through Moluccas — first European ship to approach them from Pacific.

1537–52 Fernão Pinto arrived in India at start of his travels in the East; probably first European to visit Japan.

1542–51 Francis Xavier undertook missionary travelling after arriving at Goa in 1542. In 1549 he was first Christian missionary to visit Japan.

1553 Hugh Willoughby led first English attempt to find North-east Passage to Orient, but later died in shipwreck west of Novaya Zemlya.

1554 Richard Chancellor's ship survived storm in Willoughby expedition, and he landed at Colmagro (Archangel). Went into largely unknown

Muskovy (Russia) to Moskva and opened Anglo-Russian trade with agreement of Czar Ivan.

1557 Anthony Jenkinson travelled from Moskva to Volga River, Astrakan and Caspian Sea, but prevented by Mongol ruler from going beyond Bukhara.

1561 Jenkinson began second expedition from Moskva, travelled down Caspian Sea to Qazvin in Persia, and became first European to open trade links with Persia.

1581 Yermak Timofeyevich and Cossacks began offensive expedition into Siberia against Mongols, and captured capital of Sibir. Tobolsk established nearby in 1587.

1583 John Newberry, Ralph Fitch and William Leeds left England for India seeking alternative to Dutch-dominated Cape route. Leeds joined court of Mogul Emperor at Fatephur Sikri (near Agra); Newberry headed back for England, but disappeared.

1585 Fitch left Fatephur Sikri and began six-year exploration of northern India, the Irrawaddy valley into Shan State, and travelled to Malacca and Ceylon.

1589 Jan van Linschoten retired from service with Portuguese in Goa and provided information and impetus for Dutch to challenge Portuguese trading supremacy in the East.

1591 James Lancaster made first English voyage to East Indies via Cape of Good Hope, and plundered shipping in Strait of Malacca.

1595 Cornelius Houtman led first

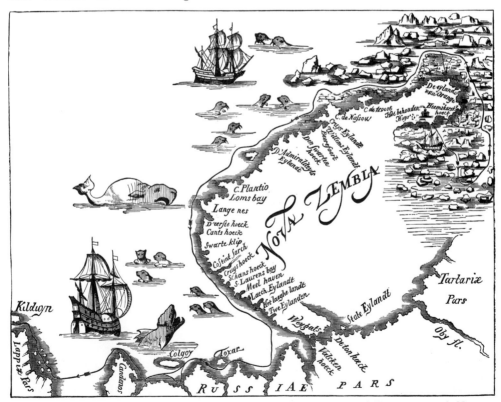

A contemporary map showing the route taken by Barents and his followers around Novaya Zemlya. (Mary Evans Picture Library)

Dutch trading expedition to East Indies under commission to group of Amsterdam merchants.

1596 On third attempt to find North-east Passage, Willem Barents discovered Bear Island and Spitzbergen and sailed around northern end of Novaya Zemlya before ship became icebound. Barents supervised heroic survival on the islands, but died in 1597 on the journey to safety.

1598–1601 Oliver van Noort made fourth circumnavigation of the world – the first by a Dutchman.

1600–1750

1601–3 First voyage on behalf of East India Company led by Lancaster, who established first English trading post, on Java.

1602 Dutch East India Company formed, forcing Portuguese decline in Moluccas.

1603 Bento de Goes began overland journey from Agra to Lahore, Kabul, through Hindu Kush and Pamirs to Yarkand. Visited jade mines at Khota (Ho-tien) and in 1605 reached Suchow, sending messenger to Peking. Return of messenger in 1607 established positive identification of all areas visited by land and sea since Marco Polo's journeys. This was first overland journey to China for some 300 years.

1604 Henry Middleton led second East India Company voyage to East Indies, but increased Dutch opposition made voyage unsuccessful.

1614 English trading post established at Surat.

1615 Dutch occupied Moluccas. Thomas Roe sent as first English ambassador to Mogul court.

1616 Invasion of China by Manchu Tartars.

1617 Elisei Busa, a Cossack, discovered Yana River in Siberia.

1619 Dutch founded Batavia and Java.

1622 English captured Hormuz.

1624 First English settlement formed in East India. Antonia de Andrade left Agra on mission to Tibet, via Badrinath and Mana Pass to Tsaparang, where he established a church.

1626 Cacella and Cabral travelled from mouth of Ganges to Cooch Behar, through Bhutan to Tibet, and founded mission at Shigatse.

1627 Thomas Herbert wrote popular account of Persian travels, including journey from Bandar Abbas to Isfahan. Foreigners excluded from Japan.

1631 Francisco de Azevado travelled from Agra to Tsaparang and then to Leh in bid to set up permanent mission in western Himalayas.

1639 English factory and settlement founded at St George, later Madras.

1641–6 Expeditions led by Stadukhin and Poyarkov which pushed Russian frontiers further east to discover Kolyma, Aldan and Amur Rivers. Portugal surrendered Malacca to Dutch.

1644–9 Deshnef and Stadukhin travelled down Kolyma River, sailed through Strait to Kamchatka, but no credit given for this discovery (subsequently Bering Strait).

1644 End of Ming dynasty in China; Manchu dynasty began.

1656 Dutch began trading with China, and took Colombo in Ceylon from Portuguese.

1661 Bombay ceded to England by Portugal; Dutch retained rule over Ceylon.

1661 Albert d'Orville and Johann Grueber travelled from Peking across Ordos Desert and reached Lhasa, going on to Shigatse, through Nepal and Ganges plain to Agra. Journey provided valuable up-to-date information about Eastern and Central Asia.

1683 Formosa conquered by China and Dutch traders established in Canton – two years before all Chinese ports were opened to foreign trade.

1690 Calcutta established as English trading post and factory.

1700 France backed her growing interest in the East with despatch of first legation to China.

1714 Desideri and Emmanuel Freyre travelled from Delhi to Lahore and across Himalayas to Leh, then east up Indus valley and Matsang Tsangpo to Shigatse and Lhasa. Desideri remained in Tibet until 1721.

1719–27 Extensive scientific exploration of Siberia by Messerschmidt and Strahlenberg. Travelled from Moscow to Tobolsk, Tomsk and the Ob, and reached Turukhansk in the north, and Irkutsk on Lake Baykal in the south.

1725 Vitus Bering left St Petersburg to determine existence of Deshnef's strait between Asia and America, for Czar Peter. Built ships at Okhotsk and Kamchatka and in 1728 sailed north through strait, briefly west, and back to Kamchatka, though he never sighted North America.

1739 Nadir Shah, Persian king, sacked Delhi and conquered the Punjab.

1740 Bering sailed from Okhotsk and Kamchatka to explore Alaskan coast and seas around Kodiak Island; continued to discover and map many Aleutian islands before he died on Bering Island.

1746 French took Madras. Persecution of Christians in China began.

1750–1850

1757 Clive defeated Bengals at battle of Plassey, NE India.

1761 Expedition of five scientists sent to Arabia by King of Denmark during a lull in Islamic fanaticism. Although all but Carsten Niebuhr died, a great deal of information was obtained about Yemen and south-west Arabia.

1774 First British mission to Tibet, under George Bogle, to establish trade and defence alliance. Bogle, the first Englishman to go beyond Nepal and Bhutan, met Tashi Lama at Shigatse.

1783 Samuel Turner commanded second British mission to Tibet, at Shigatse.

1793 French settlements in India seized by Britain.

1795 Ceylon surrendered to British by Dutch.

1807 Harford Brydges led British mission to Persia to counter Russian influence; travelled from Bombay to Bushire in Persian Gulf, and then to Isfahan, Teheran, Qazvin and Tabriz.

1808 Hyder Hearsey began explorations in Western Himalayas north and east of Dehra Dun, on headwaters of Ganges.

1810 Christie and Pottinger sailed from Bombay to Baluchistan coast west of Karachi and added greatly to knowledge of much of Persia.

1811 Thomas Manning became first Englishman to enter Lhasa and meet Dalai Lama, having travelled from Calcutta through Bhutan.

1812 Hearsey joined by Moorcroft

97

Hong Kong harbour in the 19th century. (The National Maritime Museum, London)

and travelled to Tibet through northern slopes of Himalayas.

1812 Burckhardt discovered ruins of Petra (in Jordan) while travelling from Syria to Cairo. Later visited both Mecca and Medina and gained great knowledge of southern Hejaz region of Arabia.

1819 Singapore founded by British.

1834 Sikhs captured Peshawar. James Wellsted first sighted ruins on South Arabian coast near Bi'r 'Alī. Also made extensive journeys in Oman 'bulge',

and to border of Empty Quarter desert.

1839 Evariste Huc arrived in Macao and lived in South China, then Peking. 'Opium War' fought against China.

1842 Hong Kong ceded to Britain. British forces in Afghanistan massacred.

1844 Huc and Joseph Gabet left Peking, crossed Ordos Desert to Koko Nor and to Lhasa, but were escorted out by Chinese in 1846.

1849 Sikhs surrendered at Rawalpindi, and Britain annexed Punjab.

1850 Onwards

1856 Britain and France at war against China, and Britain against Persia.

1857 Indian Mutiny broke out;

massacre of Cawnpore. England and France captured Canton.

1858 Indian Mutiny suppressed. China war halted, and number of ports opened to European trade.

1860 Vladivostok founded.

1862–7 Kropotkin carried out detailed geological and geographical survey of large parts of Eastern Asia, especially Siberia.

1865 First survey in Himalayas and adjacent regions by 'pundit-explorer' Nain Singh.

1869 Suez Canal opened.

1871–3 First of Przhevalsky's long journeys that eventually brought him to Plateau of Tibet.

1873–4 Long surveying expedition by Nain Singh and Kishen Singh from Leh to Khotan and Yarkand, Pamirs, and Taklamakan.

1876 Przhevalsky located Lop Nor, and discovered Astin Tagh mountains – which prevented him reaching inner Tibet.

1876–8 Charles Doughty made extensive journey in Arabia and was able to describe large areas of the country.

1878–9 Nils Nordenskjöld made first navigation of North-east Passage, sailing from Tromsø to Port Clarence, in Alaska. (He returned via Canton, Ceylon and Suez Canal.)

1878–82 Long surveying expedition by Kishen Singh provided information on country from Darjeeling to Shigatse and Lhasa, Tsaidam Depression and part of Gobi Desert.

1879–80 Przhevalsky made his closest approach to Lhasa, but was turned back when still 170 miles (275 km) from the holy city.

1879 In attempt to make east-west navigation of North-east Passage, Washington de Long's ship, the *Jeanette*, was caught in ice near Herald Island in East Siberian Sea. Most of the expedition perished, but wreckage of the *Jeanette* was eventually brought ashore on Greenland.

1880 End of Afghan war against Britain.

1886–7 Younghusband made extensive exploration of Burma and went on expedition to Peking. Travelled from Peking to western end of Taklamakan and discovered Mustagh Pass through Karakoran Mountains. Later explored and surveyed Karakorans, Pamirs and part of Hindu Kush.

1893–7 First of Sven Hedin's journeys in Central Asia, during which he found valuable archaeological remains, particularly in the Taklamakan. Further expeditions occupied him intermittently until 1928.

1893–1910 Extensive exploration and surveying of Persia and part of Afghanistan carried out by Percy Sykes, principally in connection with Perso-Baluch boundary disputes.

1897–1927 Aurel Stein followed up many of Sven Hedin's finds in Central Asia, and made many valuable archaeological discoveries before China again banned Europeans from the area.

1900 Boxer rising in China. International army entered Peking. Russia occupied Manchuria.

1903–4 British military intervention in Tibet; Younghusband led force to Lhasa, the first European in the city for 60 years.

1930–1 Bertram Thomas made first crossing of the Rub 'al Khālī, Empty Quarter desert, in Arabia.

1953 First ascent of Mount Everest.

Australia, Oceania and the Pacific

1400–1600

1520 Magellan led three remaining ships out of Magellan Strait into Pacific, but no land sighted until the fleet reached Ladrones (now Marianas islands). Sailed on to Philippines, where Magellan and many others were killed. Sebastian del Cano took command and in *Victoria* completed circumnavigation to Spain via Moluccas and Cape of Good Hope.

1527 Cortes sent de Saavedra to Moluccas from west coast of Mexico, but adverse prevailing winds prevented him returning across Pacific.

1529 Treaty of Saragossa defined Spanish-Portuguese division in Pacific, and Spain gave up Moluccas.

1567 Mendaña sailed from Peru in search of Terra Australis but eventually discovered Solomon Islands, although he wrongly fixed their position. Returned to American coast sailing north of Tropic of Cancer.

1578 Drake in *Golden Hind* entered Pacific through Magellan Strait; was blown back in storm to discover Drake Passage.

1579 Drake left North American coast and sailed west across Pacific, sighting Ladrones 68 days later. Concluded

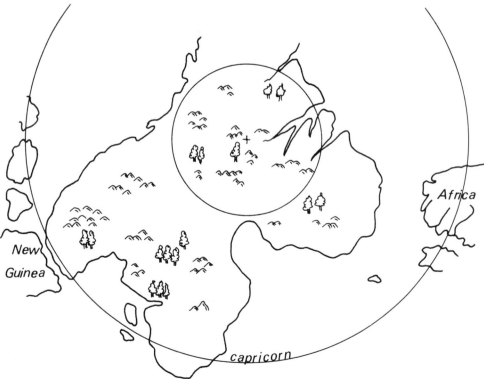

Part of the southern continent – after Cornelius Wytfliet's map of 1597. Terra Australis joins on to Terra Incognita, where trees grow well inside the Antarctic Circle.

trade treaty in Moluccas before sailing to Java, Cape of Good Hope and England.
1595 Mendaña's second voyage across Pacific; unable to locate Solomon Islands again, and died on Santa Cruz Islands. Pedro de Quiros continued voyage to Philippines.

1600–1750

1605 De Quiros sailed from Peru with three ships, but expedition broke up in New Hebrides.
1606 Willem Janz arrived via Indian Ocean to explore southern New Guinea; sailed east along coast but turned south just before Cape York Peninsula, and wrongly concluded that this was part of New Guinea.
1606 After break-up of de Quiros expedition, Luis de Torres sailed west and discovered Torres Strait between New Guinea and Australia's Cape York Peninsula.
1615–17 Schouten and Le Maire first to reach Pacific from Atlantic through Drake Passage, discovering Le Maire Strait and naming Cape Horn. Reached Juan Fernandez Islands, discovered some of Tuamotu Islands, Friendly (Tonga) Islands, and Horn Islands. Sailed to Moluccas via north coast of New Guinea.
1616 Dirk Hartog first to discover and land on Australia's west coast, at Dirk Hartog's Island off Shark Bay.
1618 Dutch mariner Jacobszoon landed at North-west Cape, Western Australia.
1619 Frederick Houtman made landfall at Rottnest Island, off present-day Perth; numerous Dutch landings resulted in Western Australia being known as New Holland, and in 1622 Leeuwin named south-west point of continent Cape Leeuwin.
1627 Thyssen sailed south of Cape Leeuwin, past Point Nuyts and into Great Australian Bight, before turning back for East Indies.
1629 First European settlers (Dutch) landed on Western Australia near present-day Northampton.
1642 Abel Tasman sailed south of Australia, discovered Van Diemen's Land (Tasmania), and continued east to discover west coast of Staaten Land (New Zealand). From Tonga and Fiji Islands sailed to New Britain. 1644 sailed along southern coast of New Guinea and into Gulf of Carpentaria, unaware of Torres Strait discovery. Tasman altogether missed four straits that had a very great bearing on the presentation of maps of south-west Pacific – the Bass, Cook, Dampier and Torres Straits.
1700 William Dampier discovered true north coast of New Guinea, and Dampier Strait west of New Britain.
1721 Roggeveen discovered Easter Island.

1750–1850

1764 Voyage through Pacific by Byron, Carteret and Clerke in search of Terra Australis.
1766 Wallis and Carteret, separated in storm after sailing through Magellan Strait, travelled independently across Pacific. Wallis discovered Tahiti, sailed through Society Islands and discovered

Tasman's carpenter goes ashore at Storm Bay, Tasmania, to choose timber for ship repairs.
(Mary Evans Picture Library)

and named Wallis Islands. Carteret discovered Pitcairn and Admiralty Islands and rediscovered Santa Cruz Islands found by Mendaña.

1767 Bougainville entered Pacific on circumnavigation and search for Terra Australis; turned north by Australia's Barrier Reef; sailed through the 'missing' Solomons, but did not identify them as Mendaña's islands. Discovered Louisiade Archipelago.

1769 On first voyage, Cook discovered east coast of New Zealand, circumnavigated both islands, discovering and naming Cook Strait. Continued west to discover and claim 'New South Wales' at Botany Bay, and sailed up Australia's east coast, inside Great Barrier Reef, rounding Cape York and rediscovering Torres Strait.

1772 Cook's second, longest voyage, during which he explored southern regions of Pacific, was the first to cross Antarctic Circle, and provided proof that no further large land mass (except for any beyond Antarctic Circle) could exist. Rediscovered Marguesas Islands. On this voyage Cook showed that scurvy could be prevented.

1776–9 Cook's third voyage, mainly to search for North-west Passage by approaching it from the west. Discovered Christmas Island and Sandwich Islands (Hawaiian Islands), where he was killed in dispute with islanders. Clerke, and later Gore and King, completed survey of northern Pacific, Aleutians and Kamchatka.

1785–8 Jean de la Pérouse sailed in search of Solomons and whaling and fur prospects in North Pacific. Crossed Pacific from Monterey to Macao, and later from Kamchatka to Friendly Islands, then sailed to Port Jackson, New South Wales. Finally set off to look for Solomons, but was never heard of again.

1788 Penal colony founded at Botany

Captain Cook's Endeavour *off Eastern Australia.* (Mary Evans Picture Library)

Explorers on the River Teramakau in New Zealand, using a raft made from bundles of reeds. (Mary Evans Picture Library)

Bay, New South Wales; later moved to Port Jackson (Sydney).

1791 On expedition to find trace of de la Pérouse, d'Entrecasteaux finally identified and correctly located position of Solomon Islands.

1791 Vancouver and Broughton surveyed portion of New Holland's southern coast, and of Dusky Sound in New Zealand. Broughton discovered Chatham Islands. Vancouver, from base on Sandwich Islands, made extensive survey of America's north-west coast.

1795 George Bass and Matthew Flinders made first inland expedition from Australia's east coast, up Georges River near Botany Bay.

1797–9 Bass discovered Bass Strait, and with Flinders explored Tasmania's coasts and Derwent River.

1801 Nicolas Baudin surveyed New South Wales coast from Port Jackson to Encounter Bay, where he met Matthew Flinders.

1801–2 Matthew Flinders carried out accurate survey of almost all Australian coast, apart from area mapped by Baudin, and coast within Great Barrier Reef.

1813 Gregory Blaxland became first to cross Australia's Blue Mountains from Port Jackson.

1814 Samuel Marsden took Christianity to New Zealand, forming mission at Bay of Islands, and made three major expeditions on North Island.

1818 Hamilton Hume discovered Lake Bathurst, south-west of Port Jackson.

1824 Hume followed course of Murrumbidgee, crossed Murray, and arrived at Port Phillip Bay, site of present-day Melbourne.

1828 Charles Sturt and Hume crossed Blue Mountains, followed Macquarie and discovered Bogan River.

1829 Sturt led expedition down Murrumbidgee and Murray to Encounter Bay, and proved that not all westward-flowing rivers reached a central lake.

1831–6 Thomas Mitchell made number of expeditions to establish relationship of westward-flowing rivers on southern part of Great Dividing Range.

1839 New Zealand proclaimed a colony, and incorporated with colony of New South Wales. Wellington founded by first settlers.

1839 Edward Eyre first saw Lake Torrens, from Mt Eyre, and explored coast between Streaky Bay and Eyre Peninsula. 1840 foiled by salt lakes in attempt to travel to centre of Australia from Spencer Gulf. 1841 arduous journey from Fowler's Bay along Bight coast to Albany and Fremantle.

1840 Maori chiefs handed over sovereignty of New Zealand to Britain.

1841 William Colenso began first of three explorations of New Zealand's North Island.

1844–8 First Maori rising in New Zealand. (Others in 1860–1, 1863–5, 1868.)

1845 Mitchell investigated upper Culgoa and Condamine Rivers in eastern Australia, and discovered northern part of Cooper's Creek-Barcoo River.

1845 First main expedition into New Zealand's South Island, by Thomas Brunner with Heaphy and Fox, down central valley to Lake Rotoroa. Major expedition by Brunner in 1846 as far south as coast due west of Mt Cook.

1847–8 Edmund Kennedy determined direction of Barcoo River, and after returning to Port Jackson set out to explore Queensland. Most members of expedition died of exposure and starvation, and Kennedy was killed by Aborigines.

1850 Onwards

1855–8 Augustus Gregory carried out important exploration of eastern Australia in expeditions between Gulf of Carpentaria and Gulf of St Vincent. His brother, Frank Gregory, discovered number of places suitable for settlement in Western Australia.

1858 Peter Warburton disproved Eyre's 'horseshoe of lakes' theory by travelling between Lakes Torrens and Eyre.

1859 John Stuart discovered The Neales River, west of Lake Eyre. In 1860 began two-year journey in which he crossed Australia from Adelaide to site of present-day Darwin; his route,

via Alice Springs, was later followed by Central Telegraph Line.

1860–1 Expedition led by Burke, with Wills, Grey and King, travelled from Victoria to salt marshes of Gulf of Carpentaria, but only King survived the journey.

1865 Convict transportation to Australia ended.

1870 John Forrest reversed Eyre's epic journey, and travelled from Perth to Yorke Peninsula.

1873 Warburton became first to travel from south Australia to centre and on to west coast, arriving near present-day Port Hedland.

1873 William Gosse discovered Ayers Rock.

1874 John Forrest made first west-to-east crossing of Australia, from Perth, through Gibson Desert, Musgrave Range and Alberga River to Lake Eyre.

1875 Ernest Giles made first inland east-to-west crossing of Australia from Spencer Gulf, round Lake Torrens across Great Victoria Desert to Perth.

1896 Wells and Carnegie (independently) made south-to-north crossings of Western Australian Deserts.

1901 Commonwealth of Australia formed.

North and South Polar Regions

The Arctic — based on an inset in Mercator's world chart of 1569. Both North-east and North-west Passages are shown (probably through hope rather than expectation) and a large rock conveniently tops the world.

1750–1850

1773 Cook in the *Resolution* became first person to cross Antarctic Circle, and crossed it twice more on this voyage (his second major voyage), reaching southernmost point of 71° 10′, and sighting mountain peaks.

1774 Cook discovered South Georgia and South Sandwich Islands.

1818 David Buchan and John Franklin attempted to take advantage of diminished Arctic ice to sail north, but only reached just north of Spitzbergen.

1820–1 Bellingshausen became first to circumnavigate Antarctica, his ship remaining south of 60° for almost the entire voyage. Discovered the first land inside Antarctic Circle, naming it after Peter I and Alexander I.

1823 On sealing expedition, and after surveying South Georgia and South Sandwich Islands, James Weddell crossed Antarctic Circle and reached 74° 15′.

1839–42 James Clark Ross with F R M Crozier, in *Erebus* and *Terror*, made first major scientific voyage to Antarctica. Discovered Ross Sea, Ross Ice Shelf, active volcano Mt Erebus, Victoria Land and Possession Island and Franklin Island. Reached 78° 10′S in Ross Sea.

1840 Jules d'Urville discovered Adélie Land.

1840 On world circumnavigation, Charles Wilkes sailed into number of Antarctic regions.

1850 Onwards

1893 Fridtjof Nansen and Otto Sverdrup made attempt to reach North Pole by drifting with ice pack in the *Fram*, on expedition suggested by fate of Washington de Long's *Jeanette*. Nansen made bid by sledge when *Fram* did not go close enough, and reached 86° 14′.

1900–4 Robert Scott's first expedition to Antarctica with Shackleton, provided first knowledge of plateau. Reached 82° 17′S, and explored 300 miles (480 km) into Victoria Land.

1906 Robert Peary made bid for North Pole, but unable to pass 87° 6′.

1907–8 Shackleton led expedition to McMurdo Sound, made Polar bid, and came within 97 miles (156 km) of South Pole.

1909 In April Peary's expedition became first to reach North Pole.

1911 In December Roald Amundsen's team became first to reach South Pole.

1912 Scott and four companions arrived at South Pole one month after Amundsen.

1914 Douglas Mawson and companions rescued from Antarctica after Mawson had made a 100-mile (160 km) journey on his own to get back to base camp after his colleague died.

1915 Shackleton's expedition in *Endurance* caught in ice. Shackleton managed to get to South Georgia, from where he set out to rescue his crew.

1925 Amundsen and Lincoln Ellsworth attempted to fly over North Pole, but only got within 170 miles (274 km) of it.

1926 Amundsen, Ellsworth and Umberto Nobile crossed Arctic from Spitzbergen in dirigible and flew over North Pole. Byrd claimed to have flown over Pole in conventional aircraft, but evidence casts increasing doubt on

Scott's expedition – Cherry-Garrard, Bowers, Oates, Meares and Atkinson in 'The Tenements'. (Mary Evans Picture Library)

validity of this claim.

1928 Byrd made first flight over North Pole.

1957–8 Vivian Fuchs led first expedition to cross Antarctica, travelling from Shackleton base, Weddell Sea, to McMurdo Sound, Ross Sea.

1958 US nuclear-powered submarine *Nautilus* first to sail under North Pole.

1968–9 Wally Herbert led British Trans-Arctic Expedition, first to make surface crossing of Arctic ice-cap.

1979 After years of trials and preparation, Transglobe Expedition 1979–82, led by Ranulph Fiennes, set out from Greenwich on first ever attempt to circumnavigate world via North and South Poles.

Explorers
and Their Discoveries

ALARCÓN, Hernando de. (fl 1540)

Spanish Conquistador in charge of the supply ships for Coronado's 1540 expedition into North America. He sailed from the mouth of the Rio Grande de Santiago, on the west coast of Mexico, into the Gulf of California, discovering the mouth of the Colorado River and proving that the long promontory was the Californian Peninsula, and not an island. That was the end of his usefulness, however, for when Coronado's men arrived at the Gulf, Alarcón had already sailed back to Mexico.

ALBUQUERQUE, Alfonso d'. 1453–1515

Francisco de Almeida laid the groundwork for European supremacy in the East, and he was succeeded by D'Albuquerque (often known as Alfonso the Great) who completed the structure that enabled Europe to control India and South-East Asia for over 400 years. In 1506 he explored the coast of East Africa with Tristao da Cunha, and in 1507 built a strong fortress on the island of Socotra at the mouth of the Gulf of Aden, before going on to capture Hormuz, a vital island-port where the Persian Gulf bends into the Gulf of Oman. D'Albuquerque was appointed governor of Portuguese India in 1508 and eventually gained control of the trade routes of the western Indian Ocean in 1510, when he conquered Goa. For the Moslem traders, access to the East was then practically impossible and the rest of the major ports quickly fell into the lap of Portugal. Her conquest of Malacca and the Strait

109

Alfonso d'Albuquerque receiving Persian ambassadors who demand a tribute, only to be told that the King of Portugal pays his tribute in cannonballs. (Mary Evans Picture Library)

of Malacca in 1511 gave her final dominance over Eastern trade although later moves against the Arabs and Egyptians in the Red Sea and around Arabia were not successful.

ALEXANDER III, 'The Great', King of Macedonia. 356–323 BC

One of history's most successful conquerors whose brief life was inspired by visionary concepts, an insatiable curiosity and a passionate sense of adventure. Alexander was the son of King Philip II of Macedonia (northern

Greece), and between the ages of 13 and 16 was tutored by Aristotle. After his father was assassinated in 336 BC Alexander inherited the Macedonian kingdom – and also the long-standing confrontation with Persia. He organized a combined Macedonian and Greek force of some 30,000 infantry and 5,000 cavalry, and in 334 BC crossed the Hellespont (Dardanelles) into Asia Minor, determined to conquer Persia and liberate the Greek colonies recently captured by Persia. With considerable ease he established Greek-styled territorial kingdoms, stormed the island city of Tyre (now Sur, between Haifa and Beirut), and crossed the Sinai Desert to conquer Egypt.

He then returned to Asia Minor and advanced across Mesopotamia, defeating the Persian army at Guagamela – though King Darius managed to escape. Continuing south, he crossed the Tigris near present-day Baghdad and before the end of 331 BC had occupied Babylon. Hearing that Darius had been murdered, the Macedonian king proclaimed himself king of Persia as well (he was then only 25 years old). By 327 BC he had occupied Sogdiana and Bactria (parts of what is now Afghanistan and Pakistan), and was prepared to invade India. But a large number of his troops rebelled, longing to begin the homeward trip after seven years of fighting and fearful that they were almost at the 'end' of the world. Alexander reached the Indus River, and from some way down river sent home the sick and wounded on an overland expedition led by Craterus.

(Mary Evans Picture Library)

With the remainder of his expedition, Alexander sailed the rest of the way down the Indus in the spring of 326 BC (Karachi was once known as Alexandria Portus); while the fleet sailed along the Arabian Sea coast, and up the Persian Gulf, the still-faithful part of Alexander's forces began the homeward journey along the Makran coast (now Pakistan's coastal area), eventually turning inland near Gwadar and heading north-west towards Mesopotamia. Throughout his conquests, Alexander had taken the opportunity to explore and make observations, and in the years of consolidating his empire he despatched two major expeditions. One went overland to explore the southern coast of the Caspian Sea, while the other sailed down the Persian Gulf from the Euphrates to explore the Arabian coast of the Gulf.

In the same year Alexander died in Babylonia, ten days after falling ill following a prolonged bout of feasting and drinking. His body, instead of being taken to Macedonia, was sent to Egypt, and was eventually sealed in a gold coffin in Alexandria.

ALMAGRO, Diego de. 1475–1538

One of the first Spanish Conquistadores to carry the conquest into South America. After Pascual de Andagoya's enticing reports of probable wealth south of Panama, Almagro, Pizarro and Hernando de Luque (a priest whose contributions were mainly financial) formed a partnership to explore the country. Pizarro headed the first expedition but Almagro soon followed and accompanied Pizarro on further voyages in 1526–8. The first expedition was disappointing and was forced to return for further assistance from the Governor of Panama. More was accomplished on the second expedition which reached the city of Tumbes on the Gulf of Guayaquil and sailed south to the Santa Pau River. Although the wealth of the Incas was now confirmed, the authorities in Panama were reluctant to finance further exploration. Pizarro eventually got support from the King of Spain, together with the promise of governorship of any lands he conquered. Almagro felt slighted by Pizarro's sudden acquisition of power: he considered that the original 'equal-share' agreement had been broken and resented his now subordinate status. The animosity between the two captains soon contributed to the instability of the new colonies.

While Pizarro was on inland expeditions in Peru in 1533, Almagro was sent to prevent Pedro de Alvarado from attacking Quito (in present-day northern Ecuador). He succeeded in this by buying off Alvarado with the assistance of Sebastian de Benalcazaar, governor of San Miguel – who had himself already captured Quito and its riches. Partly as a reward for this service, and partly as a sop to his resentment over Pizarro's authority, Almagro was given governorship of a southern area stretching some 500 miles (800 km) beyond Pizarro's territory. In July 1535 he left the Inca capital of Cusco (north-west of Lake Titicaca) in Peru to explore his land, made up mainly of what is now Chile.

There was little to enthuse about in that poor and desolate area, and although he claimed the country as far south as Santiago for the King of Spain, Almagro set off on his return journey to Cusco in 1537 disappointed and embittered. When he approached Cusco he found it under siege by the Incas with the Spaniards in considerable danger from the rebels, who had

In a multiple-scene picture, Almagro is captured by Hernando Pizarro, garrotted and publically beheaded. (Mary Evans Picture Library)

prevented relief forces from Lima reaching Cusco. Almagro's arrival was therefore timely, and he managed to drive off the Incas. But it was not long before he decided to use force to get the rewards he considered his due, and he in turn seized Cusco, claiming the old capital for his territory instead of Pizarro's. In 1538, however, his hold on the city was broken, and he was executed by Hernando Pizarro, half-brother of the conqueror of Peru. But three years later Almagro was still so well remembered by his followers that a group of them took revenge and killed Francisco Pizarro.

ALMEIDA, Francisco de. c 1450–1510

The first Portuguese representative in India, appointed by King Manuel in 1505. Leaving Lisbon with 21 ships, Almeida sailed around the Cape of Good Hope. He constructed a fort at Kilwa on the east coast of Africa and then destroyed much of Mombasa – the purpose of both actions being to break up Arabian trade. He then established himself at Cochin in India, but although he forced a trade agreeement with Malacca, the strong hold and hostility of the Moslems there prevented the Portuguese from establishing themselves. When the Arabs and Egyptians began to rise against the growing European challenge, Almeida burned and raided their established ports in India and defeated their combined fleet in the battle of Diu, north-west India, in 1509. His son Lourenco headed the first Portuguese expedition to Ceylon, and founded a settlement at Colombo. Almeida was succeeded by Albuquerque, who completed the Portuguese conquest of the Indian Ocean routes.

ALVARADO, Pedro de. c 1485–1541

A Spanish Conquistador who commanded one of the ships in Grijalva's expedition from Cuba to the Yucatan in 1518, and was subsequently a captain under Cortes in the expedition that landed near present-day Veracruz in April 1519. When Cortes temporarily left the Aztec island capital of Tenochtitlan (now Mexico City and no longer surrounded by water), Alvarado took command of the Spanish expedition – and shattered the uneasy alliance Cortes had established with Montezuma.

Incensed by the pagan rituals of an Aztec ceremony (they usually involved massive human sacrifice), Alvarado ordered an attack on the Aztecs, massacring thousands. Cortes returned to an embittered and hostile capital in 1520, and it was not long before the Spaniards were attacked. Montezuma attempted to intercede on behalf of the invaders, but when he was killed the Spaniards' last hope was gone. They made a desperate attempt to escape to the land surrounding Lake Texcoco, and Cortes and Alvarado were among the few who survived.

Alvarado took part in Cortes' siege and destruction of Tenochtitlan in 1521, and in the exploration into Guatemala. In 1533 he decided to seek his own fortune and sailed to South America, intending to conquer Quito, a kingdom on the equator (in present-day Ecuador). This unilateral action was very much against Spain's colonial policy, and Diego de Almagro was sent to stop Alvarado. With the assistance of the Governor of San Miguel, Sebastian de Benalcazaar, the rebellious Conquistador was bought off for 100,000 pesos and he then continued southwards to join Francisco Pizarro at Cusco, the Inca capital. To dissuade further attempts on Quito, Benalcazaar was put in charge of that area as well, and thus Spanish influence was pushed north of the Incas' old frontier.

Explorers and Their Discoveries
AMUNDSEN, Roald. 1872–1928

Norwegian explorer and navigator, famous for being the first to navigate the North-west Passage, and the first to reach the South Pole. Amundsen studied medicine and gained his initial knowledge of polar regions as first mate on a Belgian expedition to Antarctica in 1897. He and his companions were the first to experience the rigours of a full Antarctic winter, and it was only the combined skill of Amundsen and the expedition surgeon that prevented scurvy from taking a terrible toll of many lives.

By 1903 Amundsen was organizing his own expedition, and sailed from Oslo in the 47-ton sloop *Gjöa* to attempt the North-west Passage. From Greenland's Melville Bay he crossed Baffin Bay into Lancaster Sound, and at the beginning of Barrow Strait sailed south through Peel Sound, Franklin Strait and James Ross Strait, between Boothia Peninsula and King William Island. The *Gjöa* then headed west into Queen Maud Gulf, through Dease Strait and the Dolphin and Union Straits between Victoria Island and the mainland. An open area, now called Amundsen Gulf, led towards Banks Island and the Beaufort Sea – and on reaching the Bering Strait and Alaska's Seward Peninsula, Amundsen had at last confirmed the North-west Passage. (Modern ice-breakers, and certain other ships in favourable conditions, can take a much more direct route by passing through Barrow Strait and following the uninterrupted lane south of the Parry Islands, then entering the Beaufort Sea by passing north of Banks Island.)

Amundsen then hoped to succeed where Nansen in his *Fram* had failed, planning to drift across the Arctic's ice pack and reach the North Pole – but the news that Peary had reached the Pole in April 1909 caused him to try for the South Pole instead. Interest in that distant continent was high: the year before, Shackleton had been within less than 100 miles (160 km) of the South Pole. Amundsen sailed for Antarctica and wintered (mid-1911) in the Bay of Whales, at the opposite side of the Ross Ice Shelf from Scott's McMurdo Sound base, and some 60 miles (95 km) closer to the Pole. As soon as the weather permitted, Amundsen set out with four companions and over 50 sledge dogs, and after a direct and comparatively trouble-free journey reached the South Pole on 14 December 1911. Scott was already on his way, but did not reach the Pole until more than a month after the Norwegian. The drama and tragedy of Scott's expedition, however, which was as much a scientific exploration as a 'record book' effort, has always tended to detract from Amundsen's Antarctic achievement.

After an unsuccessful voyage to the Arctic and the North Pole in 1918, Amundsen next attempted to fly over the North Pole. In 1925, with the American aviator Lincoln Ellsworth, he came within 170 miles (275 km) of his goal. The following year they were joined by an Italian aeronautical engineer, Umberto Nobile, and successfully completed the crossing in a dirigible. Two years later Amundsen was killed in a crash while flying to Nobile's rescue, after the Italian's dirigible had crashed near Spitzbergen.

ANDAGOYA, Pascual de. c 1495–1548

The Spaniard who commanded the ships that carried out the first official survey of the Pacific coast-line south of Panama. The survey, in 1522, was not extensive and did not even reach Cape Corrientes on Colombia's west coast; but Andagoya returned with enticing accounts of a rich kingdom called Biru that was said to lie further south. From this report came the Spanish name for the Inca kingdom, Peru – and its destruction by the Conquistadores.

ANDRADE, Antonio de. c 1580–1634

A Jesuit priest in India who, intrigued by rumours that there were Christians in remote Tibet, disguised himself as a Hindu on a pilgrimage and in 1624 set out from Agra, heading via Delhi for Tibet. He crossed the upper Ganges River, continued to Srinagar and entered the Himalayas proper towards Badrinath, crossing the Mana Pass (18,000 ft/5,500 m) to the regional capital of Tsaparang. There were of course no Christians to be found, but the Buddhist ruler's reception of the Christian stranger was warm and encouraging. Andrade returned the following year to set up a church in Tsaparang, but in 1630 he was sent by his Order to Goa and the Buddhists overthrew the mission.

ARMSTRONG, Neil. 1930–

American astronaut and commander of the US Apollo 11 mission launched on 16 July 1969. With Edwin Aldrin, Armstrong flew the lunar module from the orbiting command module (piloted by Michael Collins) to a pre-determined landing point, and on 21 July 1969 became the first person to stand on the moon.

AZEVADO, Francisco de. 1578–1660

After Buddhists had overthrown Antonio de Andrade's Jesuit mission at Tsaparang in the Tibetan Himalayas, Azevado went to the site in 1631, travelling along the same Delhi-Srinagar-Mana Pass route which Andrade had used. From Tsaparang he went to Leh, and obtained the King of Ladakh's assent to re-establish the Church. The hostility of the Tsaparang Buddhists was more persuasive than Ladakh's magnanimity, however, and the mission was finally abandoned in 1635.

BACK, George. 1796–1878

Explored the North American continent's far northern regions with John Franklin. (SEE FRANKLIN, 1819–22, 1825–7.) In 1833 Back mounted an expedition to search for John Ross, who had disappeared in 1829 while on an Arctic voyage. The Great Fish River was explored at this time (thereafter known as Back River) and in 1836 Back returned to Canada to explore the Arctic coastal region eastwards from the mouth of the Back River.

HMS Terror, *commanded by Back, in the ice of Frozen Strait.* (Mary Evans Picture Library)

BAFFIN, William. 1584–1622

Sailed in 1615 with Robert Bylot to look for the North-west Passage. Bylot had been on Hudson's expedition, and on this occasion they sailed up the Hudson Strait and into Foxe Basin. Baffin judged correctly that there would be no exit, so they returned to England. In 1616 Baffin and Bylot made a second voyage together, this time sailing to Greenland's southern tip and following its west coast almost into Kane Basin, before heading down the west side of Baffin Bay, along the coast of Ellesmere Island and Devon Island. They discovered Jones Sound and Lancaster Sound but failed to realize that the latter was the starting point of the North-west Passage. Instead, they continued south and explored Baffin Bay. Some years later Baffin made extensive surveys of the Red Sea while he was with the East India Company; he was killed during an Anglo-Persian attack on the Persian Gulf island of Queshm. Baffin is believed to have been the first person to determine a degree of longitude at sea by lunar observation.

BAKER, Samuel. 1821–1893

An explorer of the Nile who went about seeking its source the long but potentially foolproof way – by systematically exploring it and its tributaries, heading upstream. Baker was accompanied by his wife on all his expeditions. On their first, they met Speke and Grant near Juba on the White Nile. Baker entirely believed Speke's claim that he had solved the dispute over the Nile's source, and so changed his objective, searching instead for Luta Ngize, a substantial lake Speke spoke of but had not himself seen. Baker and his wife continued south along a more easterly route than Speke and Grant had taken on their journey north, crossing the Nile just east of the Karuma Rapids. Eventually turning due west, the Bakers came to Luta Ngize in March 1864 – the first Europeans to see it. Baker renamed it Lake Albert in honour of Queen Victoria's Prince Consort, sailed to its northern end, and discovered the Murchison Falls before returning to his camp near Juba.

Baker's discoveries allowed a lot more detail to be added to maps of that region, but his ready acceptance of Speke's assertions had stopped his steadfast following of the White Nile; and since Speke's assertions were partly based on assumption, the Nile's source had still not been positively identified. After Baker's return the Royal Geographical Society sought to end the dispute and asked David Livingstone to head an expedition to complete the mapping of the Nile source area. Baker himself later returned to the equatorial regions of the White Nile when he commanded a military expedition for the Ottoman Viceroy of Egypt, into whose service he had

The Bakers travelling at leisure in North Africa. (Mary Evans Picture Library)

gone in 1869. He annexed a number of territories for the Viceroy, was appointed governor-general of them, and also played a substantial role in the ending of the slave trade.

BALBOA, Vasco Nunez de. c 1475–1519

Spanish Conquistador and explorer who was the first person from Europe to see the Pacific Ocean, and with Cortes and Pizarro was one of the principal founders of Spain's empire in the New World. Balboa sailed to the West Indies in 1500, initially to explore with Rodrigo de Bastidas what is now the coast of Colombia. He then settled in Hispaniola (now Haiti and Dominica), where he plunged heavily into debt. To avoid his creditors Balboa stowed away on an expedition which was taking relief supplies and new settlers to a colony that had been founded on the east side of the Uraba Gulf (which leads into the Gulf of Darien). Unfortunately the original settlers had abandoned the site, but Balboa saved the expedition from failure by convincing the settlers to begin a new colony themselves. He selected a far more pleasant site for them on the Panamanian side of the Gulf of Darien. The settlement on the isthmus was named Santa Maria, and it became the first stable, established European community on the mainland of the newly discovered continent.

Balboa discovers the Pacific Ocean. (Mary Evans Picture Library)

Balboa's organizational abilities outweighed the slur of abandoning his creditors, and in 1511 King Ferdinand appointed him the interim governor and captain-general of Darien. Balboa's methods, however, were violent, and the colony's considerable wealth in gold and slaves was obtained only at the cost of great suffering by the Indians. It was not long before Balboa heard rumours of the gold of the Incas far to the south in present-day Peru. The highly organized and industrious life-style of the Incas probably led to exaggerated stories, but their wealth was nevertheless substantial.

Balboa, as tempted by riches as any Conquistador, put together an expedition of almost 200 Spaniards and a great number of Indian bearers, and left Santa Maria in September 1513. The Darien part of the isthmus contains some of the world's most impenetrable and hostile jungles and swamps, but the expedition struggled south across it, and on 25 or 27 September 1513 Balboa climbed a rise higher and less overgrown than others, and for the first time saw the vast expanse of the Pacific Ocean. The expedition eventually reached the Pacific shore, but returned to Santa Maria in January 1514. Although the Incas were still many miles away, they were safe for only another ten years.

Balboa stepped further into royal favour with his declaration that he had claimed the new ocean for the Spanish King, calling it Mar del Sur (the South Sea). His area of governorship was consequently increased, but a cloud appeared on his horizon in the form of a new arrival, Pedrarias, who was appointed to a superior position. The lure of the south then beckoned the explorer ever more strongly, and after building a fleet of ships he had them dismantled and carried in pieces across the isthmus to the Pacific shore. As it turned out, Pedrarias really did deserve Balboa's condemnation: realizing that he was about to be replaced and that Balboa's testimony could further harm his case, he charged the Conquistador with many transgressions, most of which were spurious. Nevertheless Balboa was arrested before he could sail away, and in January 1519 he was beheaded.

BALDAYA, Alfonso Gonclaves. (fl 1436)

Portuguese who joined Gil Eannes' second journey (1435) past Cape Bojador on the West African coast. A landfall was made at the Bay of Rio de Oro, almost on the Tropic of Cancer, and the party saw the footprints of people and camels. In 1436 Baldaya led his own expedition, sailed south beyond the extremity of the Moslem territories, and reached Cape Blanc. His attempts to contact the local inhabitants were in vain, but he did bring back thousands of seal skins – the first commercial cargo from the West African coast.

BAPTISTA, Pedra. (fl 1804)

Portuguese explorer who in c 1802–4 carried out a gruelling west-to-east crossing of Africa between 10° and 18° S. Travelling with Amaro José, he left the Angola coast at the mouth of the Cuanza River and headed east-north-east, meeting the Kasai River at about 21° E and following its upper reaches until turning east again, eventually crossing the Lualaba River near Kolwezi. The expedition continued east to Lake Mweru, and then headed south-east and south to cross the Luangwe River west of Lake Nyasa (now Lake Malawi), carrying on south to Tete and through the Zambezi's lower region to the Indian Ocean.

BARENTS, Willem. c 1550–1597

One of the pioneers of Arctic voyaging. Barents was commissioned by the Dutch in 1594 to attempt to find a route to China and the East by sailing north of Europe. The south-east passage round the Cape of Good Hope was proven, as was the south-west passage past Cape Horn and across the Pacific. The North-west Passage was a likely concept yet to be attempted, but a North-east Passage seemed feasible. Barents got as far as the northern tip of Novaya Zemlya, 60° E and well into the Arctic Circle, before ice forced him back. Part of his expedition, led by Jan van Linschoten, had better luck further south, and was able to round the southern tip of the islands into the Kara Sea before meeting impenetrable ice.

In 1595 Barents and van Linschoten sailed again, but the ice reached even further south and the ships were blocked at Vaigach Island, south of Novaya Zemlya. The next summer they made another attempt, this time continuing north past Norway instead of rounding the North Cape. They discovered Bear Island and, further north, Spitzbergen before turning east into comparatively ice-free waters to pass north of Novaya Zemlya, this time going well beyond 60° E.

Then the ships became ice-bound, and the crews were faced with the prospect of wintering nearer the North Pole than anyone had ever attempted. Under Barents' inspired leadership they dragged supplies to Ice Haven harbour on Novaya Zemlya, collected driftwood from up to 8 miles (13 km) away, and built a large hut. Practically the whole expedition survived the hardship of that unprecedented winter, but Barents died soon after the expedition began its struggle south in the spring thaw of 1597. The weakened survivors eventually reached the Kola Peninsula, south of the Barents Sea. (In 1871 the hut that the expedition had built was found, and part of Barents' journal was discovered in 1875.)

BARTH, Heinrich. 1821–1865

German linguist and traveller who probably did more to bring Central and West Africa and the Sahara Desert to the attention and understanding of the world's geographers than any other man. His was the first really good scientific expedition into these huge areas, and his five-volume work, *Travels and Discoveries in North and Central Africa*, is still one of the most important publications on these areas, containing an enormous amount of historical, geographical, linguistic and anthropological information.

Heinrich Barth. (Mary Evans Picture Library)

In 1845–7 Barth travelled in North Africa, mostly in present-day Tunisia and Libya, and early in 1850 he and Adolf Overweg joined a British-sponsored expedition to Central and West Africa led by James Richardson. (SEE RICHARDSON.) After leaving Agadez, the three men separated to travel independently to Lake Chad. Barth took the most westerly route, but Richardson died before he reached the lake and Barth took over leadership of the whole expedition. He made extensive explorations south and south-east of the seasonal lake, along the Chari Basin, and to the headwaters of the Benue River, a tributary of the Niger. Overweg concentrated on the western and northern regions of the lake, and on its immediate boundaries, while Barth ranged further afield, sweeping far east as well. The expedition was due to travel on to West Africa, but before a start could be made Overweg too fell ill and died.

Barth then left Lake Chad and travelled west through Kano, Katsina, and Sokoto, across the Niger and north-west to Timbuktu. On leaving the legendary and usually hostile city, he travelled down the Niger to the point where he had first crossed it, and was therefore the first to be able to describe the middle region of the mystifying river (its huge, inverted U course initially caused frequent confusion). Barth retraced his steps to Lake Chad, recrossed the Sahara (practically through the middle), and passed well to the east of the Ahaggar Mountains to reach Marzūq and finally Tripoli, in 1855. His journey, most of it followed by extremely accurate dead-reckoning, had covered some 10,000 miles (16,000 km). (In later years Barth also travelled in Turkey and Asia Minor.)

BASS, George. 1771–1803

English surgeon turned explorer whose name has been given to the strait between Australia and Tasmania. Bass' first exploration in the newly discovered southern continent was a brief excursion up the Georges River, a few miles south of present-day Sydney. He was accompanied on that trip in 1795 by Matthew Flinders.

Two years later Bass sailed south from Port Jackson (Syndey) to determine whether Van Diemen's Land (Tasmania) was an extension of New South Wales (the name then given to eastern Australia). By sailing round to Western Port, and so discovering Bass Strait, he all but positively established that the land discovered by Abel Tasman was an island; and this was proved beyond doubt in 1798–9 when, once more in Flinders' company, Bass sailed anti-clockwise round Van Diemen's Land from Flinders Island and back. From the southern coast the explorers followed the Derwent River almost to the centre of the island.

BATES, Henry. 1825–1892

British entomologist whose finds and studies in the Amazon gave considerable support to Darwin's theory of evolution. In 1848, with Alfred Wallace, Bates explored the Pará (Belém) area and the Tocantins River (SEE WALLACE), and in 1850 he joined Herbert and Alfred Wallace at Manaus, halfway up the Amazon. The Wallace brothers went up the Negro River, while Bates continued up the Amazon and gathered specimens in the region of Ega (now Tefé). But in 1851, after his money had been stolen, he made his way back to Pará where he was able to be of some comfort to

Herbert Wallace, who was dying of yellow fever. Later that year Bates journeyed back up the Amazon to Santarém and explored far south along the Tapajós River, remaining in the region until 1855 when he went back to Ega. This time, his travels in the region took him further up the Amazon (or the Solimoes, as it is also called in these upper reaches), but eventually he headed back down the massive river on his way home to England, which he reached in 1859. His decade of observations and selections had gathered a collection of some 14,700 specimens, at least 8,000 of which were then unknown.

BAUDIN, Nicolas. c 1750–1803

Nicholas Baudin. (Mary Evans Picture Library)

French navigator who contributed to the mapping of the Australian coast. His voyage in *Le Géographe* from 1800 to 1803 took him to the west coast of Van Diemen's Land (Tasmania), and he sailed south round the island to Port Jackson (Sydney). Baudin began a survey of the south-east coast and continued westwards through Bass Strait until he met Matthew Flinders at Encounter Bay, who was charting the coast from the west. (When Flinders was imprisoned by the French at Mauritius, France and Britain then being at war, Baudin claimed the Englishman's great feats of mapping and discovery as his own.)

BEATUS of Valcavado. (fl AD 776)

An 8th-century Spanish Benedictine monk and 'religious' cartographer whose main achievement was to subtract a considerable amount from the sum of discovery and reverse the growth of geographic knowledge in a manner that was quite characteristic of the Dark Ages. In his *Commentary on the Apocalypse* (AD 776), Beatus drew a world map which was widely copied between 900 and 1200. Inspired by religious belief rather than by geographic knowledge, his map was essentially symbolic, and it was probably not his fault that others took it so seriously. Since Palestine was the

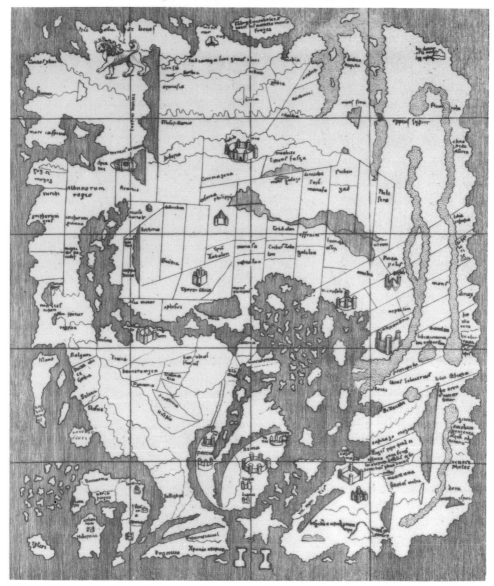

A late 10th-century Cottonian manuscript map of the world, with the Dark Ages orientation of Jerusalem in the central, north position. (Mary Evans Picture Library)

location of so much of the story of Christianity, east appeared at the top of Beatus' map – and consequently at the top of all 'Beatus' maps. A measure of their unsuitability for geographers is the fact that there was far more information on the map drawn over 1,000 years earlier by Herodotus.

BEHAIM, Martin. c 1436–1507

German navigator, geographer and cartographer who made the earliest surviving globe of the world. Behaim was an adviser and navigator to Portugal's King John II, and in about 1484 he sailed along the north-west coast of Africa. In the Azores he recorded, in German, the dictation of Diogo Gomes, one of the leading mariners fostered by Henry the Navigator. Behaim's writings were translated into Latin, lost for some 400 years, and then found in the Munich Royal Library. It is believed that he was the first to replace the wooden astrolabe – a simple forerunner of the sextant – with one made of brass. He began the construction of the Nürnberg Terrestrial Globe in 1490.

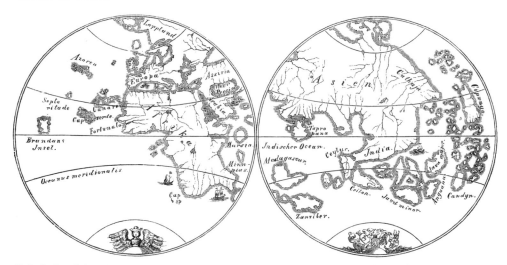

Behaim's globe of the late 15th century. The Americas do not yet exist and there is not even conjecture about Terra Australis. (Mary Evans Picture Library)

BELL, Gertrude Margaret. 1868–1926

Foremost woman explorer who was also an influential administrator in Arabia. In 1913–14 she attempted to travel to Riyadh in central Arabia, but after reaching Hā'il from Damascus the hostility of the Moslems forced her to abandon the attempt. She went to Baghdad instead, before returning to Damascus. The routes Bell took between the three centres differed substantially from those used by the few Europeans who had travelled before her, so her detailed observations were of considerable value.

BELLINGSHAUSEN, Fabian Gottlieb von. 1778 –1852

A Russian explorer whose native name was Faddey Faddeyvich
Bellingsgauzen, and who was the first person to circumnavigate Antarctica.
He led a Russian expedition which sailed in 1819, and in 1820–1 sailed
round the world, practically every mile being covered south of 60°. The
expedition arrived first at the South Georgia Islands and sailed eastwards
round the continent, only once leaving the polar regions, to replenish in
Australia. Bellingshausen discovered the first land (which could be
identified as land and not simply snow and ice) inside the Antarctic circle,
and named his discoveries after Peter I and Alexander I. Alexander I Land
is the western side of the Palmer Peninsula south of Cape Horn, but Peter I
Land was later changed to Peter I Island when it was discovered that the
Bellingshausen Sea (usually ice-covered) separates it from the continent.

BENT, James Theodore. 1852–1897

British archaeologist who excavated Zimbabwe in what was then Rhodesia
in 1891, and described the fascinating ruins in *The Ruined Cities of
Mashonaland*. As well as making expeditions into Turkey, the Aegean Islands,
Ethiopia and Sudan, Bent and his wife Mabel carried out three journeys in
southern Arabia. In 1893–4 they were in the Hadramaut region, going
inland from Al Mukalia to Shibam, and then eastwards along the coast.
Their next expedition was into the Qara Mountains in the Dhofor region,
and in 1897 they made a brief excursion into the coastal area east of Aden.

BERING, Vitus Jonassen. 1681 –1741

Although Czar Peter I had a map showing a narrow gap between Siberia
and the North American continent, it was not widely known, or else not
fully believed, that Ivanov Deshnef had already navigated the strait. In
1725, the Czar commissioned the Danish navigator Bering to resolve the
uncertainty. That year Bering set out from St Petersburg (Leningrad) on the
traditional and very long overland route to Okhotsk. While one ship was
being built there, another was under construction on the east coast of the
Kamchatka Peninsula, and in 1728 the expedition was ready to sail from
Kamchatka. Accompanying Bering were Alexei Chirikov and Martin
Spanberg. The ships sailed north through the strait, following the Asian
coast until it swept west. Certain that the strait did exist, Bering returned to
Russia – but since he had not sighted America at any stage, some were still
sceptical of his claim.

In 1740 Bering was once again in Okhotsk with Chirikov, and they rounded Kamchatka on an expedition to sail eastwards to the north-west coast of America. The ships were separated but both eventually reached the American continent, discovering many of the Aleutian Islands on the way. Bering explored the Kodiak Island area, and reached the Gulf of Alaska coast off Mt St Elias – which is almost on the same latitude as Okhotsk, his starting point. By the time he was able to head back to the Siberian coast, Bering had fallen very ill with scurvy, and he was unable to maintain proper command of his ship. The vessel was duly wrecked, and he died on Bering Island, close to Russia and in the sea that now carries his name.

BEUTLER, August. (fl 1752)

In 1752, a hundred years after the Dutch founded the first settlement at the Cape of Good Hope, Beutler led a group eastwards along the southern coast of Africa, away from the increasing bureaucracy at the Cape. They passed Algoa Bay and eventually crossed the Great Kei River into what is now the Transkei, where they met increasing signs of resistance from the tribes that were simultaneously moving south towards the tip of Africa.

BLAEU, Willem. 1571–1638

Dutch geographer, astronomer and cartographer whose map of the two American continents displayed the great amount of knowledge gained since Ortelius represented the New World. By 1630 – the approximate date of the map's publication – the outlines and many interiors were well-known. Tierra del Fuego, for instance, was no longer shown as part of the imaginary 'Terra Australis', but as an island. Blaeu also published a good map of Asia in about 1617 (when he used to sign his maps 'Janszoon'), and it was included in the 1623 edition of the Mercator-Hondius atlas.

BLASHFORD-SNELL, John. 1936–

British army officer who has led three especially significant expeditions (among many others) in which British Armed Forces have played major roles. Apart from gathering a vast amount of scientific and geographic knowledge, the expeditions have been outstanding examples of how team work, courage and meticulous organization and planning can combine with sophisticated and often *avant garde* technology to tackle and overcome extreme obstacles. The first to claim widespread public interest was an expedition down the hazardous course of the Blue Nile, in which inflatable rubber boats played a major role. Blashford-Snell led the British Trans-Americas Expedition of 1971–2, in which two Range Rover vehicles made the first ever Alaska-to-Cape Horn journey – after other members of the large force involved had blazed a trail through the inhospitable and previously unconquered Darien Gap in Panama and Colombia. In October 1974, using two enormous inflatable rubber boats as the principal means of transport, the Zaïre River Expedition began a 2,700 mile (4,300 km) journey from near Lubumbashi, in south-east Zaïre, mainly to gather scientific information through the participation of the Scientific Exploration Society, but also to

John Blashford-Snell. (The Scientific Exploration Society)

commemorate the centenary of Stanley's expedition during which the Zaïre River, formerly the Congo River, was first traced.

BLAXLAND, Gregory. 1778–1853

The first to cross Australia's Blue Mountains behind Sydney. In 1813 he went almost due west from the town – then called Port Jackson – for some 130 miles (210 km) inland, stopping approximately between present-day Bathurst and Portland. As with most 'firsts', his expedition seemed to open the way for others, and it was not long before the west-flowing headwaters of the Macquarie and Lachlan rivers were discovered.

BLOCK, Adriaen. (fl 1614)

A Dutch explorer and trader who had been with Hudson when the latter was exploring the north-east American coast in the service of the Dutch East India Company. In 1614 Block sailed between the American mainland and Long Island and then discovered the Connecticut River (named more or less phonetically after its Indian name). He sailed some 50 miles (80 km)

129

upriver, and was so taken with the promising countryside that on his return to Holland he strongly urged the Dutch to establish a settlement there. However the first Dutch colonists chose the mouth of the Hudson River instead, mainly Manhattan Island which they called New Amsterdam. (In 1664 the English captured it and renamed it New York.)

BLUNT, Wilfrid Scawen. 1840–1922

English poet, traveller, and breeder of Arab horses who in 1878, accompanied by his wife Anne, travelled from the Iskenderun Gulf (north-east of Cyprus) to the Euphrates and down to Baghdad. They went north again along the Tigris River before turning south-west to Damascus, and on to the Mediterranean. In 1879 the Blunts returned to Damascus and under the guardianship of an authoritative Arab sheik they began an expedition into the An Nafūd region to buy horses and study the Arabians. They returned safely to Baghdad (the safety of Christians, and especially female Christians, was considerably at risk in those Moslem areas), and followed the Tigris for a while before boarding a ship on the north-east shore of the Persian Gulf, at Būshehr.

BOGLE, George. 1746–1781

The first Englishman to venture beyond Nepal and Bhutan into Tibet, being sent there in 1774 by the Governor General of India (Warren Hastings) in the hope of establishing Tibet as a British East India Company trading partner. Britain's commercial motives were compounded by her expectation that the alliance would form a protective buffer on India's northern border.

Bogle journeyed north from Calcutta through Bhutan to Shigatse, and was the first European to be seen there for 100 years. He formed good relations with the Tashi Lama, who was the second most influential Buddhist in Tibet. All Bogle's endeavours and extensive reports on trade possibilities and other aspects of the area were of little immediate value, however, as the authorities in the capital city of Lhasa forbade the entry of any more foreigners into Tibet.

BORMAN, Frank. 1928–

American commander of the 1968 Apollo 8 space mission who, with James Lovell and William Anders, was the first to make a lunar orbit, and see the 'back' of the moon.

BOUGAINVILLE, Louis-Antoine de. 1729–1811

French navigator and leader of the first French naval force to sail around the world. Bougainville sailed from France in 1766 for the South Atlantic where his first duty was to hand over the Falkland Islands to the Spanish to whom France had sold them, only two years after they had taken the trouble to settle them. (Seven years before, Bougainville had been an eyewitness to the eclipse of French rule in Canada.)

His next task was to look for Terra Australis, the 'lost' southern continent. He entered the Pacific through the Strait of Magellan, and followed the usual wind-favoured course to beyond the Tropic of Capricorn, before heading almost due west to Tahiti. From there his ships went via Samoa to the Great Barrier Reef off Australia's north-east coast.

Bougainville did not realize just how close he was to the missing continent, saw no land beyond the impenetrable reef, and so went north to the Solomon Islands, discovering the Louisiade Archipelago in the Coral Sea on the way. The Solomons were also 'lost': no European voyager had located them since Álvaro de Mendaña had incorrectly plotted them in 1567, but Bougainville failed to identify them. (The largest, westernmost island was named after him.)

The French ships then passed north of New Guinea to the Moluccas where scurvy and essential ship repairs caused some delay, before they returned to France via the Cape of Good Hope. Bougainville's voyage

Louis-Antoine de Bougainville. (The National Maritime Museum, London)

failed to find Australia mainly because he had so closely duplicated the voyages made before him. No one had yet managed a radical approach, and few had ventured further south than 40° anywhere west of the 80th meridian.

BRENDAN. 484–578

Irish monk variously known as Saint Brendan, Brendan the Voyager, Brendan the Navigator, and Brendan of Clonfert. By the 8th century he had become the hero of a legendary Christian story of the sea, the 'Voyage of Brendan'. Monastery records were said to indicate that he travelled on missionary trips to Scotland, Wales and Brittany, but legends have him far more widely travelled – to the Sheep Islands, for instance, which were perhaps the Faroes. The 'Voyage of Brendan' can be interpreted fairly loosely, but a thread of reality runs through it. Brendan and other Irish monks are described making a fantastic journey to a 'Promised Land of the Saints' that might have been the Canaries or even Bermuda but gave rise to the myth of a 'Saint Brendan's Island' somewhere in the Atlantic, as fervently believed in as was the lost city of Atlantis. During Columbus' period there were accounts that many inhabitants of the Azores had seen this island, but it has always been as elusive as a mirage.

BRUCE, James. 1730–1794

James Bruce. (The National Maritime Museum, London)

The first to make a scientific exploration of the Blue Nile, and to claim discovery of the Nile's source – though it was later discovered that the White Nile was much longer. His expedition from 1768 to 1773 took him through some of the worst hazards of man and nature; but at first his claims were disregarded in Britain, for he had made the mistake of telling the French of his discoveries before he told the British.

Bruce arrived at Cairo in 1768, went down the east coast of the Red Sea, and crossed from the northern Yemen to Massawa and present-day Ethiopia. From there he travelled south to Aksum and then to Gondar, and he soon confirmed the Blue Nile's source as the Springs of Geesh and Lake Tana. From his Gondar camp Bruce went west to join the river at Sennar, and then followed it north to its junction with the White Nile at Khartoum, continuing with the mainstream past Shandi and Berber and the Fifth Cataract. Where the Nile loops west, Bruce continued north across the Nubian Desert, joining the river once more at Aswan and following it to Cairo where he made his premature declaration of discovery. It was to be almost 100 years before the true source of the Nile was finally proven.

BRULÉ, Etienne. 1592–1633

French-Canadian protégé of Champlain, and discoverer of four of the five Great Lakes. Brulé lived with a tribe of Huron Indians from 1610 to 1612, and discovered Georgian Bay, the north-east extension of Lake Huron. In 1615 he accompanied Champlain on part of his journey to fight alongside the Huron Indians against the Iroquois at Lake Oneida, just south of the eastern end of Lake Ontario. After leaving Georgian bay, Brulé and Champlain took separate routes. Brulé arrived first at the western end of Lake Ontario, crossed the narrow neck of land and discovered Lake Erie. By the time he arrived at Lake Oneida, the battle was over and the Hurons defeated, and he continued down the Susquehanna River to Chesapeake Bay. In 1620 Brulé returned to Georgian Bay and made a journey westwards, discovering the full extent of Lake Huron. He missed the narrow entrance to Lake Michigan, but carried on to discover Lake Superior. It is possible that Brulé travelled the full length of this lake to Chequamegon Bay, in 1622.

BRUNN, Anton. 1901–1961

Led a Danish scientific expedition in the *Galathea* to look for forms of marine life at extreme depths. Many extraordinary specimens were brought up by trawling depths of more than 34,000 feet (10,500 m) in the Pacific's Mindanao Trench.

BRUNNER, Thomas. 1821–1874

The principal explorer of New Zealand's South Island. In 1843 Brunner made a brief expedition south from the site of Motueka in Tasman Bay, travelling up the valley west of Richmond Range. Two years later, joined by Charles Heaphy, William Fox and a Maori guide named Ekuhu, he travelled from the east side of Tasman Bay up the Richmond valley and circled Lake Rotoroa. In 1846 Brunner, Heaphy and Ekuhu crossed Tasman Bay to Golden Bay on South Island's north-west corner. Travelling overland, they followed the west coast, crossing Grey River and briefly venturing up Taramakau River.

From 1846 to 1848 Brunner undertook a 'Great Journey' with Ekuhu, and travelled south from Tasman Bay, down the course of the Buller River to its mouth near Cape Foulwind. He explored the Grey River, continued north and east into the foothills of the Southern Alps and up the valley east of the Paparoa Range to rejoin the Buller River. Further south Brunner made his second journey up the Taranakau, and discovered Lake Brunner between it and the Grey River. He continued south along the rugged west coast, past the many fjords and beyond Mount Cook to Tititira Head, due west of New Zealand's highest point.

BRYDGES, Harford Jones. 1774–1829

Headed a British diplomatic mission to Persia in a move to counter the growing Russian influence in that area at the beginning of the 19th century. Brydges left Bombay in 1807 and travelled to the Persian Gulf, disembarking at Bushire (Būshehr). Over the next four years he visited Isfahan, Teheran, Qazvin and Tabriz, from where he sent expeditions towards the Caspian Sea and northwards to the Araxes River, establishing trade and diplomatic contacts. Brydges was received by the Shah in 1809.

BUCHAN, David. 1790–1845

Britain had displayed little curiosity about high northern latitudes since the tragedy of Hudson and the unsuccessful North-west Passage exploration by Baffin. Then, some 100 years later, a significant decrease in the amount of Arctic ice revived interest and two expeditions were sent out in 1818 – John Ross to look for the North-west Passage, and Buchan to get as near to the North Pole as possible. John Franklin accompanied Buchan, but they encountered very thick ice north of Spitzbergen, and were forced to abandon their attempt.

BURCKHARDT, Johann Ludwig. 1784–1817

The re-discoverer of the ancient city of Petra (in what is now Jordan). Burckhardt was under the patronage of the Association for Promoting Discovery of the Interior Parts of Africa (the 'African Association'), and he spent quite a time in Syria learning the language and customs of Arabia and making himself accustomed to Islamic life, adopting the name Ibrāhim Ibu 'Abd Allāh. His patrons instructed him to cross the Sahara, and on his way from Syria to Cairo in 1812 he discovered the Petra site.

In Cairo Burckhardt eventually gave up waiting for a caravan that would take him through the Fezzan (in western Libya), and instead began a two-year journey travelling up the Nile, and exploring both sides of the Red Sea, discovering the extraordinary rock temple at Abu Simbel. Burckhardt used his Moslem training to enter Mecca and its twin holy city,

Medina, providing the first comprehensive information on this part of the
Hejaz region. He then returned to the Red Sea and explored the Sinai
peninsula before going back to Cairo – where he died, still hoping to join a
caravan across the Sahara.

BURKE, Robert. 1820–1861

In 1860 the Government of South Australia offered a prize of £2000 for the
first south-to-north crossing of Australia. Burke led the expedition that
achieved the crossing, but it cost him his life and others'. With three
companions, Wills, Grey and King, Burke set out from Menindee on the
Darling River in October 1860, and headed north to the southern end of the
Bulloo River. The expedition crossed the northern part of Sturt Desert to
Cooper's Creek (or Barcoo River) and then north to the Cloncurry River. In
February 1861 the Flinders River was crossed, almost at its mouth in the
Gulf of Carpentaria, but the four men were prevented by swamps and

*John King, sole survivor of the Burke and Wills expedition across Australia, is rescued just in
time.* (Mary Evans Picture Library)

anxiety over their diminishing supplies from finding a way to the coast. On the return journey across the deserted plains and deserts, Grey died; and when the three survivors reached their intended supply camp at Cooper's Creek, they found it deserted – the group waiting with supplies for the expedition had in fact left that very morning. Although food had been left to enable the group to reach the nearest town, Burke and King foolishly decided to carry on south to Adelaide, leaving Wills at Cooper's Creek. After two days, Burke died. King returned to the Barcoo River, where he found Wills dead; King himself was rescued just in time.

BURTON, Richard. 1821–1890

One of the most famous and colourful characters in the history of exploration, Burton was enormously talented – though by no means universally liked or respected. He was a great 19th-century scholar, prolific author (43 volumes and 100 articles written, 30 volumes translated), soldier, poet, botanist, geologist, an extremely able linguist (25 languages, mounting to 40 with dialect variations), translator, a foremost ethnologist, and eventually an absorbed translator and student of Eastern erotica and folk literature.

In 1853 Burton journeyed from Alexandria to Arabia, where in the guise of an Afghan Moslem he travelled the hazardous route to Mecca – a favourite hunting ground for bandits. He entered Mecca undetected, and even took the great risk of measuring and sketching the mosque and the holy Moslem shrine, the Ka'bah. (Burton was not the first European or non-Moslem to enter the 'forbidden city', but his observations were far more numerous and superior to any made before.) In 1854 he went to Harer in East Africa, an equally forbidden Moslem city, and was the first European to enter it – and leave it alive.

Burton was becoming steadily more and more intrigued by the mystery of the Nile's source, and in 1855 he began an expedition with three officers of the British East India Company, among them John Hanning Speke. Their camp near Berbera was attacked, Burton was injured, and the attempt was called off. The Crimean War then intervened but in 1857, following rumours (strengthened by Johann Krapf's report of what he had learnt in Mombasa) about an 'inland sea' in the equatorial region of East Africa, the Royal Geographical Society commissioned Burton to find it. Accompanied once more by Speke, Burton returned to Africa, calling at Zanzibar on the way to Bagamoyo.

The expedition encountered enormous difficulties and hardships but forged steadily inland, first in an arc south, west and then north to Tabora, then travelling west until Burton and Speke discovered Lake Tanganyika, meeting it a little south of Ujiji. Burton and Speke travelled up the lake's east coast, but turned back before sighting the northern end and so were unable to determine in which direction it drained. They returned to Tabora after learning from Arab traders that there was another lake north-east of Lake Tanganyika.

By this stage (it was then 1858) Burton was seriously ill, mainly with malaria; Speke, too, had been suffering a great deal, and could only see with considerable difficulty. Of the two, Speke was healthier, however, and when his sight began to improve he left Burton at Tabora and went due north, so discovering Lake Victoria. Perhaps the immense size of the lake gave Speke the instinct that it was the Nile's source – at any rate he returned to England ahead of Burton and claimed the lion's share of the glory for himself. So began a vicious life-long feud with Burton, whose criticism of Speke led him to dispute Lake Victoria as the Nile's source, even after Speke had strengthened (though not proved) his claim by a second expedition to the area.

Burton contined to travel in Africa and Arabia, though he made no further discoveries. His studies of African tribal and other foreign customs kept him in the public eye, however, for his approach to anthropology had more in common with present-day attitudes than with those of Victorian England. His years with the British Foreign Office were only mildly successful; his outspoken attacks on the hypocrisy of Victorian society, and the frankness of his anthropological writings were hardly in keeping with the niceties of diplomatic service. Nevertheless his contributions earned him a knighthood in 1886, a royal acknowledgement which neither made Burton a tame conformist nor encouraged others to think more favourably of him. He and his weak and bewildered wife lived in Trieste for the last few years of his life, during which his literary output scarcely abated.

After Burton died, his wife, from a mixture of wifely concern and Victorian prudery, carried out a tragic desecration by burning all Burton's working papers. Practically all his journals and diaries – a collection that covered some 40 years – were also reduced to ashes.

BYLOT, Robert. (fl 1610)

Sailed on Hudson's 1610 voyage which discovered Hudson Bay in Canada. After the mutiny in 1611 that left Hudson and eight others adrift in the bay, Bylot sailed the ship back to England. He returned to those regions with Baffin in 1615 and 1616, seeking the North-west Passage (SEE WILLIAM BAFFIN).

BYRD, Richard E. 1888–1957

American Rear-Admiral who pioneered polar aviation and made the first flight over the South Pole. He also achieved considerable fame in 1934 when he endured an Antarctic winter entirely on his own.

Byrd's polar career began in 1924, when he participated in an Arctic-Greenland expedition as commander of a small naval aviation unit. In 1926 he was navigator in a plane piloted by Floyd Bennett that supposedly flew over the North Pole during a flight from Spitzbergen. The US Congressional Medal of Honour was awarded to Byrd, but years later controversy arose over his records and whether he had in fact crossed the Pole. The southern summer of 1928–9 saw Byrd in the Antarctic, head of the most expensive, biggest, best-equipped expedition to land on the continent (Byrd was the first American to cross the Antarctic circle since Wilkes, 90 years before). He established a base called 'Little America' in the Bay of Whales, and made a number of flights. He discovered a range of mountains which he named the Rockefeller Mountains, while the unknown land beyond them was named Marie Byrd Land. On 29 November 1928 Byrd navigated his plane, carrying three companions, over the South Pole and back to Little America on a flight that took 19 hours.

Five years later Byrd made another trip to the Antarctic. The most important period of this expedition was the winter of 1934, which he spent alone in his winter research camp – 123 miles (198 km) nearer the Pole than the Bay of Whales. During the long dark months the temperature often plunged as low as –60°C, and when relief came after almost five months, Byrd was extremely ill, suffering mainly from frostbite and carbon monoxide poisoning. (After World War II Byrd made further mapping flights over Antarctica.)

BYRON, John. 1723–1786

Like many in England at that time, Byron believed implicitly in the existence of Terra Australia – a huge southern continent whose bulk was considered necessary to balance the known land masses north of the equator. In 1764 he left England with Philip Carteret and Charles Clerke on a commission to find the continent. Contemporary and earlier maps placed the northern shores of the undiscovered land well into the South Atlantic, but the only land Byron saw was the Falkland Islands. He then rounded Cape Horn into the Pacific Ocean, following much the same route as previous mariners – and one which would also be followed by others after him, such as Bougainville.

Byron called at Juan Fernandez Island, the Tuamotu Islands (on

140° W) and went via the Gilbert, Marshall and Ladrones (Marianas) Islands to near Formosa, making no major discoveries but at least adding a number of islands to the slowly emerging map of the Pacific. One of the ships used in this circumnavigation, the *Dolphin*, sailed again in 1766 with Carteret leading the expedition (SEE PHILIP CARTERET). Byron – nicknamed 'foul weather Jack' in memory of his survival of a particularly fierce Atlantic storm – was later made Governor of Newfoundland. He was the grandfather of the poet Lord Byron, who used some of his reminiscences in 'Don Juan'.

CABOT, John. c 1450–1498?

Considerable conjecture surrounds both the early and later years of John Cabot, a highly skilled Venetian navigator who might so easily have been the discoverer of the New World. He arrived in Venice with his parents before 1461 and in due course worked for a Venetian merchant, on whose behalf he sailed to the eastern shores of the Mediterranean and visited Mecca. His understanding and expertise in navigation made it quite probable that he deduced, independently of Columbus, that the Orient could be approached by sailing west. Cabot and his sons went to England in 1484, and soon began looking for someone to sponsor a westward passage to the East. Eventually, in March 1496, England's King Henry VII gave them his authority, and also granted them a monopoly on any trading rights that they established.

An expedition was hurriedly mounted and was almost as quickly abandoned, but in May 1497, in the small ship *Matthew* and with 18 men, Cabot sailed from Bristol, westward bound. It is not known exactly where he landed, but he rediscovered for Europe (for the first time since the Vikings) Nova Scotia and Newfoundland. Although signs of habitation were apparent no people were seen ashore, and after raising both the English and Venetian flags Cabot sailed north to the northern tip of Newfoundland.

On his return to England Cabot gave highly enthusiastic accounts of the agreeable climate and the appearance of the land he'd seen – which he too firmly believed to be part of Asia. He also reported on the abundance of fish in those waters, but without the evidence of even a small box of the riches and luxuries usually associated with the East, let alone an ambassador or a single captive from the lands of the Great Khans, Henry VII was reluctant to take further interest.

John Cabot, however, remained convinced and announced an expedition to Japan. Five ships and 200 men sailed in 1498, but what happened after then has never been established. At least one report states that the whole expedition was lost at sea, but there is also evidence that suggests he not only reached North America again and explored much further south, but then returned safely to England. Nothing certain is known of him after 1498.

CABOT, Sebastian. c 1476–1557

Navigator, cartographer and explorer, and son of John Cabot. His early life is obscure, but it is likely that he accompanied his father on his first voyage to North America in 1497 on behalf of England's King Henry VII. In 1509 Sebastian Cabot sailed from Bristol, headed up the west coast of Ireland, and then voyaged west to Greenland's southern tip. He crossed to the Hudson Strait but turned back before reaching the huge bay, and sailed south past Newfoundland, Nova Scotia and Long Island, before returning to England.

Cabot apparently never returned to Venice, his birthplace, but he served both English and Spanish royalty. In 1512 he was cartographer to King Henry VIII, but in 1525 the Spanish court put him in charge of three ships to pursue trade with the East. Cabot believed that there was no northern route to the Orient – at least not westwards – so he took the southerly route, and after leaving the Cape Verde Islands headed south-south-west across the Atlantic to Cape São Roque on South America, and sailed on to the Rio de la Plata. Unfortunately he heard rumours of extensive wealth in the area, disregarded his original intentions and orders, and spent three years searching in vain for treasure. On returning to Spain he not surprisingly found himself out of favour, and was banished to Africa. After two years he was pardoned, went to England once again and was instrumental in organizing attempts to find a North-east Passage – attempts which resulted in increased trade with Russia.

CABRAL, João. 1599–1669

(SEE ALSO ESTEVÃO CACELLA.) A Jesuit missionary who arrived in India at the mouths of the Ganges in 1626 with Cacella. They headed north-east, crossed the Brahmaputra River, and went west to Cooch Behar before turning northwards and travelling through Bhutan into Tibet. At Shigatse they founded a Christian mission. Cabral returned to India for supplies via a westerly route through Katmandu and the course of the Ganges, and met Cacella again at Cooch Behar, the latter having failed to reach the mission at Tsaparang. In 1631 Cabral returned to the Shigatse mission, but was recalled to India the following year.

CABRAL, Pedro Alvares. c 1467–1519

One of the foremost Portuguese navigators of the Age of Discovery, appointed Admiral by King Manuel and put in command of Portugal's second expedition to India. Cabral sailed from Lisbon in March 1500 with thirteen ships, but over-reached da Gama's advice to give a wide berth to the becalming waters surrounding the Gulf of Guinea. As a result, he sighted South America, and was probably the first European to set foot on the continent, at Caravela, about 18° S. Unaware that he was in fact on a great land mass, Cabral named the land 'island of the true cross', and it was some years before Brazil got its name from *pau-brasil*, a wood used in making dye. Under the Treaty of Tordesillas, this land fell within '370 leagues west of the Cape Verde Islands' and consequently belonged to Portugal; Cabral therefore claimed it for Manuel, and sent a ship back to Lisbon with the news (which led to Vespucci's expedition).

Cabral then continued his voyage to the East, but his early landfall was the last of his good fortune. He lost four ships in a storm off the Cape of Good Hope, and all on board them perished as well – among them Bartolomeu Dias. Eventually the expedition reached Malindi on the east coast of Africa, and then sailed north-east to Goa, on the west coast of India. At Calicut – Cabral's destination and then India's leading trading post – a dispute with the Moslems escalated rapidly and the Moslems attacked the Portuguese post, killing most of its defenders before reinforcements from the ships could reach them. Cabral retaliated by bombarding Calicut, after which he captured ten ships belonging to Moslem traders and slaughtered all their crews. Antagonism towards the disruptive newcomers was far less pronounced further south at Cochin, and Cabral acquired a passable cargo for the return journey. But more ships foundered on the voyage back to Europe, and only four reached Portugal.

Initially Cabral was chosen to lead the third, and by far the most powerful, expedition to India, but eventually Manuel selected Vasco da Gama. Choosing Cabral before the senior Admiral was not a decision da Gama would have tolerated lightly.

CACELLA, Estevão. 1585–1630

(SEE ALSO JOÃO CABRAL.) In 1626 Cacella travelled to Tibet with his fellow Jesuit missionary João Cabral and founded a missionary at Shigatse. When Cabral went back to India for supplies, Cacella tried to reach the mission at Tsaparang by following the Himalayas on their northern slopes; but heavy snow forced him to give up the attempt. He then went to India, and by following the route taken on the way to Tibet, met up with

Cabral in Cooch Behar. In September 1629 Cacella set out once more for Shigatse. By the time he arrived in February 1630 he was dangerously ill, and he died within days.

CADAMOSTO, Alvise. 1432–1488

A Venetian mariner who shared with Diogo Gomes the discovery and accurate charting of much of Africa's west coast in the Senegal-Gambia River area. It is not clear which of the two were the first Europeans to discover the Cape Verde Islands and the Azores. Cadamosto entered the service of Henry the Navigator in 1455 and made his first voyage along the African coast the same year, reaching the Gambia River, but hostile natives forced him back and he sailed further south to the Geba River. On returning from this voyage he claimed discovery of the Cape Verde Islands.

CAESAR, Gaius Julius. 101–44 BC

The Roman emperor merits brief mention among explorers for his role as historian, since among his few surviving writings is one of the earliest accounts of Gaul and of Britain, which he invaded in 55 BC.

CAILLIÉ, René-Auguste. 1799–1838

Explored north-west Africa and was the first European to visit Timbuktu and to live to tell about it. Caillié made two expeditions from Dakar, in 1816 and 1824 – one north-east to the Senegal River, and one south-east to the Gambia River. He began preparations for the Timbuktu expedition in 1824, and in 1827 sailed north from Freetown, landing again at Conakry. Posing as an Arab trader, Caillié travelled inland to Tieme, then north-east to Djeuné on the Niger River. Serious illnesses delayed his journey by some five months, and he eventually reached Timbuktu in April 1828, a year after leaving the Atlantic coast. Caillié stayed for two uneasy weeks before he followed caravan routes north across the Sahara, crossed the Grand Atlas Mountains to Fez, and travelled via Rabat to Tangier.

CAM, Diogo. ?–1486

(Also known as Diogo Cão.) Portuguese navigator who paved the way for

Bartolomeu Dias' discovery of the sea route to the Indian Ocean. Cam led the first voyage of exploration commissioned by King John II, a year after he ascended to the Portuguese throne in 1481. The southernmost point reached on the African coast by then was Point St Catherine which had been sighted by Gomes. Cam went beyond this to discover the mouth of the Congo River in August 1482. He set up a *padroa* there (a stone pillar bearing the Portuguese royal arms), and carried on south to Cape Santa Maria (latitude $13° 26'$ S) where he erected a second *padroa*. Thinking he had reached the southern tip of Africa, Cam returned to Portugal.

In 1485 he sailed on his second journey, finding that there was still a lot of Africa left. He placed a *padroa* on Monte Negro north of the Cunene River, another on Cape Cross north of Walvis Bay, and continued south, almost reaching the Tropic of Capricorn. Cabral returned to Portugal once more, but the leadership of the next voyage was given to Bartolomeu Dias, who at last reached Africa's southernmost Cape.

CAMERON, Verney Lovett. 1844–1894

British explorer who was the first to cross equatorial Africa from coast to coast. Cameron was chosen by the Royal Geographical Society in 1872 to lead an expedition taking supplies to Dr Livingstone, after which he was to explore the unknown equatorial regions. But not long after Cameron reached the African mainland from Zanzibar, and was heading inland, he met Livingstone's servants carrying the body of the missionary. He continued west from Tabora and made the first maps of much of Lake Tanganyika's shoreline.

During this operation Cameron discovered the Lukuga River and determined that it was the outlet of the Lake, while at Ujiji he recovered some of Livingstone's papers. From Lake Tanganyika Cameron contined westwards and travelled extensively in the Congo–Zambezi watershed. Arab hostility prevented him from getting hold of a suitable boat to prove his contention that the Lualaba River was an early part of the Congo system, and he had to complete his journey on foot, reaching Benguela in November 1875. Cameron was later to be the instigator and ardent promoter of the 'Cape to Cairo' railway concept.

CAMPBELL, John. 1766–?

One of the many British missionaries to arrive at the Cape of Good Hope after the British take-over in 1806. From 1812 to 1814 Campbell travelled from Cape Town eastwards to beyond Algoa Bay, and then turned inland to cross the bare highveld to Kuruman and Lattakoo, at that time the capital of the Botswana region. He then turned east to the Hartz River and followed it to its junction with the Vaal River, keeping to its course until it joined the Orange River and led him to Namaqualand. From there he returned to Cape Town. Six years later, in 1820, Campbell returned to the southern edge of the Kalahari and discovered the source of the Limpopo River.

CANO, Juan Sebastian del. ?–1526

(Also known as Juan Sebastian de Elcano). Magellan is naturally credited with being the first to circumnavigate the earth, but he died in the Philippines, and did not actually complete the journey. As captain of the *Victoria*, Cano took command of the expedition's two ships after Magellan's death. In the Moluccas the ships parted: one sailed back across the Pacific, while the other, under Cano, continued the circumnavigation and reached Spain in September 1522, three years after setting out on the historic voyage.

CÁRDENAS, Garcia Lopez de. (fl 1540)

Spanish discoverer of the Grand Canyon who travelled with Francisco Coronado in 1540–1. Coronado was searching for the supposed riches of the Seven Cities, expecting them to be in the region of Cibola in southern North America. After the expedition from New Spain (Mexico) failed to find the treasures, Coronado directed Cárdenas to explore westwards. For a while he followed the Colorado River, and eventually came to the spectacular canyon.

CARNEGIE, David. 1871–1900

In 1896 Carnegie attempted a south-to-north crossing of Western Australia – the same year that Lawrence Wells made his crossing. Carnegie's route from Lake Barlee was more to the east than Wells' and he crossed the Gibson Desert, Great Sandy Desert and Sturt Creek, before deciding to turn back.

CARPINI, Giovanni da Pian del. c 1180–1252

Wrote the first important and responsible general work on Central Asia, following a long and hazardous journey from 1245 to 1247. The Mongols of Asia had spread their empires rapidly westwards in the first half of the 13th century, but their approach was halted in 1241 by the death of the Great Khan and the procedure to elect his successor. Pope Innocent IV hoped to take advantage of the temporary lull to arrange a more lasting peace, and he chose Carpini to try to dissuade the Mongols from war. For Carpini – already over 60 – it must have been a daunting assignment. The journey itself was across a largely unknown land whose natural hazards were only exceeded by the widespread hostility of its peoples. The Pope also enjoined Carpini to make as many converts to Christianity as he could, and on Easter Sunday 1245 the expedition set out from Lyon. Carpini's route took him through Kiev, and along the north of the three great inland seas of Asia – the Black Sea, Caspian Sea and Aral Sea.

Batu, the Mongol conqueror of East Europe, directed the Christians to the royal court at Syra Orda, near Karakoram on the northern borders of the Gobi Desert, and the difficult journey continued eastwards at Easter 1246. The delegation finally arrived at Syra Orda in time for the crowning of Güyük, the new Great Khan, but they were no more able to obtain promises or concessions from the Mongols than they were to make converts to Christianity. In November 1246 Carpini and his group began the long, hazardous journey back to Europe and they eventually reached Kiev in June 1247. Nothing had been heard of them since they entered Mongol territory two years before, and they had long been given up for dead.

CARTERET, Philip. ?–1796

British explorer who sailed on two voyages with Byron in search of Terra Australis, in 1764 and 1766 (SEE JOHN BYRON and SAMUEL WALLIS). On the second expedition Carteret and Byron in the *Swallow* became separated from Wallis in the *Dolphin* after passing through the Strait of Magellan. Carteret sailed north, closer to the South American coast than Wallis, searching for islands believed to be in the vicinity of the Juan Fernandez Islands. When he did not find them, he began the journey westwards across the Pacific – a journey of considerable difficulty, for illness among the crew was rife and the ship was by then scarcely seaworthy. Despite the hardships, the explorers discovered Pitcairn Island and the Admiralty Islands, and rediscovered the Santa Cruz Islands east of the Solomons, unvisited by any Europeans since their discovery by Álvaro de Mendaña in 1595. Carteret sailed through the Solomon Islands, passed north of New Guinea to Mindanao in the Philippines, and eventually crossed the Indian Ocean to round the Cape of Good Hope and head north up the Atlantic, arriving back in England in 1769.

Cartier offering prayers at Gaspé Peninsula. (Mary Evans Picture Library)

CARTIER, Jacques. 1491–1557

The French mariner who initiated France's hesitant interest in the New World. Cartier was commissioned to find a western route to Asia, and ordered to return with the usual spices and gold. In 1534 he discovered the Gulf of St Lawrence, having sailed into it from the northern shores of Newfoundland, through the Strait of Belle Isle. He also briefly explored the Gaspé Peninsula; but instead of gold, Cartier took two Indians back to France.

Nevertheless, he persuaded King Francis to finance another two expeditions, and on the first of these, in 1535, Cartier established a base at present-day Quebec, before sailing upstream as far as the Lachine Rapids at Hochelaga (now Montreal). He returned to the St Lawrence in 1541 and made an inland expedition a little way beyond Hochelaga. The winter of 1541–2 was very severe, and many of Cartier's expedition died. Not much went right, in fact, and Cartier and his undisciplined crews treated the local Indians with mindless cruelty. Against Francis' orders, the explorer abandoned the base at Quebec in 1542 and spoke so ill of the land on his return home that the French were to find little enthusiasm for settling North America for some 50 years. French fishing fleets and some fur traders, however, profitably visited the area of the Gulf.

CHAMPLAIN, Samuel de. c 1567–1635

Far more than Cartier, Champlain was the true founder of 'New France' and of Quebec. The French explorer first went to North America in 1603, when he reached Hochelaga (Montreal) after entering the Gulf of St Lawrence through the Cabot Strait, south of Newfoundland. In 1604 he began his second journey and sailed along the coast of Nova Scotia, founding the first French colony in the New World at Port Royal on the peninsula's Bay of Fundy coast. Champlain continued south along the American coast, rounded Cape Cod and Nantucket Island, but turned back before reaching Long Island.

In 1608 he returned to the St Lawrence and founded a permanent colony at Quebec, initially as a fur-trading base. In contrast to Cartier, Champlain became friendly with the local Indians, the Hurons, and joined with them against the belligerent Iroquois. On one expedition with the Hurons he discovered Lake Champlain, south of Montreal. In 1610 he met Etienne Brulé, who was living with an Indian tribe, and learnt a great deal more about North America's first inhabitants. An account of a 'great sea' by its alleged discoverer, Nicolas Vigneau, took Champlain on a search up the Ottawa River in 1613; possibly Vigneau had seen or heard about one of the

147

Great Lakes, but Champlain abandoned the expedition half-way up the river and returned to Montreal. In 1615 he joined the Hurons in an unsuccessful raid against the Iroquois' stronghold at Lake Oneida, and on the way crossed Lake Ontario.

CHANCELLOR, Richard. ?–1556

The English pilot on a three-ship expedition led by Hugh Willoughby that sailed in 1553 from Deptford to seek a North-east Passage to the East. The ships became separated in a storm near the Lofoten Islands and Chancellor found himself alone at the pre-arranged rendezvous at Vardø, east of the North Cape. He sailed on through the Barents Sea and into the Beloye More (White Sea), landing at Colmagro (Archangel) where he discovered he was in little-known Muscovy (Russia). Chancellor abandoned the North-east Passage attempt and instead went overland to Moskva (Moscow), where he met Czar Ivan and formed an agreement for Anglo-Russian trade. This achievement was greatly praised when he returned to England, and he was sent back to Moskva in 1555. On that visit he arranged a monopoly of trade through the White Sea for the hastily formed Muscovy Company, but on his return voyage Chancellor was shipwrecked and drowned off the coast of Scotland.

CHANG CH'IEN. ?–114 BC

The Chinese ambassador during the early Han dynasty who was sent by Emperor Wu Ti to seek allies in Central Asia to counter the threat of the Huns from northern Asia – mainly against whom the Great Wall of China had been built some 100 years earlier. Chang Ch'ien set off in 138 BC hoping to get assistance from the Yue-Chi nomads, but he was captured by the Huns and spent ten years as their prisoner. Eventually, however, he did reach the Tashkent region, and although he was unable to enlist any allies in defence of China's northern borders, his knowledge of the land and the people between China and Afghanistan was soon to help establish the Silk Route. Eleven years after his return he was again sent on a mission, this time to the Wu-sun tribe in the Tarim Basin region, in what is now Russia. Chang Ch'ien travelled through lands that are now the Sinkiang province, Afghanistan and west Turkistan. He therefore brought China into contact with the outer limits of the Hellenistic cultures set up by Alexander the Great, and this led to the first exchange of envoys.

CHRISTIE, Charles. ?–1812

Together with Henry Pottinger discovered and mapped a great deal of land in the area now forming Iran, Afghanistan and Pakistan. In 1810 Christie and Pottinger set out on a two-year journey from Bombay and landed on the Baluchistan coast, just west of Karachi. In the guise of horse traders they travelled north to Nushki, south-west of present-day Quetta. Christie then went westwards across the Dasht-i-Margo Depression, and north to Herat in Afghanistan. He then crossed into Persia and rejoined Pottinger in Isfahan, from where they went north to Teheran and Qazvin. Once again their routes separated and Christie continued to Tabriz, eventually heading north-east to Baku on the Caspian Sea.

CLAPPERTON, Hugh. 1788–1827

The first European to see the huge varying lake in north Central Africa, Lake Chad, and the first to give a first-hand description of the region now

A ferry point on the Upper Niger River. (Mary Evans Picture Library)

described as northern Nigeria. In 1822 Clapperton, accompanied by Dixon Denham and Walter Oudney, left Tripoli and travelled south across the Fezzan to Marzūq. Clapperton and Oudney explored the region west of Marzūq and visited Ghat, north-east of the Ahaggar Mountains. The expedition completed the crossing of the Sahara to Lake Chad, where Denham was left to explore the region while the other two travelled west to Kano. Oudney died there and Clapperton continued westwards on his own to Sokoto. Unable to find a suitable guide, he returned to Kano by way of Katsina, and eventually retraced his steps to Tripoli, arriving there in 1825.

Later that year Clapperton made another expedition to Nigeria, accompanied by Richard Lander. On this occasion Clapperton approached from the south, landing on the coast on the Bight of Benin in the Gulf of Guinea. The two explorers travelled north to Bokani, crossing the Niger River, and went on to Kano and west to Sokoto – the intention being to reach the Niger again further upstream, and then sail to its mouth. However, in 1827, Clapperton died at Sokoto, and Lander returned to Kano and the Gulf of Guinea – though he was to return in 1830.

CLARK, William. 1770–1838

Explorer of North America. (SEE MERIWEATHER LEWIS.)

CLERKE, Charles. ?–1780

An officer in James Cook's voyages of 1768–71 and 1772–5. On the third voyage, which left England in 1776, he was promoted to captain of the *Discovery*, which accompanied the *Resolution*. After Cook was murdered in the Sandwich Islands (Hawaii) in 1779, Clerke assumed command of the expedition and sailed north-west to Asia's Kamchatka Peninsula. He completed the charting of the Bering Sea (the North American side having already been accomplished under Cook). While sailing past Kamchatka on the return trip, Clerke died and the journey home was completed by John Gore and James King, going by way of Japan, the Malaya Peninsula and the Cape of Good Hope.

COLENSO, William. 1811–1899

An early explorer of New Zealand's North Island who arrived at Poverty Bay in 1838. In 1841 he travelled westwards inland to Lake Waikaremoana, then headed north-west past Lake Rotorua and up North Island to the Bay of Islands. In 1843 Colenso explored south from Poverty Bay to about 41° S, returning via an inland route to circle Hawke Bay and revisit Lake Waikaremoana. Four years later he travelled from Hawke Bay to Lake Taupo, in the centre of North Island, and crossed the Ruahine Range before returning to Hawke Bay.

COLLINSON, Richard. 1811–1883

Explored North America's Arctic areas while searching for Franklin. (SEE JOHN FRANKLIN, 1850–4.)

COLUMBUS, Christopher. c 1451–1506

There can be few people who have never learnt the name Christopher Columbus, but perhaps the braggardly, foul-tempered mariner does not warrant such immortality. He is remembered for a discovery he did not realize he had made, and which was made almost by accident – and yet he had vision, unswerving faith in his convictions, and the ability to lead men onwards when all their instincts urged them to turn back.

Columbus was born in Genoa of Spanish-Jewish ancestry and is thought to have gone to sea at 14. His early seafaring was passed in piracy and other dubious activities, and eventually he was shipwrecked while fighting on the Portuguese side in a conflict with his home port of Genoa. The shipwreck was one of the most fortuitous events of his life, for it happened off the Portuguese coast and he swam ashore near Sagres, the site of Henry the Navigator's school for mariners. He was therefore plunged into the bustling focus of maritime exploration and authoritarian trade. Since his cartographer brother, Bartolomé, was also in Lisbon, it was natural that Columbus should remain – he never returned to Genoa. (He also wrote almost exclusively in Spanish, and called himself successively Colombo, Colomo and Colom, before settling on the Spanish Cristóbal Colón. He never used the name by which he is remembered.)

Soon after he arrived in Lisbon, Columbus went on a voyage to Iceland, and the idea that the East could be reached by travelling west (inspired by the writings of the cosmographer Toscanelli) probably matured into the beginnings of a plan on this journey. Columbus then lived for some time in the Madeira Islands, and sailed extensively in the central and south Atlantic, going as far as Mina on the Gold Coast – as far south as had been reached at that time. From the flotsam sighted on one of his voyages, he deduced that vegetation was growing somewhere not too far away, the direction of the current indicating that there should be land to the west.

Columbus added observations such as this to the deductions he made from the writings of Marco Polo, Ptolemy, and others. But he felt that he existed on a higher plane, and derived most of his conceptions from the apocryphal prophet Edras, so becoming absolutely certain that the world was indeed round. (It was characteristic of Columbus that after any successful endeavour, he would labour to find a Biblical text which 'prophesied' his discoveries; thus in 1502 he claimed that his discovery of 'An Other Land' was due more to prophecy and divine guidance than to navigational skill. It was not in his nature to be as self-deprecating as this remark seems to indicate, and modesty was doubtless not the reason for it.)

The prophet Edras not only vouched for the shape of the earth, but gave Columbus guidance on distances. The distance by land from the West to the East (which Columbus took to mean from Spain to India) was, Edras said, very long; and it was logical for Columbus to deduce that the sea route would therefore be shorter. With this guideline the mariner was able to get down to calculating specific distances, and brought into play a series of coincidences which were to have everlasting effect. Columbus reckoned that a degree of latitude at the equator spanned $56\frac{2}{3}$ miles, but he used Italian miles, whereas the longer Arabic mile, also then in use, would have given a figure much closer to reality. This meant that Columbus had an equator, or an earth, some 4,500 miles (7,240 km) smaller in circumference than its true size.

About 1,300 years earlier Ptolemy had also represented the earth as being considerably smaller than it really is, while he also allocated far more relative space to Europe and Asia (and consequently far less to the seas). Columbus took some satisfaction from Ptolemy, and followed Edras more closely. But Edras was an extremely inaccurate prophet, for he allocated six parts of the earth to land, and only one part to sea. Columbus calculated that 282° lay between Spain and India by land, which left only 78° for the journey the other way, by sea. The final outcome of all these prophecies and calculations was that India would be found about 3,900 miles (6,300 km) west of the Canaries. Unfortunately, this happens to be about the distance between America and the Canaries.

When Columbus had worked out the theory of his belief to his satisfaction, he took his proposal to the King of Portugal – who rejected it out of hand. Columbus then went to Spain, and began the long climb up the ladders of society and influence until, in spring 1486, he was granted an audience with King Ferdinand and Queen Isabella. They duly set up a commission to investigate Columbus' extraordinary claim that India, many thousands of miles across difficult land to the east, could also be found a few thousand miles away to the west, and was readily attainable by sea. Columbus did not help his case by cloaking some of his theories in secrecy and blanketing others beneath elaborately obscure statements, and his proposal to lead an expedition was turned down. Shortly afterwards, he met the shipowner and pilot Martin Pinzón, and the astronomer Antonio de Marchena, both of whom had worthwhile contacts in Spanish royal circles. Once again Columbus' proposal was put to the King and Queen, and early in 1492 they gave their assent – and even approved the exorbitant rewards he demanded should the expedition succeed.

Once he had the go-ahead Columbus moved swiftly, aided considerably by Pinzón who was part-owner of the two 50ft (15 m) caravels, *Pinta* and *Niña*, that were to accompany the 117ft (36 m) *Santa Maria*. At dawn on 3 August 1492 the three ships left Cape de Palos on Spain's Mediterranean coast and sailed to the Canaries, where fresh supplies were taken on board and modifications made to the riggings of the vessels. At last, on 6 September, the journey into the completely unknown Atlantic began, most of the sailors fearing that before long they would reach the end of the world and plunge into eternity, oblivion, or somewhere worse. By his confident bearing, however, and by his daily strategy of convincing the crews that they had sailed further than they in fact had, Columbus prevented any serious unrest. As the three ships continued westwards, further than any European had yet been, Columbus and the Pinzón brothers (commanding the two small caravels) noticed the growing difference between true north and

The Pinta – *a picture of a 19th-century reconstruction, hence the US flag.* (Mary Evans Picture Library)

Columbus' ships encountered strange seaweed in the Sargasso. Sea and many birds were seen before land was reached – after a 1599 engraving.

magnetic north, a phenomenon that did nothing to allay the unease that repeatedly overcame bouts of conviction and confidence.

It was Martin Pinzón who eventually persuaded Columbus to change to a more southerly course, and early in October they began to see numerous birds. Excitement mounted on the night of 11 October when endless flocks of birds could be heard flying overhead, and the next morning they were picking pieces of cut wood out of the sea. Early on 12 October 1492 a lookout sighted land, and soon Columbus stepped ashore on Guanahani in the Bahamas. He raised the Spanish flag, took possession of the island for the King of Spain, renamed it San Salvador (it is also known as Watling Island), and immediately set off in search of the major parts of the East Indies, for that is where Columbus believed he was – and why the islands came to be called the West Indies.

Columbus named the next two islands Fernandina and Isabella after his patrons (now Long Island and Crooked Island) and eventually came to a very large island, which he became convinced was either Cipango (Japan) or the coast of China, but which was in fact Cuba. Next to it was another large island of such appeal that Columbus named it Hispaniola, or Española (now Haiti and Dominica): he decided that this must be Japan, if the previous island (Cuba) was China.

Columbus had already met a number of natives, many wearing gold

154

ornaments, but he mishandled relations with them from the start. He brusquely removed seven inhabitants from Guanahani, and the goods he had brought with him for barter were so inferior that the islanders could see little benefit to be derived from these arrogant visitors. The Europeans were able to gather that warlike peoples lived somewhere to the south, and these Columbus equated with the people ruled by the Khans, about whom Marco Polo had written. Strangely, no serious attempt was made to find the source of the gold ornaments displayed by many inhabitants, although when Martin Pinzón and the *Pinta* suddenly disappeared one day, Columbus was convinced that the navigator had slipped off to find the gold for himself (the *Pinta* rejoined Columbus a few weeks later). His worries increased on Christmas Day 1492 when the *Santa Maria* was wrecked on Hispaniola. Eventually 40 men were left behind, euphemistically to form a settlement, but more realistically because they could not all fit on board the *Niña* and the *Pinta*.

On 16 January the two small ships set off for home, but a storm that struck in mid-Atlantic was so fierce that once again the *Pinta* went on alone – while Columbus wrote an account of his voyage, put it in a cask, and threw it overboard. He eventually reached Portugal in March, was honoured by King John, and went on to Spain to report to King Ferdinand, telling him that he had found the eastern extremity of the Asian mainland (in fact the northern coast of Cuba), and the island of Japan (in fact Haiti and Dominica).

Christopher Columbus – after a portrait attributed to Ghirlandio, c 1525, reputed to be a close likeness of Columbus in middle age.

Columbus duly received the numerous honours and titles, and the wealth and power he had insisted on, and even pocketed the money that had been promised to the first man to sight land – the rightful recipient, an angry and embittered sailor, went to live in Morocco. A second voyage was planned almost immediately, amid much acrimony over whether the principal aim should be missionary, settling, exploration or exploitation. Eventually, in September 1493, Columbus sailed in command of an expedition of 17 vessels which reached the West Indies in November. Arriving further south than before, he discovered some of the Lesser Antilles and Puerto Rico, but hastened to the spot on Hispaniola where he had left behind members of his first expedition – only to find that they had all been killed by the islanders. On this

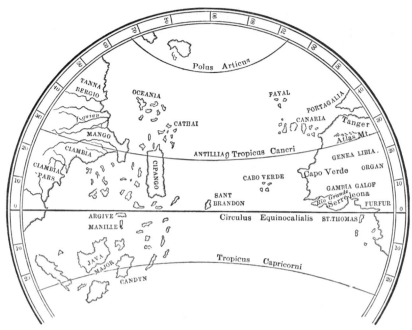

Behaim's view of the Atlantic in 1492, showing that it was not only Columbus who expected to find the East where in fact the Americas were. The island of Saint Brandon in the middle of the ocean may have been a mythical island, like Atlantis, or rumours of its existence may have come from voyages to the West Indies long before Columbus – by Phoenicians, Carthaginians, Irish monks, Vikings, and perhaps others. (Mary Evans Picture Library)

occasion, however, Columbus was properly prepared for founding a colony, and the first European settlement in the New World, Isabella, was established – today it is only a ruin on the north coast of Dominica. Whatever his abilities as a mariner, Columbus began to earn a decidedly unsavoury reputation as a governor and administrator. The settlers at Isabella quickly grew discontented with his harsh and uncompromising authority: it was his habit to settle disagreements by hanging the dissenters, and it was not only the native islanders whom he treated inhumanely.

Columbus again went to Cuba, from where he was duly directed to Jamaica; but he was there only briefly, being determined to establish Cuba as the Chinese mainland. Perhaps he began to suspect that he had been wrong all the time: well before he reached the western end and the Yucatan Channel (and thus before he had any definite proof) he announced to his crew that he was entirely satisfied that he had found the mainland, and that anyone who disagreed or later claimed that his leader had not gathered conclusive evidence, would pay for such effrontery by having his tongue cut out. Stifling criticism was not so easy, however, and discontent in the expedition was matched in Spain where Columbus' detractors were enjoying his absence. Anxious to redeem his standing, Columbus had two caravels built and sailed back to Cadiz in April 1496 – the first ships built in the New World to sail to the Old World.

The disfavour in which Columbus found himself was gradually overcome by his enthusiasm and confidence, and six ships sailed on his third voyage in May 1498. With part of the fleet Columbus took a south-west course from the Cape Verde islands, hoping to find more islands that he had heard of. He found none, but when he turned northwards again he was only a few days distant from the Amazon and South America. What he discovered instead on the way to the Caribbean was Trinidad. He sailed round the island into the Gulf of Paria and even landed on the South American mainland. To Columbus, however, this was yet another island, though later it seemed to gain significance when he attributed the relatively low salinity of the water in the Gulf of Paria (it receives the discharge of the Orinoco River) to its being the mouth of one of the four 'Rivers of Paradise'. He carried on to Cuba, unaware that the Spanish court, alarmed by reports of the increasing unrest in the new colonies, had appointed a governor in his place. On his arrival the new governor arrested Columbus (whose efforts to put down a revolt on Hispaniola succeeded only in inflaming it) and returned him in irons to Cadiz.

Although disgraced, humiliated and stripped of political power, Columbus still managed to persuade the King and Queen to moderate their displeasure, and he was able to undertake yet another voyage to the New World. His chief objective this time was to find gold that would finance his new obsession of 'liberating' Jerusalem. He sailed on his fourth voyage in May 1502 – by which time a considerable number of ships were crossing the Atlantic. He again sailed through the Lesser Antilles, discovering Martinique, went on to Jamaica and then across the Caribbean Sea to the Panamanian isthmus. May 1503 found Columbus in Panama's 'Mango Province', which was, according to him, 'next to that of Cathay' (Cathay being the old name for China). His expedition was plagued by fierce storms, a mutinous crew and a decaying ship, which was finally made derelict in a small Jamaican cove. Columbus was duly rescued and returned to Spain in September 1504. After that his mental and physical health declined rapidly, and he died in May 1506. His remains, after being exhumed and moved four times, at last came to rest beneath the Columbus Memorial Lighthouse on a cliff in Dominica.

CONDAMINE, Charles Marie de la.
SEE LA CONDAMINE.

CONTI, Niccolo dei. c 1395–1469

An Italian merchant who lived in Damascus and learnt Arabic at a very early age, and whose account of 25 years travelling in southern Asia from 1419 to 1444 provided geographers, cartographers and historians with a tremendous amount of information. Conti travelled overland from the eastern Mediterranean to Baghdad, went down the Persian Gulf to Hormuz, and learnt the language and habits of coastal Persians before he went on to India. He crossed the sub-continent from west to east and then travelled extensively in Burma and the Malaya Peninsula, went as far as Java, explored areas on both side of the Bay of Bengal and sailed along both the Ganges and the Irrawaddy. His journey back to Europe was via southern Ceylon, India, Aden and Jidda and he arrived in Venice in 1444. During his long wanderings Conti had neglected and renounced Christianity – as a penance he recounted his adventures to the Pope's secretary, who recorded the valuable account in Latin.

COOK, James. 1728–1779

The son of a Scottish farmhand, whose discoveries gave cartographers more valuable and accurate information about the world than had – or has since – been provided by any one man. He was born in Yorkshire and went to sea on the Whitby coal barques that plied the North Sea. His advance was rapid, but he joined the Royal Navy as an able seaman and was a master in the Seven Years' War. Later he carried out meticulous surveying of the Newfoundland coast and gained further recognition by his superiors when he sent details of his observation of an eclipse of the sun in 1766 to the Royal Society. By 1768 Cook had shown himself to have outstanding qualities of leadership, ability and zeal, and in that year he was chosen by the Royal Society and the Admiralty as commander of their first scientific expedition to the Pacific. The main task was to observe a transit of Venus on 3 June 1769 from Tahiti, which was the best place for its observation, but Cook also received orders to search for a sourthern continent.

He arrived at Tahiti by way of Le Maire Strait (at the tip of Tierra del Fuego), then sailing north-west and west through the Pacific. After the Royal Society's planetary observations were carried out, Cook sailed the *Endeavour* south to 40°S. By this single act, Cook demonstrated his superiority, for previous searchers had without fail followed favourable winds westwards or north-west, individual routes varying little from each other. On reaching 40°S Cook sailed two long legs north-west and then south-west, and so reached the east coast of New Zealand's North Island, again almost on the 40th parallel. He then sailed north round North Island,

Cook and members of the 1768–71 scientific expedition, on Tahiti. (Mary Evans Picture Library)

down its west coast, discovered Cook Strait between North and South Islands, and circumnavigated South Island. He thus proved that Tasman's Staaten Land was in two parts, and that neither of them had any connection with a southern continent.

From New Zealand Cook sailed west, and in April 1770 a Lt Hicks sighted land. This was the south-east corner of Australia, whose western coast was then known as New Holland. Cook headed slowly north and discovered Botany Bay – named for the great number of botanical specimens found there. Only a few miles further north lay the inlet into what was to become Port Jackson, and later Sydney, but its size was not fully appreciated and Botany Bay was marked for settlement. On 23 August Cook claimed the land for Britain and named it New South Wales. He then continued north, surveyed 2,000 miles (3,200 km) of the east coast, and sailed between the shore and the Great Barrier Reef – an undertaking which even today is attempted only by the most skilled navigators. The *Endeavour* rounded Cape York, rediscovered Torres Strait and then passed through the Timor Sea to Java. Cook anchored at Batavia (Djakarta) and proved the separation of Sumatra and Java; but there illness struck his previously healthy crew, and 30 died of fever and dysentry contracted ashore. Cook's humane and dignified bearing had already won him his crew's respect, a respect which grew every day as scurvy, the dread of long sea voyages, was kept from his ship. By prescribing a diet that included sauerkraut, cress and a kind of orange extract, and by insisting on cleanliness and adequate ventilation below decks, Cook never lost a member of his crews from scurvy, an achievement as notable as his discoveries and surveys.

The *Endeavour* arrived back in England in July 1771, Cook was promoted to commander, and planning began for what was to be one of the greatest voyages undertaken by sailing ships. In 1772 Cook set sail with the *Resolution* and the *Adventure*. Early in 1773 he became the first to cross the Antarctic circle, at about 35° E, and began the first west-to-east circumnavigation of the world in high latitudes. Keeping far south, mostly in the region of the 60th parallel, Cook sailed eastwards, but at about 145° E he turned north-east to sail up the west coast of New Zealand's South Island. In July 1773 he passed through Cook Strait and began a long loop north past Tahiti. He came back to chart the Friendly Islands (Tonga), and sailed down New Zealand's east coast, continuing south-east until he again crossed the Antarctic Circle. Further east at about 110° W, he crossed it for the third time and on this occasion reached 71° 10′, the highest southern latitude achieved.

Cook was by then approaching the western end of the Atlantic, but he headed north back into the Pacific and surveyed Easter Island before heading north-west to rediscover the Marquesas Islands, unvisited by European mariners since Mendaña's second voyage of 1595. Easter Island presented Cook with as intriguing a mystery as it presents to modern scientists. A Spanish expedition that had visited the island four years previously, in 1770, reported a thriving population of some 3,000, apparently of very mixed appearances – yet Cook found only about 400 men and 30 women, stricken by considerable starvation and sickness. He reported that the gigantic stone figure-heads were no longer venerated by the islanders, and that a number of them had been toppled over.

The *Resolution* and the *Adventure* then sailed back to Tahiti, past the Friendly Islands and headed north-west, enabling Cook to fix the exact position of the Santa Cruz Islands (where Mendaña had died). Cook then sailed south again, charted the New Hebrides and discovered New Caledonia, surveying its east coast before returning to New Zealand – by then a familiar watering place. In November 1774 he sailed east through Cook Strait and crossed the Pacific yet again, but on this occasion he continued through Le Maire Strait into the South Atlantic. Even then he was not ready to return home. He discovered the South Atlantic island of South Georgia and the South Sandwich Islands and called at Table Bay, before at last heading north to arrive back in England in 1775.

Cook's systematic voyages and highly accurate surveying of vast areas of the Pacific had at last broken the myth of a huge southern land mass, the

160

imaginary Terra Australis. Long-lost islands had been rediscovered, many new ones found, and much of Australia and all of New Zealand firmly placed on the map. The world map could now also feature higher southern latitudes with greater confidence than before, though Cook's sighting of mountain peaks when he crossed the 70th parallel indicated that one mysterious land did still exist. Once again, none of Cook's crews had died of scurvy, and this, and a paper he presented to the Royal Society on scurvy, earned Cook a fellowship of the Society and its highly prized gold Copley Medal.

With the southern Pacific Ocean now largely mapped and Terra Australis outlined, the next major challenge Cook took up was to discover a northern route from the Atlantic to the Pacific – the North-west Passage, or, if necessary, the North-east Passage. In July 1776 he sailed on this mission in the *Resolution* and the *Discovery*, hoping to find the North-west Passage from the Pacific, an approach that would also enable him to chart much of the northern part of the ocean. Cook was by now a full captain; the *Resolution* was commanded by William Bligh (who was to become captain of the *Bounty*) and the *Discovery* by Charles Clerke, who had been with Cook on the previous two voyages as well. Cook swept wide down the Atlantic and approached South America before turning to the Cape of Good Hope and heading east through the southern Indian Ocean, and then on to the southern tip of Van Diemen's Land (Tasmania). He returned to the familiar Cook Strait in New Zealand, and in turn sailed to the Cook Islands, back to the Friendly Islands, and east again to Tahiti. Then he headed into the northern Pacific Ocean and discovered Christmas Island and the Sandwich Islands (Hawaiian Islands). These he made his base, before sailing on to America's west coast, just north of 40° N. He sailed along the Alaskan coast, charting as he went, began the charting of the Bering Sea and the Aleutian Islands, and passed north through the Bering Strait before returning to Hawaii.

Early in 1779, during an argument with the islanders over the theft of one of his small boats, a scuffle broke out and Captain Cook was killed with a blow from a club. The surveying of the Bering Sea was completed by Clerke, and the voyage home, after Clerke's death, was directed by two of Cook's lieutenants (SEE CHARLES CERKE).

CORONADO, Francisco Vásquez de. 1510–1554

One of the early explorers of North America who was directed by the Viceroy of New Spain (Mexico) to search for the gold that Alvar de Vaca alleged existed in profusion in areas north of New Spain – allegations made more tempting by the legend of the wealthy Seven Cities of Cibola. In 1540

Coronado set out up the east side of the Gulf of California, and eventually found Cibola on the Colorado Plain (near present-day Gallup). Rather than being a golden city, however, it was a far from prosperous Indian village. Coronado then sent one of his companions, Melchior Diaz, back to the Gulf of California to meet Hernando de Alarcón, who was bringing supply ships up the Gulf. Diaz, however, only found a note from Alarcón at the mouth of the Colorado River, saying that he was abandoning his wait. Another of Coronado's colleagues, Garcia de Cárdenas, was sent westwards to look for possible riches, while Coronado himself led a search for another supposedly wealthy area called Quivira. He followed a fruitless trail north-east to beyond the Arkansas River, before returning to New Spain. Although Coronado's journey provided a vast amount of important geographical and anthropological information, as far as the Conquistadores were concerned success was measured in gold alone, and Coronado found himself disgraced and ignored.

CORTE-REAL, Gaspar. c 1450–c 1501

Portuguese mariner who, presumably having learnt of John Cabot's claim to have found the land of the Great Khan by a westerly route (this was actually Cabot's 1497 voyage to Newfoundland), sailed in 1500 and retraced Cabot's path to the southern tip of Greenland. Ice packs along Greenland's west coast forced Corte-Real to turn back; but in 1501, accompanied by his brother Miguel Corte-Real in a second ship, he returned to Greenland, sailed directly west and reached the coast of Labrador. Later on they captured some Indians on Newfoundland whom Miguel took back to Portugal while Gaspar continued south. By May 1502 Gaspar had still not returned to Portugal, and Miguel sailed again to the new land to search for him. Nothing was heard of either of the Corte-Real brothers again.

CORTES, Hernando. 1485–1547

Conqueror of Mexico, and the best known of the Spanish Conquistadores. Cortes grew up in a tough peasant province in Spain, and was distantly related to another famous Conquistador, Francisco Pizarro. He had a brief and unsuccessful sojourn at the University of Salamanca, but it was enough for him to be regarded as a 'man of letters' in the primitive early settlements on Hispaniola (Haiti and Dominica), to which Cortes sailed in 1504 at the age of 19. He was consequently made notary of a small village, but in 1511 he joined the 300 men under Diego Velasquez who sailed to conquer Cuba. Cortes swiftly made himself prominent and was appointed King's Treasurer in Santiago. Despite his office and responsibility, he was unable to temper his compulsive womanizing, and his position grew rather precarious. An ideal and timely escape presented itself when he was appointed the leader of an expedition to follow up indications of Aztec wealth arising from Juan de Grijalva's expedition. The new venture comprised 11 ships, over 500 soldiers, 100 sailors, 16 horses, and a considerable supply of guns; it was largely paid for by Velasquez, who hoped to get a profitable return in the way of gold, but Cortes also put all his savings into the expedition and thus secured the leadership.

The ships sailed in February 1519 – none too soon for Cortes, whose behaviour in Santiago was also threatening his relationship with Velasquez. Having at last escaped from the opponents among his colleagues, Cortes totally committed himself and his men to the Mexican venture by the irrevocable step of burning his ships on the Mexican beaches. Then he started the march inland, and so began the destruction of the Aztecs. The devastation was not entirely caused by military action, though in a two-hour battle at Cholula some 3,000 Indians died. Cortes' losses were relatively low, despite the hardships of the jungle, and at last the column arrived at Tenochtitlan, where Cortes was met with rare humility by Montezuma, the

Cortes meets Montezuma at the Aztec capital, Tenochtitlan. (Mary Evans Picture Library)

Aztec Emperor. Considerable superstition surrounded Cortes' arrival, for Aztec mythology predicted the arrival of a god and Cortes seemed to fulfil the prophecy. The luxurious welcome afforded him, and the magnificence of Tenochtitlan (an island city, then in the huge Lake Texcoco, and now Mexico City), together with the sight of a great deal of gold, must have fired Cortes' imagination, but his initial approach was cautious. In countering the astute Montezuma Cortes was helped considerably by the devotion of a captured Indian princess who spoke the Aztec language.

Mutual respect and peaceful co-existence between the Spaniards and Aztecs was a false situation with little hope of endurance. Montezuma must have seen Cortes as a threat to his power and his people, while Cortes could not have believed that he would get the gold he wanted without considerable cost. He must also have felt very vulnerable among the vast numbers in the city – there was a great deal of evidence that the elaborate culture of the Aztecs was interwoven with a fearsome barbarity. But before the situation could develop into conflict, Cortes had to rush to the Mexican coast to put down an attempt, organized by Velasquez, to usurp his position in Mexico, and to gain a greater share of the Aztec riches which Cortes considered his due. During his absence from Tenochtitlan, Pedro de Alvarado and the Spaniards massacred thousands of Aztecs during a festival, and Cortes returned to find the atmosphere decidedly antagonistic.

The Aztecs duly attacked the Spanish invaders, Montezuma was killed by stones flung by his own people, and Cortes, Alvarado, and a minority of the Spaniards managed to escape by night over the causeway, while the battle raged. In May 1521 Cortes returned to besiege Tenochtitlan, and after 80 days the city fell. Yet it was not guns and soldiery or military tactics that caused the final collapse and annihilation of the Aztec civilization. Along with their missionary zeal, their lust for power, their avaricious scavenging for gold and their mechanisms of killing, the invaders brought smallpox, measles, scarlet fever and respiratory illnesses to a civilization that had not the slightest inbuilt immunity. (Christians of that era liked to believe that it was their God who arranged the 'visitations' which decimated populations without a pistol being fired – eventually even well in advance of their arrival in areas they wished to conquer.) The toll was horrific. Before Cortes stepped ashore, the population of Central America was in the region of 20,000,000. Twenty years later it was little more than 6,000,000, and 60 years after Montezuma's death it had fallen to below 2,000,000.

It is unlikely that Cortes was anything but pleased to see the population shrinking dramatically – Spain, and Velasquez, were giving him enough trouble as it was. He constantly nursed an ambition to establish an independent kingdom, but the urge to explore and his remaining loyalty to Spain overcame this dream, and instead he sent out expeditions and put down local uprisings. A journey to Honduras damaged his health and also his reputation, for once again the deputies he left behind proved needlessly cruel. His standing in Spain was also much diminished, and in 1528 Cortes returned to affirm his loyalty and redeem his reputation.

In 1530 he returned to New Spain only to find it virtually in anarchy. Cortes managed to restore a degree of control, and began to build a palace at Cuernavaca, 30 miles (48 km) south of Mexico City. He dreamt of an exploratory voyage into the Pacific, despatched an expedition to the Moluccas (SEE ÁLVARO DE SAAVEDRA), sent aid to Pizarro in Peru, but was compelled to return to Spain in 1540. His fortunes continued to decline; and eventually, pursued by his debts and with no more standing than a commoner, he begged to return to Mexico, but died before he could leave Spain.

COSA, Juan de la. ?–1509

A cartographer whose maps show how the world looked in Columbus' time,

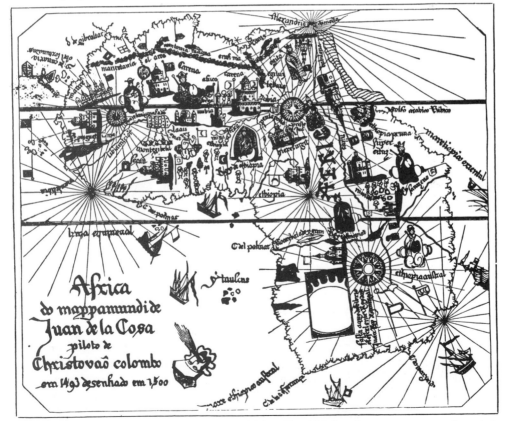

Juan de la Cosa's late 15th-century map of Africa. Fanciful drawings, compasses and symbols were ideal for covering areas about which the cartographers knew nothing. (Mary Evans Picture Library)

though they leave many questions intriguingly unanswered. Cosa was a pilot on Columbus' second voyage to the New World, and in 1499–1500 accompanied Amerigo Vespucci to the north coast of South America, the Caribbean, and the Bahamas. Cosa depicted the Americas fading off to the edge of his parchment, thus avoiding making a judgement on Columbus' claim that he had found the East. Cuba, strangely, was drawn by Cosa as an island though Columbus argued that it was mainland, and it was not proved to be an island until 1508. Some say that this is evidence that Portuguese mariners might have preceded Columbus to the New World.

COSMAS.

SEE INDICOPLEUSTES.

COVILHÃ, Pedro da. c 1450–c 1540

Rumour reached Portugal in 1486 about a great Christian ruler in the East, and this was taken to be yet another reference to the legendary Prester John, then generally supposed to be in the region of Abyssinia (Ethiopia). King John II despatched Covilhã to look for Prester John and to try to find a sea route around Africa from the east (Portuguese mariners were then pressing further and further down the west coast of Africa). Covilhã, accompanied by Afonso de Paiva, sailed east through the Mediterranean in 1487 and went down to the Red Sea. Paiva disembarked to search for Prester John in Abyssinia while Covilhã sailed to India, and crossed the Arabian Sea to the entrance of the Persian Gulf. He returned to the Gulf of Aden and sailed far down the African coast to Sofala (now Nova Sofala, just south of Beira). Not knowing how much of Africa remained, Covilhã turned back for Europe, but at Cairo he learnt that Paiva was dead. He sent a lengthy report to King John and went back down the Red Sea to Abyssinia (which practised Coptic Christianity) to continue the search for Prester John in 1490. Covilhã remained in the service of the Emperor of Abyssinia until his death, and his report on the east coast of Africa greatly aided Vasco da Gama on his first voyage round Africa.

CRESQUES, Abraham. (fl 1375)

Cartographer whose world map, drawn in about 1375 on eight panels, was the first to show the new knowledge gained from the travels of Marco Polo and Odoric. The map became known as the Catalan Atlas.

CROZIER, F R M. ?–1848

Polar explorer who accompanied James Ross to the Antarctic from 1839 to 1843, and took part in Franklin's ill-fated expedition to find the North-west Passage, taking command after Franklin's death. SEE JAMES CLARK ROSS, 1839–43, and JOHN FRANKLIN, 1845–8.

DAMPIER, William. 1652–1715

An English pirate who set off on a voyage in 1683, rounded South America into the Pacific, and sailed north to the Gulf of California. He followed Álvaro de Saavedra's 1527 route from Mexico to the Moluccas, an area offering rich pickings for a seasoned pirate like Dampier. In 1688 he sailed south from the Moluccas and came to the unknown northern part of New Holland (Western Australia), where he enjoyed the safety of a refuge in King Sound. He explored the promontory of Dampier Land and made copious notes on some 1,000 miles (1,600 km) of Australia's north-west coast. The substance of his findings was published in his *Voyages* in 1697, and although he had little good to say about the land, he was commissioned (by the Admiralty, no less) to lead an expedition to New Holland.

Dampier sailed in 1699, and decided to find New Holland's east coast by another Pacific approach. Atlantic storms eventually forced him to take the Cape of Good Hope and Indian Ocean approach, however, and so he missed the chance to discover the richer side of the continent. Instead he reached New Holland at Dirk Hartog's Island, but stopped following the coastline at Dampier Land and continued across the Timor Sea to make an extensive voyage around the Moluccas and nearby islands. Two narrow passages off New Guinea were named after him; Dampier Strait separates New Guinea from New Britain, and Selat Dampier is at New Guinea's western extremity.

DARWIN, Charles. 1809–1882

The English naturalist who became one of the most famous scientists in history through his deductions on evolution. He joined HMS *Beagle* as official naturalist when it sailed on a round-the-world surveying voyage in December 1831. The *Beagle*'s first task was to carry out an intensive survey of the Patagonian and Tierra del Fuego coasts, and Darwin was regularly left ashore on land expeditions while the ship was making its slow survey. By March 1834 the ship and Darwin had reached the Falkland Islands, and

Dampier meets aborigines in Australia. (Mary Evans Picture Library)

from April to May he crossed the South American mainland from east to west on the 50th parallel; by then his collection of specimens was already formidable. In January 1835 the *Beagle* was off the southern coast of Chile, and Darwin explored Isla de Chiloé and later the inland region near Valparaiso. The expedition eventually left South America half-way through 1835, Darwin's last collections being made in Peru. Despite the vast amount of material gathered in South America, it was in the Galápagos Islands that Darwin found the richest variety of unknown creatures, insects, birds, and plants, and was able to gather the evidence and conviction he needed to present his revolutionary statements. The *Beagle* returned to England in 1836 and in 1859 Darwin published his *On the Origin of Species by Natural Selection, or the Preservation of Favoured Races in the Struggle for Life.*

DENHAM, Dixon. 1786–1828

Travelled with Hugh Clapperton and Walter Oudney across the Sahara desert from Tripoli to Lake Chad (SEE CLAPPERTON), 1822–3. Denham remained in the vicinity of Lake Chad until 1824, explored the south and east areas bordering the depression, and followed the course of the Chari River until it crossed 10° N.

DESHNEF, Semen Ivanov. c 1605–1673

Led the 1644–9 expedition during which the first known passage through the Bering Strait between Siberia and Alaska was made. Deshnef was accompanied to the Kolyma River (meeting it on about the 150th meridian, in eastern Siberia) by Mikhailo Stadukhin, who had discovered it on an earlier expedition (SEE STADUKHIN). Near the coast Deshnef founded Nizhiye Kolymsk, and at the river's mouth the expedition took to the sea and sailed eastwards, south of Vrangelya Island, and then south through the then unknown 'Bering' Strait. A landing was made at the northern end of the Kamchatka Peninsula, and Deshnef went north to pick up Stadukhin's old trail to the Anadyr River, which flows into the Bering Sea. The river was followed upstream until its turn to the north, when Deshnef continued east to rejoin the Kolyma, following its upper course as the expedition headed south-east towards Okhotsk. Some time passed before news filtered back to high offices that Deshnef had found an 'end' of the Asian continent, but he was not widely believed and even Bering's commissioned voyage of 1728 left some in doubt.

A view of the Ganges River in the early 19th century. (Mary Evans Picture Library)

DESIDERI, Ippolito. 1684–1733

A Jesuit missionary who travelled from Goa to Delhi in 1713, and the following year set out for Tibet, accompanied by Emmanuel Freyre. The pair initially followed Bento de Goes' path to Lahore, but on about 74° E they continued north, and then crossed the Himalayas in an eastwards loop to Leh. Although they were warmly welcomed there, and even encouraged to establish a mission, Freyre was anxious to return to India and they set off eastwards in the hope of finding an easier crossing of the huge mountain range. After travelling high in the valley of the Indus River to Gartok, Desideri and Freyre followed the Matsang Tsangpo (the upper reaches of the Brahmaputra River) for some distance, crossing the Shigatse-Katmandu road to reach Shigatse, and eventually, in 1716, Lhasa, the mysterious capital of Tibet.

Freyre returned to India after only a brief stay in Lhasa and by-passed

Shigatse to the south before entering Nepal and going on to the Ganges River and to Agra. For some time Desideri was the only European living in Lhasa, and it was not until 1721 that he followed Freyre's route to Agra. In 1725 he returned down the Ganges and embarked on a ship bound for Rome. Desideri's attempt to establish a Christian mission in the heart of Tibet was unsuccessful, and so isolationist and steadfast were the Tibetans that some 200 years were to pass before further Christian missionaries followed the footsteps of these early travellers.

DIAS, Bartolemeu. c 1450–1500

Portuguese navigator whose discovery of the southern tip of Africa led to Vasco da Gama making the first sea voyage from Europe to the East. King John II of Portugal had been made responsible for the southward exploration of Africa's west coast in 1474, and when he succeeded to the throne seven years later he ordered a new series of voyages to determine Africa's southern extremity, the mariners being required simultaneously to claim coastal lands for Portugal by erecting *padroas* – stone pillars bearing the royal arms of Portugal. Most successful of these mariners was Diogo Cam, who had reached Cape Cross; following Cam's last voyage, King John directed Dias to find the route to India round Africa (at the same time despatching Pedro da Covilhã on an overland expedition to look for other new routes to the East).

Dias sailed in August 1487 with three ships and some of Portugal's leading pilots – one of whom had sailed with Cam. The expedition reached Walfisch Bay (Walvis Bay) on 8 December and passed the Gulf of St Stephen (Elizabeth Bay) just after Christmas. Then, early in January 1488, a series of fierce storms struck and Dias could do no more than keep heading south, though he was soon swept out of sight of land. Several days later better weather allowed him to head west again, and when he had sailed well past the longitude at which he had last seen land, he realized that he must have reached the end of the continent. Dias turned north, sighted land on 3 February, and landed at Mossel Bay on Africa's southern coast, where he put up his second *padroa* (the first was erected at present-day Luderitz).

A group of inhabitants fled when the expedition arrived but later attacked the shore party. In due course, Dias sailed further east to Angra da Roca (Algoa Bay – the site of Port Elizabeth). With his crew strongly urging him to turn back for home, Dias sailed still further east and reached the Rio do Infante (probably the Great Fish River), but then turned about. As he reached the Atlantic, Dias got his first sight of Africa's magnificent southern cape; according to legend, Dias, remembering the earlier storms which had swept him from it, named it the Cape of Storms. King John hoped that it would be a better portent if he renamed it the Cape of Good Hope, but he

The lateen-rigged caravels that took Diaz further and further down the coast of Africa. (Mary Evans Picture Library)

died before da Gama's voyage saw his ambition fulfilled. Dias had perhaps named it aptly, however, for he perished in a storm off the Cape in 1500, commanding a ship in Pedro Cabral's ill-fated voyage.

DIEFFENBACH, Ernst (fl 1839)

In 1839, the year in which New Zealand's first settlers arrived in the *Tory* to establish Wellington, Dieffenbach explored the central Taranaki region on North Island and became the first to climb Mount Egmont.

DOUGHTY, Charles. 1843–1926

An Englishman who travelled extensively in Arabia, one of his principal achievements being that he managed this without concealing his

Christianity, or his nationality. In 1874–5 he travelled with Bedouin tribesmen through Petra, and east of the Dead Sea to Damascus. Doughty heard about some ancient ruins at Medā'in Sālih, from there going to Taymā and the Hā'il area. He also saw Buraydah and Unayzah in central Arabia, and then travelled on to Jiddah on the Red Sea. Entrance to Mecca was impossible since he made no effort to disguise himself, but his writings, *Arabia Deserta*, provided a valuable and absorbing picture of his travels, and described his many hardships and dangers in a harsh land especially hostile to European Christians.

DRAKE, Francis. c 1540–1596

English Admiral, conqueror of the Spanish Armada and the greatest of England's Elizabethan mariners. He was the son of a tenant farmer in Devon and went to sea at 13, serving an apprenticeship on a small vessel in the North Sea. Ten years later Drake joined the substantial Plymouth-based fleet of the Hawkins family, to whom he was distantly connected, and gained the experience of sailing across the Atlantic to the New World – principally on slave ships between West Africa and the West Indies. Above all else he developed a dislike of the Spanish, and this turned to a burning hatred after he experienced an attack by Spanish ships during his second expedition to the West Indies. Many Englishmen were killed, and as John Hawkins himself had been on the expedition, Queen Elizabeth duly heard about the disaster, and about the fierce and talented Drake.

In 1572 Drake was given a 'privateering commission'. This was a dignified way of telling him to go out and raid Spanish ships for any cargoes that would benefit England. Drake could have wished for nothing more, and with two ships he had a successful voyage to the West Indies. During this expedition he crossed the Isthmus of Panama and was so moved by the sight of the Pacific, that he determined that England should benefit from it as much as anyone else.

Drake's chance to fulfil his vow came in December 1577 when, on Elizabeth's orders, he sailed to explore South America for possible English interests, capture what bounty he could, and attempt a circumnavigation of the world. He sailed with only 200 men in five small ships – his own, which he renamed the *Golden Hind*, was a mere 100 tons. At the tip of South America the two food-supply ships had their cargoes transferred and were left behind while the expedition made its way to the Magellan Strait. The narrow, winding route took 16 days to navigate. As the ships entered the Pacific they were caught in a severe storm, during which the *Golden Hind* was separated from the others. When the storm abated the leader of the other ships presumed Drake to be lost, and returned to England; Drake,

Francis Drake. (Mary Evans Picture Library)

meanwhile, discovered that he had been blown back eastwards beyond Tierra del Fuego's meridian, proving that this most southerly known land was an island, and not a promontory of the supposed Terra Australis. The 600-mile-wide gap (965 km) below Tierra del Fuego was then named

Drake's Passage, though Willem Schouten was the first to use it deliberately to enter the Pacific in 1615.

Undeterred by being left on his own, Drake sailed up the Chile coast and enjoyed wreaking havoc as the first hostile ship the Spanish had ever encountered in the Pacific. He plundered every Spanish ship he met, and for good measure the ports of Valparaiso and Callao as well. With the *Golden Hind* heavy with gold, prizes and provisions, Drake sailed northwards in the hope of finding a Pacific entrance to a North-west Passage, but by 48° N, when he was off present-day Vancouver Island, the cold forced him to turn south. For a short while he anchored off what is now San Francisco, named the country New Albion, and claimed it for Queen Elizabeth. In July 1579 Drake set off across the Pacific, missed discovering Hawaii, and after 68 days sighted islands that probably were the Ladrones (Marianas). Drake landed in the Philippines and concluded a trade treaty in the Moluccas before going on to Java (where some reef damage to his ship was repaired). He crossed the Indian Ocean and arrived back in England in September 1580. Only 56 of the original 100 on the *Golden Hind* completed the voyage, but Drake had become the first leader of an expedition and first ship's captain to circumnavigate the world (Magellan was killed in the Philippines), as well as the first Englishman to do so; he was also the first Englishman to sail into the Pacific, Indian and South Atlantic oceans.

The amount of wealth that Drake brought back, and the apparent ease with which he got it, had considerable influence on English policy, and the rigours, expense and uncertainty of exploration were ruled out in favour of a more piratical campaign. Drake was knighted by Queen Elizabeth on board the *Golden Hind*, and he was made Mayor of Plymouth. His lifelong hatred of the Spanish had its culmination in his defeat of the Spanish Armada in 1588, but he had already wrecked Spain's influence, her Empire, and much of her wealth by other crushing defeats in the West Indies and the Cape Verde Islands. A later expedition to the West Indies was unsuccessful, however; fever struck his crew and little could be accomplished. A great number died, and eventually Drake, too, succumbed. He was buried at sea off Portobelo, Panama.

DUVEYRIER, Henri. 1840–1892

From 1859 to 1861 this young Frenchman travelled in the northern Sahara among the Tuareg, gradually gaining their confidence after overcoming their habitual hostility to foreigners. His wanderings with these nomads included the northern region of the Grand Erg Oriental from Ouargla to Biskra and east to the Gabés Gulf, and also the eastern region of the Grand Erg Occidental at El Goléa. Duveyrier travelled as well to

Ghudāmis, to Ghāt, Marzūq, and across the Fezzan to Tripoli. His book, *The Tuareg of the North*, is still one of the most authoritative works about these daunting people, whose traditional life-style has been forced into rapid change.

EANNES, Gil. (fl 1434)

A Portuguese of some wealth who was in the service of Henry the Navigator (the third son of King John I) and who broke one of the substantial barriers to Portuguese exploration of Africa's west coast – although not easily. In 1433 Eannes sailed to Tenerife in the Canaries, but turned back instead of continuing south past Cape Bojador. This point was the legendary 'end of safe journeys', beyond which lay the terrors of a boiling sea, where all white men turned black and from whence it was impossible to return. His apprehension seemed a good deal less understandable to Eannes once he got back to Portugal, however, and he was so ashamed of having let Henry down that he immediately planned another voyage. In 1434 he safely passed Cape Bojador, broke the dreaded spell, and proved it totally redundant with another voyage the next year, when he sailed well south of the cape to the Bay of the Rio de Oro, just north of the Tropic of Cancer.

ELCANO, Juan Sebastian de.

SEE CANO, JUAN SEBASTIAN DEL.

EMIN PASHA. 1840–1892

A brilliant but frequently eccentric German turned Moslem, born Eduard Schnitzer. As an official of the Egyptian Government Emin rose to become the Governor of the Equatoria Province. Following the Mahdi's revolt in 1885 he retreated up the Nile with the Equatoria 'garrison', a somewhat unwieldy gathering of 10,000 soldiers, women and children. He was the last to hold out against the rebels, his remoteness working in his favour, although this very remoteness prevented him from communicating with the rest of the world. Emin, however, knew the area well – since 1876 he had made a number of expeditions, and had thoroughly explored the Nile–Congo watershed west and north-west of Juba. He also explored a wide area between Juba and Lake Victoria, though Lake Kyoga escaped his notice.

In 1888 a fund was gathered to rescue Emin Pasha, and Stanley was appointed to head the expedition – an expedition that became a nightmare for Stanley and the 700 who began the journey with him from the mouth of the Congo (SEE HENRY MORTON STANLEY). Emin was reasonably secure with his garrison at Lake Albert, and in the end he was the one to save Stanley. There was little rapport between the two highly dissimilar men, but after a good deal of argument and acrimony, Emin left his stronghold – as is recounted in the entry on Stanley.

Having reached Bagamoyo comparatively unscathed, Emin once again set off for Africa's interior, heading a German expedition that was initially intended to seize the Nile source area for Germany. This intention was soon changed, however, though Emin ignored orders to return to the coast, and Germany eventually had to disown him. In 1891 he made contact with soldiers of his Equatoria garrison who had remained at Lake Albert, but they no longer regarded him as their leader. Emin then pushed deeper into Africa, doing a fair amount of scientific work but losing half his force from smallpox. One October night in 1892, less than 100 miles (160 km) south of Stanley Falls in the depths of the Congo, a group of Arab slavers attacked Emin's camp, burst into his tent, and cut his throat. For all his eccentricities and occasional foolhardiness or delusions of grandeur, Emin Pasha is regarded by many as one of the greatest explorers of Africa, for, unlike many who are better known, he made highly intelligent and determined efforts to understand and discover all aspects of life in the continent.

ENTRECASTEAUX, Bruni d'. 1737–1793

In 1791 d'Entrecasteaux led an expedition to try to find Jean de la Pérouse, who had disappeared in 1788 after sailing from Port Jackson (Sydney) in an attempt to locate Mendaña's Solomon Islands. No trace of Pérouse was ever found, but d'Entrecasteaux did manage to identify and pin-point the Solomon Islands, 'missing' since their discovery in 1567. He explored these islands, as well as the Louisiade Archipelago on the eastern tip of New Guinea, where a group is known as the d'Entrecasteaux Islands.

ERIC the RED. c 940–c 1010

A Norseman who was expelled from the Viking colony on Iceland in 982 and then sailed west to land on Greenland, which had been discovered by Irish monks some 100 years earlier. Eric gave the country its name, and soon left for Norway to prepare a colonizing expedition. This sailed to Greenland in 985, and the colonists settled in two main groups on the southern end of Greenland's west side, though Eric extensively explored the east coast as well as the west.

ERICSSON, Leif. (fl AD 1000)

The son of Eric the Red, and the discoverer of Vinland in c AD 1000. The expedition left the southernmost Norse settlement on Greenland's west coast and sailed northwards past their second settlement (which was on approximately the same latitude as Reykjavik) before sailing west to land at Helluland (probably Baffin Island). The Vikings then sailed south along Markland (Labrador and Newfoundland) to Vinland (the coastal area between Cape Cod and Nova Scotia). Ericsson arrived in Vinland in winter, and enjoyed the comparatively mild weather before returning to Greenland in 1001.

EYRE, Edward. 1815–1901

Australian explorer who was the first, in 1839, to sight the huge Lake Torrens north of the head of Spencer Gulf in South Australia. Eyre later explored the coast of the Great Australian Bight from Port Lincoln on Eyre Peninsula north-west to Streaky Bay. In 1840 he tried to travel into central Australia, but kept coming up against the numerous lakes that periodically cover so great an area of eastern South Australia (the largest of these is Lake Eyre). This led him to conclude that an impenetrable barrier of lakes curved round Spencer Bay – a theory that remained credible for 18 years. Eyre undertook his most arduous exploration in 1841 when he travelled west from Fowlers Bay along the practically waterless coast of the Bight, as far as Albany, from where he cut across the south-western tip of Australia to Fremantle.

FAWCETT, Percy. 1867–1925?

British explorer whose disappearance in South America is one of exploration's many intriguing mysteries. Fawcett's involvement with the continent began in 1906 when he sailed down its west coast to determine the boundaries of Bolivia, Peru and Brazil. His expedition went ashore at Mollendo in southern Peru, crossed the Andes and Lake Titicaca, and

Eyre meets a party of French whalers on the coast during his 1841 crossing of Australia. (Mary Evans Picture Library)

followed the Beni River to the Bolivia–Brazil border, just past the junction with the Madre de Dias. Brazil's Peruvian and Bolivian borders in the Madeira River source areas were surveyed before the expedition headed back across the mountain range.

Fawcett returned to the Lake Titicaca area in 1910 to survey the Andes north of the lake, but before that, in 1908–9, he travelled from Buenos Aires up the Paraná and Paraguay rivers to the Chapada dos Parecis, the watershed which partly drains south in the Paraguay River, and partly into the Amazon by way of the Guapore River (most of which forms the Brazil–Bolivia border). Fawcett explored this region again in 1913–14 from the west coast and a base at La Paz, after surveying in the Andes south-east of Lake Titicaca. In 1920 he was in Rio de Janeiro and went on an expedition westwards into Paraguay, from where he travelled north and followed the Cuibabá River into the Planalto do Mato Grosso. The following year Fawcett was further north up the Brazilian coast, exploring the inland region between Salvador and Vitória da Conquista.

A document Fawcett had acquired during his travels described one of the many fabled 'lost cities' of the South American jungle, and in 1925, with his son Jack and Raleigh Rimell, he set out to search for it. He retraced his 1920 route into the Mato Grosso and continued north almost to 10° S, and some distance west of the Xingu River. Fawcett's intention was then to head westwards, believing that the city lay between the Tocantins and São Francisco Rivers. The group set off towards the Xingu River, but nothing was heard or seen of the expedition again.

FIENNES, Ranulph. 1945–

Leader (with his wife Virginia as base leader) of the British Transglobe Expedition which at the time of writing is attempting the first longitudinal circumnavigation of the world. Fiennes, Charles Burton and Oliver Shepard, supported by a highly trained (and unpaid) team, plan to cross 900 miles (1,500 km) of unexplored Antarctica to the South Pole, and continue via the Scott Glacier to MacMurdo Sound, where they will rejoin the expedition's ship, the *Benjamin Bowring*.

Transglobe's next land section will begin at the mouth of the Yukon River, Alaska, where one-man inflatable boats, fitted with skids for travelling on ice, will be used to follow the course of the Yukon and Mackenzie Rivers to the gruelling North-west Passage. Travelling by the ice-boats, sledges and skis, the three-man team will then head for their overwintering camp on the Arctic coast of Ellesmere Island.

The second polar crossing, via the North Pole, is scheduled for the spring of 1982, after which the expedition will take advantage of the summer movement of ice into the Greenland Sea to meet the *Benjamin Bowring* at Spitsbergen.

Extensive media coverage will give armchair adventurers an opportunity to appreciate the rigours that polar exploration entails, even with the benefit of sophisticated modern technology.

FITCH, Ralph. ?–1606

An Englishman who travelled widely in India and the East in the late 16th century and provided valuable information about trading prospects. Fitch left England in 1583 on an expedition to find an overland route to India which might rival the long Cape of Good Hope sea route. The expedition was headed by John Newberry and included William Leeds. In Hormuz the entire group was arrested and taken to India as prisoners. They obtained their release in Goa, and Fitch went with Leeds to Fatephur Sikri (adjacent to Agra, on the Jumna River), the court of the Mogul Emperor Akbar, to whom he delivered a letter from Queen Elizabeth. Newberry, the expedition's leader, headed back for England (and was not seen again), Leeds joined Akbar's court, and Fitch began, in 1585, a six-year exploration of the East. He travelled along the Ganges and up to Cooch Behar, then down to the western edge of the Ganges delta, to the eastern edge of the Irrawaddy delta, up into the Shan States in northern Burma, to Malacca, Ceylon, and India's west coast. He arrived back in England in 1591.

FLATTERS, Paul-Xavier. 1832–1881

The commander of an ill-fated French military expedition which was sent to North Africa to survey a railroad route across the Sahara desert. The unit set out from Skikdar (on the Mediterranean coast between Algiers and Tunis) in 1880 and travelled south through Biskra and Ouargla, but got no further than the Tassili n' Ajjer, the mountain range north-east of the Ahaggar. Later that year Flatters, accompanied by Lt Dianous, led a second attempt, this time reaching Ouargla from Algiers. But soon after crossing the Tropic of Cancer in the Ahaggar region, Flatters and a small group were ambushed by Tuaregs while fetching water, and they were all killed. Lt Dianous and the main part of the expedition began the long

The awesome view that greeted explorers setting out across the Sahara from Biskra. (Mary Evans Picture Library)

journey back towards the Grand Erg Oriental, but repeated attacks by Tuareg tribesmen and the difficulty of finding water killed all but a few men.

FLINDERS, Matthew. 1774–1814

Navigator and mariner whose surveys of the Australian coast finally corrected the rumours and speculation about the continent that persisted even in the beginning of the 19th century. In 1795 Flinders explored inland from Botany Bay with George Bass, whom he also accompanied on a circumnavigation of Van Diemen's Land (Tasmania) in 1789 (SEE BASS). Flinders returned to England and in 1800 was given command of the *Investigator*, with instructions to make a study of the Australian coast. In 1801 he arrived at Dirk Hartog's Island, on the west coast, and began his two-year surveying journey by heading south, rounding Cape Leeuwin and then following the coast from King George Sound, the point where the coast again became 'unknown'. Flinders stuck close to the coast and discovered Spencer Gulf and Gulf St Vincent, which became the site of Adelaide.

At Encounter Bay he met the French ship *Le Géographe*, commanded by Nicolas Baudin, who had been charting the south-east coast from Port Jackson (Sydney). Flinders restarted his surveying at Port Jackson, only leaving the coast in order to stand well off the Great Barrier Reef, rejoining it again at Cape York and charting the Gulf of Carpentaria. By the time he reached Cape Arnhem, however, the *Investigator* was in very poor condition, and Flinders decided to return to Britain. Unfortunately he did not know that Britain and France were at war, and when he called at the French island of Mauritius for water and provisions he was imprisoned and held for $6\frac{1}{2}$ years. When he at last reached Britain, Flinders learnt that Baudin had claimed his discoveries as his own, but it was Flinders who soon gained recognition as one of the most important figures in the discovery of Australia.

FORREST, Alexander. 1849–1901

Explorer of Western Australia, and brother of John Forrest. In 1871 he followed the Swan River inland from Perth and continued eastwards to the edge of the Great Victorian Desert, returning to Perth via the south coast and the Swan River. In 1879 Forrest sailed to the mouth of the De Grey River in Western Australia (a little south of the 20th parallel), and went overland to the Dampier Land promontory. He followed the course of the

Fitzroy River, exploring its surroundings and the south-west area of the Kimberley Plateau before continuing north-east to the Daly River. On meeting the Central Overland Telegraph line, Forrest followed it across western Arnhem Land to the newly founded Palmerston (Darwin) on Darwin Bay.

FORREST, John. 1847–1918

Explorer who made the first west-to-east crossing of Western Australia. Before that, in 1869, he travelled north-east from Perth to Lake Moore, and after rounding the northern end of Lake Barlee, eventually reached Lake Raeside. Unfortunately for Forrest, he did not realize that his journey had taken him over rich gold fields, and he returned to Perth. In 1870 he made the long overland journey from Perth to Yorke Peninsula on the east of Spencer Gulf, so tracing in reverse Edward Eyre's pioneering journey of 1841. John Forrest set out on his second and biggest west-to-east expedition in 1874, beginning at Geraldton, about 250 miles (400 km) north of Perth on the coast of Western Australia, and heading north-east to the Murchison River. From there he went into the Gibson Desert, and was almost lost in that inhospitable region before following a long and meandering route to a point between the Peterman and Tomkinson mountain ranges. Forrest followed the Musgrave Ranges to the Alberga River which led him to Lake Eyre, well east of the middle point of the continent. He later became Lord Forrest, and was the first premier of Western Australia.

FOUREAU, Fernand. 1850–1914

A Frenchman whose dreams of forging a link by rail across the Sahara were not dashed by the fate that befell the Flatters expedition of 1880. In 1895–6 Foureau explored the Grand Erg Oriental south of Biskra, and in 1897 he went to Paris to seek backing for a longer expedition. The French Government had lost interest after the debacle of its 1880 venture, but it provided a military escort for Foureau under the command of Major A Lamy. Foureau initially followed Flatters' route, but crossed the middle of the Sahara by passing between the Tassili n' Ajjer and Ahaggar mountain ranges, continuing south to Agadez and so to Zinder before turning east to Lake Chad.

Until then the military escort had deterred attackers, even the Tuareg, but at Kousseri, south of Lake Chad, the expedition was attacked by a large force of Bornu tribesmen. Major Lamy was one of those killed in the fighting, and Kousseri was later renamed Fort Lamy. Foureau continued south, first along the Chari River, then overland to the Ubangi River whose course led the expedition to the Congo River and eventually to the Atlantic Ocean.

FOX, William. 1812–1893

Explorer of New Zealand – SEE THOMAS BRUNNER.

FRANKLIN, John. 1786–1847

The British explorer and mariner who mapped vast regions of Canada's northern regions, and whose disappearance resulted in remarkable and persistent attempts at rescue which eventually achieved the discovery Franklin himself died searching for – the North-west Passage. The story of the discovery of North America's Arctic regions is the story of Franklin, before and after his death.

Franklin learned his seamanship with the Royal Navy, which he joined at 14, and he served in the Battle of Trafalgar in 1805. His first voyage of exploration was when he commanded the *Trent* in the unsuccessful North Pole expedition led by David Buchan in 1818. This was Franklin's introduction to Arctic regions, and he spent from 1819 to 1822 in the area of America's Hudson Bay with George Back and John Richardson, going on an expedition from York Factory along the Nelson River. He skirted the northern end of Lake Winnipeg and followed the Saskatchewan River upstream along its northern branch before crossing overland to Fort Chipewyan on Lake Athabasca; from there he followed the Slave River to the Great Slave Lake and crossed it to Yellowknife. Franklin headed north from Yellowknife and joined the Coppermine River, which he followed to the coast in Coronation Gulf. Heading east, he mapped the coast to Bathurst Inlet, as well as Melville Sound and the Kent Peninsula.

In 1825, again with Back and Richardson, Franklin returned to the Great Slave Lake, and this time took the Mackenzie River exit at its west end. The expedition followed the river to Mackenzie Bay, and Franklin mapped the Beaufort Sea coast from there to Point Barrow. These surveying achievements earned Franklin a knighthood, and from 1836 to 1843 he was the Governor of Van Diemen's Land (Tasmania). He was then chosen to lead an expedition to find a North-west Passage, and in May 1845 sailed from England in the *Erebus* and the *Terror* (the two ships that James Ross had taken to the Antarctic six years before). Franklin was accompanied by F R M Crozier, and the rest of the expedition numbered 138 officers and men.

John Franklin. (The National Maritime Museum, London)

The ships were seen for the last time by a Scottish whaler, heading into Lancaster Sound in July, but diaries and notes found later enabled the journey to be reconstructed. Beyond the western end of Lancaster Sound, Franklin found the Barrow Strait to be blocked by ice, and so sailed north into the Wellington Channel, between Devon Island and Cornwallis

Island, to 77° N. The expedition spent the winter of 1845–6 on Beechy Island, and in spring returned along the west side of Cornwallis Island, and headed south through Peel Sound and into Franklin Strait, west of the Boothia Peninsula.

Some miles north of King William Island the *Erebus* and the *Terror* were trapped in thick ice-floes – and they were never to get free. Franklin organized the exploration of King William Island by sledge, and a cairn was built on the north of the island. The winter of 1846–7 was spent in the slowly drifting ice-bound ships, but by June 1847 Franklin and 24 other men had died. After a second winter Crozier, now the commander of the expedition, decided to abandon the ships. In April 1848, therefore, the 105 men who were still alive left the ships to go east of the Adelaide Peninsula into the adjacent gulf and the mouth of the Back River; but no-one survived the cold and starvation.

Back in Britain, anxiety over the expedition had already mounted by the winter of 1846–7, for no word of it had been heard for some 18 months. In the spring of 1847 the first search party began the long hunt for Franklin. It was led by John Richardson (who had accompanied Franklin on two previous expeditions) and John Rae, though no-one had the slightest idea where, in that vast area, Franklin might be. The plan was for Richardson and Rae to begin at Mackenzie Bay and work eastwards towards the waterway between Victoria Island and the mainland, but the thick ice that clogged Coronation Gulf forced the search to be abandoned at the mouth of the Coppermine River.

While Richardson and Rae were struggling through the ice in 1848–9, James C Ross, with Leopold McClintock and Robert McClure, was attempting to find Franklin by following the route he had intended to take. This expedition also experienced terrible ice conditions and was only able to reach Somerset Island; sledge trips made to the southern part of the island discovered nothing. Then, in 1850, Robert McClure sailed on yet another search, accompanied by Richard Collinson. On this occasion McClure intended to approach from the east, in the hope of finding either Franklin or the North-west Passage. After sailing through the Bering Strait, McClure and Collinson became separated and searched independently. McClure's party explored most of the Prince of Wales Strait by sledge, and then travelled round the west of Banks Island, reaching the northern opening of Prince of Wales Strait into Viscount Melville Sound.

McClure thus proved the existence of navigable water (dependent on ice) from the Atlantic to the Pacific. The North-west Passage had been charted although not yet navigated in its entirety, and the wide strait running north of Banks Island between the Beaufort Sea and Viscount Sound was named McClure Strait in his honour. Ice, however, was always

186

to be a major problem; McClure himself became ice-bound off Banks Island in 1851 and was not rescued until 1853.

Only ten days after McClure left Prince of Wales Strait, Collinson entered it, and having rounded the southern end of Banks Island returned to Victoria Island to winter in Walker Bay. In the spring, Collinson sailed south and east and into Dease Strait. Using sledges across the ice, search teams from his ship were able to reach Gateshead Island off the east coast of Victoria Island, a promontory thereafter named Collinson Peninsula.

A second series of search expeditions in 1850 was organized in Britain and in America, the British party being led by John Ross and Leopold McClintock. Baffin Bay, Jones Sound, Prince of Wales Island and part of Melville Island were included in the searches by sledge and by sea, but all that was found were the remains of the winter camp of 1845–6 on Beechy Island. It was not until 1853, eight years after they were last seen, that the Franklin expedition's likely fate was discovered. John Rae, who had been on the first search expedition, returned to the northern regions of the American continent in 1851, and, making observations and charts as he went, travelled overland from the Great Bear Lake and along the Coppermine River to Coronation Gulf. He then made his way to Prince Albert Sound in Victoria Island and went east to the 'X' junction of four straits and channels that lies between Victoria Island and Boothia Peninsula. Unfortunately Rae did not know how close he was to the place where the expedition foundered, but in 1853–4, after setting out from Repulse Bay on the Arctic Circle, on an expedition intended to take him up the Boothia Peninsula, Rae met an Eskimo who had witnessed the deaths of many of Franklin's expedition, and who had some items that had belonged to men in the expedition.

With this confirmation of Franklin's death the official search for him was called off; but Lady Franklin was determined to find out exactly what had happened to her husband, and in 1857 commissioned Leopold McClintock to lead a new search party. At Bellot Strait, between Somerset Island and Boothia Peninsula, the expedition took to sledges and eventually began the exploration of King William Island. There the cairn built by Franklin's team was discovered, and with it a note recording Franklin's death and the decision to abandon the ships. McClintock also found the skeletons of some of the men, and records of the expedition. After 12 years of searching, conjecture about Franklin – and about a North-west Passage – had reached a conclusion.

FRASER, Simon. 1776–1862

Fur trader, explorer, and discoverer of the Fraser River in Canada's British

Columbia. As a partner in a fur-trading company, Fraser was given charge of south-west Canada, and searched the Rockies for new trade and a route to the Pacific. In 1806 he began an expedition from Lake Athabasca and followed the route taken by Alexander Mackenzie in 1792, along the Peace River. At Finlay Forks, however, Fraser went directly to Fort George (Prince George) and then continued south down the unnavigable river which Mackenzie had taken to be the Columbia. But when Fraser reached the Pacific at Vancouver, he realized that he was well north of the Columbia River, and the new river was named after him. Fraser later fell victim to the monopolistic power of the Hudson's Bay Company and was forced out of business. He also suffered from a false accusation that he had taken part in an attack on a settlement in 1816.

FRÉMONT, John Charles. 1813–1890

With justification nicknamed 'Pathfinder', Frémont was an accurate and detail-conscious surveyor and explorer, and as a member of the US Army's Corps of Topographical Engineers was instructed to carry out expeditions in the far west of North America. In 1838–40 he surveyed the Mississippi–Missouri area; in 1841 the Des Moines River; and in 1842 he crossed the central plains and was able to disprove the speculation that there was a great desert in the centre of America. The settlement of the plains west of the Mississippi began after this.

In 1843–4 Frémont undertook an extensive expedition from St Louis to California, which also resulted in a confident flow of settlers. On this journey he went first to Great Salt Lake and from there north-west along the Snake River, across the Blue Mountains and the Cascade Range. Frémont then surveyed the inland side of the Cascades and the northern half of the Sierra Nevada before crossing the range opposite San Francisco Bay, and then continuing south. He eventually returned to St Louis by way of the Mojave Desert and Utah Lake, and returned to the California coast in 1845–7, crossing the Great Basin from Great Salt Lake. In the war with Mexico Frémont led the Californian Americans and held control of northern California.

After resigning from the Army he continued exploring and travelled down part of the Rio Grande before heading west, following the Gila River to the Colorado River, and then continuing to the Pacific coast at San Gabriel (Los Angeles). Frémont made another crossing, further south, of Nevada's Great Basin in 1853–4. After this, there were few large areas in North America which were still unknown – though detailed knowledge and comprehensive surveys only came with the pioneers and the settlers who followed them.

FROBISHER, Martin. c 1535–1594

The Englishman who was the first to search for a North-west Passage to India, having been inspired by Humphrey Gilbert's early conviction that North America was in reality 'lost' Atlantis, and must therefore be an island that could be circumnavigated. Frobisher set out in 1576, rediscovered Greenland (unvisited by Europeans since the Vikings), crossed the entrance to Baffin Bay, and landed on Baffin Island and on the Labrador coast. He sailed for some distance up a narrow inlet, thereafter known as Frobisher Bay, hoping that it was the North-west Passage, but then returned to England. He brought back what he mistakenly believed to be gold ore from Labrador, and made two more journeys to this region in pursuit of more 'gold'. On the second of these return visits, in

Martin Frobisher. (The National Maritime Museum, London)

1578, Frobisher sailed into Hudson Strait, and not surprisingly took that to be the secret of the North-west Passage, although he barely explored it. He made an unsuccessful attempt to establish a colony on Labrador, but later his naval career flourished; he was the Vice-Admiral in charge of Drake's expedition to the West Indies in 1585, and played a significant role in England's defeat of the Spanish Armada.

FUCHS, Vivian. 1908–

Fulfilled Shackleton's dream of being the first to cross Antarctica. Fuch's expedition took place during the Antarctic summer of 1957–8. A team led by Edmund Hilary made a vital contribution to his success, setting up supply depots between the South Pole and McMurdo Sound for the second half of the journey. Fuch's team set off from Shackleton Base at the south-east end of the Weddell Sea, and on the Pole to Ross Sea section took a route some 20° further west than that taken by earlier explorers, thus avoiding the Ross Ice Shelf. The expedition, which was highly

189

mechanized, carried out a great number of scientific tasks. It took place during the International Geophysical Year in which Antarctica was declared to belong to all nations in the world, solely for the purpose of peaceful observations and experiments.

GAGARIN, Yuri. 1934–1968

Russian cosmonaut who, on 12 April 1961, in the spacecraft *Vostok I*, became the first man to travel beyond the earth's atmosphere, and orbit in space.

GALLUS, Aelius. (fl 25 BC)

Roman who sailed from Cleopatris (Suez) in 25 BC down part of the Red Sea and then went overland in an unsuccessful attempt to capture the Arabian trading centre of Marib. His expedition did, however, provide information about previously unknown territories.

GAMA, Vasco da. c 1460–1524

The Portuguese navigator whose voyage to India in 1497–9 signalled the start of a new cycle in history and established Portugal as a world power. After Bartolomeu Dias had discovered the southern tip of Africa early in 1488, King John II of Portugal chose the nobleman Estevão da Gama to lead an expedition to India. The elderly da Gama died, however, and his son Vasco took his place when Manuel I became king after John's death. Four vessels sailed to find India in July 1497 – two of 120 tons, a 50-ton caravel, and a 200-ton supply-ship. Dias accompanied the small fleet as far as the Cape Verde Islands.

Da Gama left the islands in August, and by sweeping far out into the Atlantic was able to avoid the calms and slowing currents that had troubled all the previous coast-hugging voyages around the Gulf of Guinea. In early November da Gama made his first landfall on the continent, at St Helena Bay, north of the Cape of Good Hope. As on Dias' voyage, however, the expedition was greeted by storms at the Cape, and they did not round it until late November. At Mossel Bay da Gama erected a *padroa* (a stone pillar carved with the Portuguese arms) and broke up his empty supply ship.

On Christmas Day 1497 the three ships were sailing along the green sub-tropical south-east coast of Africa, and so da Gama named the land Natal. Frequent storms and counter-currents made the journey further north arduous and slow, but eventually da Gama reached Quelimane where the ships were repaired, and the crew was able to recover from attacks of scurvy. Another *padroa* was put up at Quelimane, but being unable to learn anything of India, da Gama pressed on northwards. At Mocambique, a predominantly Moslem port frequented by Arab mariners trading between Africa and India, da Gama heard much of interest, including fantastic accounts about Prester John, and saw Arab merchants dealing in gold, jewels, silver and spices. But the Portuguese became very unwelcome when it was discovered that they were Christian, and another hostile reception awaited them at Mombasa.

At Malindi, however, da Gama was able to find a pilot who was willing to guide him across the Indian Ocean, and on 21 May 1498 the Portuguese ships anchored off Calicut. Although the rulers of India were Hindus, the trading ports were dominated by Moslems and once again this proved an obstacle. The situation was aggravated by the inferior goods that da Gama had brought for trade and gifts, being more suitable for the humble West African coast than for the splendour of India. Further north, at Goa, da Gama had a greater measure of success, but he eventually left India, taking with him six Hindus in order to find out more about the people, and to learn their language. The voyage back to Malindi took three

Vasco da Gama. (The National Maritime Museum, London)

months because of unfavourable winds, and many of the crew died of scurvy before the African coast was reached. Da Gama burned one of his ships at Malindi, and then began the long trip back to Portugal. In March 1499 he rounded the Cape of Good Hope, and, after a short stay in the Azores, reached Lisbon in September.

After Cabral's ill-fated voyage in 1500, Manuel ordered a third expedition to India to be commanded by Cabral. But da Gama, by then an admiral, protested, determined that the command of his ships should not be given to someone with as disastrous a record as Cabral. Consequently da Gama was appointed to lead the fleet of 30 ships that

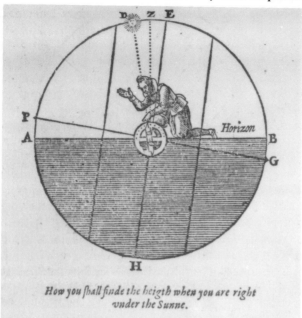

How you shall finde the heigth when you are right vnder the Sunne.

IF you vnderstand the rules before going well then this is easie to be found. If you be right vnder the Sunne, that is, when the Sunne is eleuated ninetie degrees, then you are euen as many degrees northward or southward from the line, as the Sunne hath northerly or southerly declination.

How to use an astrolabe — from a 1620 volume. (The National Maritime Museum, London)

sailed in February 1502.

On the east coast of Africa da Gama called at Mocambique and Kilwa, and skirted the Arabian coasts to Goa, rather than sailing directly across the Indian Ocean. After Goa da Gama sailed to Cannanore, north of Calicut, where he lay in wait for Arab ships. One duly arrived, laden with goods and up to 400 passengers, many of them women and children. With senseless brutality, da Gama had the passengers shut up in their ship, to which he then set fire, killing them all. At Calicut he continued his barbarous assertion of power by bombarding the town, and by killing 38 Hindu fishermen who had approached his ships to sell their produce. He then sailed on to Cochin where he formed convenient alliances with rival states, and fought off an attack by Arab ships. In 1524 da Gama was appointed viceroy in India by John III, but he very soon became ill and died in Cochin on Christmas Eve. His body was returned to Portugal in 1538.

GENGHIS KHAN. 1162–1227

The founder of the vast Mongolian empire which reached its greatest extent and influence when Kublai Khan, Genghis Khan's grandson, was the Great Khan. Genghis gained control of Mongolia in 1206, and in wars lasting from 1211 to 1215 conquered northern China. The empire expanded steadily, enveloping huge areas of central and southern Asia and Asia Minor.

GILBERT, Humphrey. c 1539–1583

Gilbert's assurance that North America was the legendary lost island of Atlantis, and could therefore be circumnavigated, led directly to Frobisher's expedition in 1576 to find the North-west Passage, and heralded expeditions spanning over 300 years before Roald Amundsen became the first to navigate the Passage. In 1583 Gilbert attempted to establish a settlement on Newfoundland, but ill-fortune dogged his efforts. One ship deserted the expedition in mid-Atlantic, another was in such a poor condition after the crossing that it had to be abandoned in Newfoundland, and the largest remaining ship grounded on Cape Breton Island. The two tiny ships that were left could hold only a

Humphrey Gilbert. (The National Maritime Museum, London)

fraction of the people, so a settlement was begun while Gilbert headed back for England in his 10-ton vessel. But the sea claimed him and his small ship, and it was not long before the colony was abandoned as well.

GILES, Ernest. 1833–1897

Explored large areas of Australia west of the Central Overland Telegraph Line, which, on its opening in 1872, left the central and western half of Australia as the only large areas still to be explored. Giles made his first expedition in 1872, travelling along the Finke River into the Macdonnel

Ranges, until a lack of water forced his return. The following year he set out from Lake Eyre with Alfred Gibson and headed north-west to cross the Alberga River before heading west, skirting the Musgrave mountains. In the bleak emptiness of the desert Gibson became lost, and Giles, unable to find a trace of him, named the region Gibson Desert.

In 1875 Giles began the daunting journey which had long been his ambition, and set out from the head of Spencer Gulf on an inland east-to-west crossing. He rounded Lake Torrens to the north, and then headed west across the Great Victoria Desert to Perth. From Perth he began a return journey by travelling northwards across the headwaters of the Gascoyne and Fortescue Rivers, turned east, crossed the Gibson Desert (where he again searched without success for his colleague), and passed south of Lake Amadeus on his way to join the Finke River.

GOES, Bento de. 1562–1607

Made the first overland journey to China for some 300 years, and positively established China's position on the world map. By 1600 geographers and explorers were still not certain that the China known to Portuguese mariners was the same as the Cathay which Marco Polo had reached by land. Goes set out from India in 1603 to establish the truth, travelling from Agra via Delhi to Lahore. Pretending to be a Moslem merchant, he continued north-west to Kabul, crossed the Hindu Kush, and then turned east through the Wakhan province in the Pamir Mountains to Yarkand, on the western end of the Taklamakan Desert.

There he waited to join a caravan which would skirt the northern edge of the desert, filling in time by a journey to see the jade mines of Khotan (Ho-tien). The caravan took Goes via Aksu (Wensu), Turfan (T'ulufan), and Hami to Suchow (Chin-chuan), at the western end of the Nan Shan mountains – the first town of Cathay to be approached from the west. Goes waited at Suchow while a messenger went to see Matteo Ricci, the head of the Jesuit mission in Peking. Ricci's affirmation that the Peking and Cathay reached from the sea were the same as those approached from the land, reached Goes at Suchow in 1607, only days before he died.

GOMES, Diogo. 1440–1482

Portuguese mariner, one of the foremost of those sponsored by Henry the Navigator. Gomes led the last fleet (1458–60) which extended Portugal's knowledge of the west coast of Africa during Prince Henry's time, and reached Cape Palmas, at the beginning of the entry to the Gulf of Guinea.

Gomes and Cadamosto explored the river systems on the coast of **Guinea**, and made the first accurate surveys of this unknown territory. Either Gomes or Cadamosto was the discoverer of the Azores. (SEE ALSO MARTIN BEHAIM.)

GOMES, Fernão. (fl 1470)

In 1469 Gomes was granted a five-year contract by Portugal's King Alfonso giving him exclusive trading rights on the African coast – on the condition that he explored at least a further 100 leagues (400 miles/645 km) of coast every year. This was a simple enough obligation, but although Gomes carried out the necessary exploration, reaching as far as Point St Catherine, the contract was never renewed. Alfonso put his son, John, in charge of exploration, and he succeeded to the throne in 1481 (as John II). Numerous wars made Fernão Gomes' final voyage the last until Diogo Cam's of 1482.

GORDON, Robert. (fl 1778)

A Scot who was one of the early explorers of South Africa. In 1777 he travelled eastwards from Cape Town, keeping some distance from the coast and initially accompanying William Paterson. Inland from Algoa Bay, Gordon turned northwards and made his way up to the highveld, the rolling grasslands of the southern African plateau, as far as the junction of the Groote (Orange) and Vaal Rivers. Gordon made a second expedition in 1779, on which he was joined by Paterson and a Dutchman, van Reenen. From Cape Town they followed the western coastal belt into Namaqualand and arrived at the mouth of the Groote River, which Gordon then renamed the Orange River. Further inland they ventured briefly into the barren land north of the river, and then followed its course eastwards into the highveld.

GOSSE, William. 1842–1881

The discoverer of the remarkable Ayers Rock in central Australia. In 1873 Gosse attempted an east-to-west crossing of the continent, starting from Alice Springs, and soon came across the enormous, rounded mountain. Near the Musgrave Mountain Ranges, however, Gosse was forced to give up his expedition.

GRANT, James. 1827–1892

Accompanied Speke on his second African trip, and was thus co-discoverer of the Nile's exit from Lake Victoria (SEE JOHN HANNING SPEKE).

GREGORY, Augustus. 1819–1905

Elder of two brothers who contributed enormously to knowledge of the Australian interior. Gregory's first expedition in 1846 was a loop northwards from Perth, reaching some 50 miles (80 km) north of the Murchison River, and returning closer to the coast. Nine years later he began a long journey at Pearce Point, on the east side of Joseph Bonaparte Gulf (approx. 15° S, 129° E), and travelled south and south-west to discover Sturt Creek whose course he traced to Lake Gregory, a seasonal lake in the Great Sandy Desert. Gregory returned north, followed much of the Victoria River, and then headed east to skirt the Gulf of Carpentaria. Reaching the Gilbert River on the Gulf's south-east corner, he followed it across the base of the Cape York Peninsula and joined the Burdekin River which flows south along the western slopes of the Great Dividing Range. The Burdekin is joined by the Belyando where its course winds through the mountains, and Gregory followed the Belyando River almost as far south as the Tropic of Capricorn. Eventually he headed south-east, crossed the Mackenzie and Dawson rivers and the Great Dividing Range, and reached Australia's east coast near Bustard Head, south of Rockhampton.

Augustus Gregory began his third major expedition in 1857, the year after he completed his crossing of northern Australia. This began at Brisbane's Moreton Bay, crossed the Great Dividing Range, and headed north-west to cross the upper reaches of the Dawson and Warrego Rivers. Gregory then explored the northern region of the Barcoo River, following it into the Sturt Desert. He continued south to pass between Lake Frome and the Flinders Range, eventually reaching Adelaide on the Gulf of St Vincent.

GREGORY, Frank. 1821–1888

The younger brother of Augustus Gregory; while he did not cover as much of Australia as did his brother, his contribution was nevertheless substantial, for he discovered, in the largely infertile Western Australia, a number of areas which were suitable for settlements. In 1846 Frank Gregory travelled inland from Perth, completing a rough circle to the north and back to Perth, passing between Lakes Barlee and Moore, and north of Lake Monger. In 1857–8 he explored the Murchison River, and crossed the Macadam Plains to the Gascoyne River, which he followed to its mouth at the northern end of Shark Bay. He also explored the Lyons River, a Gascoyne tributary, before returning overland to the Murchison River, just north of Mount Hale. In 1861 Gregory carried out an extensive exploration of the Western Australia area north of the Hamersley Range, between the Tropic of Capricorn and 20° S. The principal rivers in this area are the Fortescue and the De Grey-Oakover, but Gregory also crossed the Hamersley Mountains and the Ashburton River, reaching (from the north) the Lyons River area which he had explored from the south three years before.

GREY, George. 1812–1898

Sailed along the coast of Western Australia in 1837, from Perth, round North-west Cape and on to Brunswick Bay (approx. 15° S, 125° E). Grey abandoned his intention to return overland to Perth, but two years later he again sailed from Perth, this time to Shark Bay. Here he discovered the Gascoyne River and explored ashore until a shortage of food forced him to sail again for Perth. He was shipwrecked in a gale when just south of the Murchison River, and the expedition returned to Perth overland down the coast.

GRIJALVA, Juan de. c 1489–1527

Grijalva's voyage of 1518 marked the end of the Aztec empire. The Spaniard sailed from Santiago da Cuba, round its north coast, and crossed the Yucatan Channel to Central America. Continuing westwards, he followed the Yucatan coast across the Bay of Campeche and sailed north almost as far as present-day Tuxpan. On his forays inlands Grijalva found numerous indications of a large and civilized society, wealthy in gold and other treasures. His reports were all that were needed to inspire Cortes on his way to Tenochtitlan (Mexico City).

GROSEILLIERS, Médart Chouart, Sieur de. c 1625–1697

French trader who explored large tracts of Canada and the Great Lakes. Groseilliers and his brother-in-law Pierre Radisson spent a long time in the vicinity of Lake Superior, operating as fur traders, though without a licence. In 1661 they crossed part of the lake on their way to Lake Nipigon and James Bay, at the southern end of Hudson Bay. They returned to Lake Superior in 1663, but later that year the French authorities caught up with them and confiscated their furs in Nova Scotia. The two disgruntled Frenchmen offered their services to the English, and in due course they were employed by the New Englanders at Boston, on whose behalf they investigated the Hudson Bay area and discovered gold near Lake Superior. The reports the English received were so encouraging that they paid increasing interest to the Hudson Bay area, and in 1670 founded the Hudson's Bay Company. Radisson made other expeditions on his own, but later on both he and Groseilliers returned their allegiance to France, and served in the French Fleet.

GRUEBER, Johann. 1623–1680

A Jesuit missionary who represented the re-awakening of European interest in Central Asia. In 1661 Grueber and Albert d'Orville set out from Peking and crossed the Ordos Desert to Kumbum (now Hsi-ning) and Koko Nor (the lake also known as Ch'ing Hai). They then travelled south-west along the China–Tibet boundary area to the ancient Tibetan capital city of Lhasa, and were the first Europeans to enter the city for some 300 years. Grueber and Orville stayed in Lhasa for several weeks, and then went on to Shigatse, through Nepal into Katmandu, and up the Ganges plain to Agra. Orville died there in 1662, but Grueber later continued westwards, followed the Indus, and crossed into Baluchistan and Makran in southern Persia. He reached the Mediterranean after travelling through the Tigris–Euphrates area and sailed to Rome, bringing back a great deal of new knowledge about much of Asia's interior.

GUTIÉRREZ, Diego. ?–1554

A cartographer who drew the first authoritative map (by the standards of the early 16th century) of South America, including the Amazon, as a result of Orellana's voyage. Gutiérrez was cosmographer, under Cabot, at the House of Trade for the Indies (*Casa de la Contractación de Las Indias*), which was founded in 1503 under Amerigo Vespucci.

HAKLUYT, Richard. c 1552–1616

An English geographer whose high standing gave him considerable

Vessels of numerous different kinds painted by Brueghel, c 1560. (The National Maritime Museum, London)

influence. Hakluyt actively promoted expansion overseas during England's powerful Elizabethan period, and he also strongly favoured colonization in North America. He was well acquainted with numerous geographers, navigators, mariners and explorers and served officially in Paris (1583–8). Hakluyt was also a prolific writer, his most notable work being *The Principal Navigations, Voyages and Discoveries of the English Nation*. The Hakluyt Society is dedicated to promoting an interest in geography, and to keeping records of expeditions and geographic writings.

HANNO. (fl 450 BC)

A Carthaginian whose voyage in about 450 BC was perhaps the first ever true voyage of exploration, for exploration's sake. With a huge fleet of 60 ships, Hanno sailed through the Strait of Gibraltar down the west coast of Africa with the main intention of establishing further Carthaginian colonies. However, after founding six cities in and around present-day Morocco – including Acra (Agadir) and one on Mogador – Hanno carried on south. He established a settlement called Cerne, probably on the

Senegal River, and went as far as the coast of Sierra Leone, and perhaps even as far south as Cameroon. (Herodotus records an earlier Phoenician voyage that sailed right round Africa.)

HARTOG, Dirk. (fl 1616)

Made the first Dutch landing on the west coast of Australia. Hartog, in the *Eendracht*, was one of the first mariners from Holland who challenged Portuguese supremacy in the East Indian trade. In 1616 he was swept way off course after taking a new route round Africa. His landing was on Dirk Hartog's Island off Shark Bay, and over the next 15 years there were repeated landings on Australia's west coast by Dutch mariners (few of which were intentional, for the coast had nothing to offer), from North-west Cape to Cape Leeuwin, resulting in that part being named New Holland – though little thought was given to colonizing it.

HATSHEPSUT. Queen of Egypt c 1489–1469 BC

Commissioned one of the earliest long sea journeys, sending ships to Punt (probably on the African coast of the Red Sea, almost at the Gulf of Aden) to obtain a cargo of myrrh.

HEAPHY, Charles. 1820–1881

Explored New Zealand's South Island in 1845 and 1846. (SEE THOMAS BRUNNER)

HEARNE, Samuel. 1745–1792

An employee of the Hudson's Bay Company who was among the first to explore Canada's North-west Territories. After Hudson and Baffin, there had been few expeditions to look for a North-west Passage, though the Hudson's Bay Company maintained interest in the hoped-for route. In 1769 Hearne set out overland from Churchill on the Hudson Bay's west coast, in an attempt to find a waterway from the Bay to the Pacific, and to look for a rumoured wealthy deposit of copper. He wandered rather at random in a long loop north to Lake Dubawnt and almost to Aberdeen Lake, and then back to Churchill. Hearne set out again the following year, headed north-west, and explored the unknown area north of the Great Slave Lake.

On his way back to the lake he met an Indian with whom he struck up a friendship, and they again searched for copper north of the lake. Eventually Hearne discovered the Coppermine River and followed it to the sea; but his expeditions had fallen far short of his hopes, for he had reached the Arctic and not the Pacific, the copper was not present in appreciable quantities, and the land between Hudson Bay and the mouth of the Coppermine River was so desolate and forbidding that it was worthless from a trader's point of view.

HEARSEY, Hyder Jung. 1782–1840

Much of the first accurate information about the western Himalayas was provided by Hearsey after two expeditions in the region. In 1808 he explored the mountains north and east of Dehra Dun, before returning to Delhi via Bareilly, due east of Delhi. In 1812 he was joined by William Moorcroft and travelled again towards Dehra Dun; then, in the guise of Indian fakirs, they entered Tibet and reached the northern slopes of the Himalayas. Turning west, Hearsey and Moorcroft went to Gartok, near the source of the Indus River's first tributary, before travelling eastwards to Lake Manasarowar, and returning over the Himalayas.

HEDIN, Sven. 1865–1952

A member of the Swedish embassy in Persia whose enthusiasm for exploration was aroused in 1890 by a journey from Persia to Kashgar (on the western end of the Taklamakan Desert) and then over the Tien Shan mountains to Issyk-Kul, one of the largest mountain lakes in the world. Hedin made five more journeys in Central Asia – all long, and all contributing a great amount of valuable information. The first of these began in 1893 and lasted until 1897, when Hedin explored extensively around Kashgar before going to Yarkand on his way to Khotan (Ho-tien). At the southernmost tip of the desert, he turned north and crossed the vast drifting sands of the Taklamakan, finding invaluable archaeological remains of cities almost entirely burnt and destroyed. Hedin continued to skirt round the Taklamakan and passed Lop Nor, but after passing the foothills of the Altyn Tagh, he turned east across the Plateau of Tibet, skirting the southern tip of the Tsaidam depression towards the huge lake, Koko Nor. He then followed a route round the southern end of the Nan Shan mountains and took a long north and east loop into the southern Gobi desert before crossing the Ordos Desert to Peking. He continued his exploration into unfamiliar lands by heading north to Mongolia, on a route that took him across the eastern end of the Gobi desert.

Hedin's second great expedition began in 1899, again from Kashgar and Yarkand. He crossed the western end of the Taklamakan and followed a tributary of the Tarim River to the Tarim Basin, going on to explore the area surrounding the fluctuating lake of Lop Nor. After investigating large areas of the Altyn Tagh and the hills north of the Tsaidam depression, Hedin disguised himself as a Mongolian and headed south across the Plateau of Tibet in an attempt to reach the forbidden city of Lhasa. When he was within 150 miles (240 km) of the capital, however, soldiers turned him back; further west he was again turned back, and prevented from crossing into India. Hedin was thus forced to travel across the uncharted southern part of the Tibetan Plateau to Leh. He followed the Indus through the western extremities of the Himalayas, passed through Rawalpindi to Lahore and then crossed northern India, following the Ganges valley to Calcutta, which he reached three years after leaving Yarkand.

In 1906 Hedin began a thorough exploration of the western and southern parts of the Himalayas, adding to his discoveries the Kailas range and the source of the Tsangpo River (which becomes the Brahmaputra), and verifying the source of the Indus.

Some 20 years later, in 1927, Hedin was the leader of a joint Swedish and Chinese scientific mission into Central Asia. It lasted until 1933 and filled in most of the remaining blanks on maps of Central Asia, carrying out extensive exploration in the Taklamakan, the southern foothills of the Tien Shan, and the area between Lop Nor and Dzungaria, north of the Tien Shan. Well over 300 archaeological sites between Manchuria and Sinkiang were located, from which it was determined that the desolate steppes and deserts were once the homelands of an extensive Stone Age culture. Hedin himself concentrated on the Lop Nor–Dzungaria area, having arrived overland by way of Shanghai, Peking and the Gobi Desert.

He covered much of the same ground yet again in his sixth expedition, 1933–5, which began in Shanghai and followed the eastern end of the ancient Silk Route. This expedition concentrated on the Lop Nor–Nan Shan mountains and the Hwang Ho River.

HENDAY, Anthony. (fl 1754)

An employee of the Hudson's Bay Company in North America who left York Factory in 1754 to look for further trade. Travelling south-west, he crossed Lake Winnipeg, followed the Saskatchewan and North Saskatchewan rivers, and turned south at the foothills of the Rockies to return to Lake Winnipeg by way of the South Saskatchewan River.

Henday managed to establish good relations with the Blackfoot Indians, who occupied the territory between the North and South Saskatchewan Rivers.

HENRY THE NAVIGATOR. 1394–1460

l'Infant Don Henri

Henry the Navigator. (The National Maritime Museum, London)

Prince of Portugal and third son of King John I. Henry's enthusiasm for discovery and expansion began and maintained the Portuguese voyages of the 15th century which led to Portuguese domination of trade to the East, and which broke the Moslem hold on a large part of the world. Portugal's small size but grand ambitions compelled the royal house to look for a means of attaining greater power, and it decided to capture the North African port of Ceuta, just in the entrance to the Mediterranean. The port was duly taken in 1411; Henry took part in the invasion and was then appointed Governor.

From this sprang his awareness of Africa, and his future moves were motivated by sheer curiosity, a desire to thwart the Moslems by literally going behind their backs, and an interest in the gold and other treasures whose whereabouts seemed known to the Moors. Equally powerful was Henry's missionary zeal: he dreamed of a great Christian empire with Portugal in the west and the legendary Prester John's kingdom further south and east. In 1419 Henry retired from the main affairs of the Portuguese court, and was appointed governor of the Algarve. He founded a court, a school of navigation, and an observatory on the Sagres promontory, and from here came many of the decisions as well as the developments in cartography, shipbuilding and navigation, that were to play a major role in Portugal's discoveries.

In 1420 the Pope made Prince Henry a Grand Master of the Order of Christ, and many of his expeditions were funded by this order, his ships bearing the familiar large red crosses on their sails. The navigating and cartographic developments were important, but perhaps even more so was

Henry's patronage of the development of the caravel. Nevertheless one obstacle held up exploration of Africa's west coast: the superstition that after passing Cape Bojador any number of horrific or disastrous happenings would befall a ship's crew. It was not until 1434 that Gil Eannes sailed safely beyond this ominous point, and after that progress was so rapid that within two more years Henry's mariners had gone well beyond Moslem influence. In 1445 Portuguese ships reached the mouth of the Senegal River (then thought to be a branch of the Nile) and three years later Cape Verde was passed.

Domestic crises then held up exploration, and with the distraction of the embryonic but lucrative slave trade and other commercial interests in the areas already discovered, it was 1455 before Cadamosto reached the Gambia River. Five years later Gomes reached Cape Palmas, and in the same year the instigator of the Great Age of Discovery died.

HERBERT, Thomas. (fl 1627)

Went to Persia in 1627 with one of the Shah's English ambassadors, Robert Sherley (SEE ANTHONY SHERLEY), and wrote a highly popular account of his years there (1627–9), his journey from Bandar Abbas to Isfahan taking him through largely unknown territory. After Herbert's expedition, European interest in Persia tailed off, the British in particular being more occupied with India. While traders continued to call, little exploration took place until the early 19th century.

HERBERT, Wally. 1934–

The leader of the 1968–9 British Trans-Arctic Expedition, which made the first surface crossing of the Arctic Ocean via the North Pole – ending in considerable haste as spring thaws broke up the ice packs.

HERJULFSSON, Bjarni. (fl AD 986)

Possibly the first Viking, and the first person from Europe, to see Vinland – the North American continent. The sagas tell how in AD 986 Herjulfsson sailed south-west from Iceland and first sighted land somewhere north of what is now Long Island. Apparently, however, the Viking never went ashore, neither where land was first sighted nor at any stage during the rest of his voyage along the coastlines of Nova Scotia, Newfoundland and Labrador. After he reached Baffin Island, Herjulfsson crossed to

Greenland, sailed to its southern tip, and then returned to Iceland.

HERKHUF. (dates unknown)

A Governor of one of Egypt's southern provinces, in about 2270 BC. Herkhuf travelled up the Nile towards Africa's tropical region, and returned with ivory, ebony and frankincense. He possibly made, or directed, a number of expeditions into Africa, one apparently returning with a pygmy captured in the jungle.

HERODOTUS. c 484–424 BC

The Greek historian who reached some remarkably accurate conclusions about the size and shape of the world, although the substance of his *Histories* mainly concerns the Graeco/Persian struggles. Herodotus' early thinking on geography was largely an extension of the writings of Hecataeus, whose book is regarded as one of the earliest on geography (c 500 BC). Hecataeus depicted the earth as a flat disk bordered by water, but Herodotus queried this, and although the subject provided philosophers of the time with a source of endless argument, he eventually settled for a spherical earth. Apart from listening closely to all accounts by travellers, Herodotus himself travelled widely, visiting, among many other places, Egypt, Athens, the Black Sea and Italy (he died in an Athenian colony in southern Italy).

The map of the world drawn from his descriptions is the earliest impression of the world to bear some relation to its actual appearance. Herodotus judged Europe to be longer than Africa and Asia (an understandable habit in early years, when it would have been difficult for Europeans to believe that they inhabited only a very small portion of the earth), but he had the Caspian correctly set down as an inland sea and Africa surrounded by water – something that even Ptolemy, 500 years later, got wrong. Perhaps most interesting, however, is Herodotus' record of a Phoenician, Nechos, being commissioned to sail around Africa – a remarkable voyage which apparently took place in c 600 BC.

HILARY, Edmund. 1919–

New Zealand conqueror, with Sherpa Tensing Norgay, of Mount Everest in May 1953. He led the 1956–8 New Zealand Antarctic Expedition, and established bases between the South Pole and McMurdo Sound which he and Vivian Fuchs used for the second half of the Trans-Antarctic Expedition (SEE VIVIAN FUCHS).

HIMILCO. (fl 450 BC)

A Carthaginian and contemporary of Hanno, who is believed to have sailed from Carthage in about 450 BC, passing through the Straits of Gibraltar and heading north along the Spanish and French coasts. Himilco was possibly searching for the tin mines of Cornwall, and landed at a number of places on the coasts of England and Ireland.

HOLYWOOD, John. (fl 1230)

A Yorkshire mathematician who named himself Sacrobosco, and whose 1230 *Treatise of the Sphere* caused a considerable disturbance by expressing theories completely contrary to the Christian belief that the earth was flat. Sacrobosco's work dealt with the globe itself, the imaginary movement of stars and the real movement of planets. The accurate principles of Renaissance navigation began with his theories, and the *Treatise* was to be the standard work on the world for some 300 years.

HOOD, Robert. ?–1821

A highly talented midshipman on Franklin's expedition of 1819–21, Hood made many detailed and accurate observations and paintings of animal and human life in Canada's North-west Territories. Scientific and navigational subjects, including attempts to determine the height of the aurora borealis, were also recorded in his *Narrative of the Proceedings of an Expedition of Discovery in North America*. In 1819 Hood reached the Great Slave Lake, having come from Hudson Bay via Lake Athabasca and the Slave River. He wintered at Fort Enterprise, just south of the Hay River's entrance into the Great Slave Lake, and in summer 1820 journeyed down the Coppermine River to Coronation Gulf, then followed the northern coast of the continent eastwards as far as Point Turnagain (on the Kent Peninsula at the start of the Dease Strait). So severe were the hardships of the journey back to the Great Slave Lake, that Hood died before he reached the security of Fort Enterprise.

HORNEMANN, Friedrich. 1772–1801

Made one of the longest journeys directed towards discovering the secrets of the Niger River. In 1798, after Mungo Park's first journey, Hornemann set out from Cairo and followed a caravan route to the Siwa Oasis on the eastern edge of the Great Sand Sea. He then crossed present-day Libya to Marzūq in the Fezzan, following up this considerable achievement by heading south across the heart of the Sahara to Lake Chad. From there Hornemann followed the Hadejia River to Kano and turned north-west to Katsina, where he began the last stage – a southerly journey towards the Niger. He had almost reached his goal when he died from the rigours of the expedition, at Bida.

HOUGHTON, Daniel. c 1740–1791

Like Hornemann, Houghton died in search of the Niger's mystery (the river's great semi-circular course confused many early efforts to identify its source and its mouth). Houghton arrived at the mouth of the Gambia in 1790, followed the river inland, and later continued east and crossed the Senegal River. But Moslem tribesmen decoyed him into the desert a little east of $10°$ E, and after attacking him and stealing all his belongings, left him to die. Four years later Mungo Park found the place where Houghton died, near Nioro du Sahel.

HOUTMAN, Cornelius. c 1540–1599

Houtman's voyage of 1595 marked the beginning of Dutch interest (and Portuguese decline) in the East Indies. Cornelius Houtman was the representative in Lisbon for nine Dutch merchants, but he and his younger brother Frederick were jailed by Portugal for the attempted theft of secret charts of the Portuguese sailing routes to the East Indies. They were released in 1595, whereupon the Dutch merchants formed a company, commissioned the Houtman brothers and gave them four ships to make an expedition to the East Indies. They sailed in April that year and, using directions written by Jan van Linschoten, reached the Indies in 1596.

The Houtmans established trading agreements in Java, Sumatra and Bali, and returned the same year to Amsterdam. Although it showed that the Portuguese did not necessarily have a monopoly on that trade, the voyage was not entirely successful. Over half of the men who set out died, and the cargo of spices was modest. The Houtman brothers began a second voyage in 1598, and on the way out established a trade arrangement with Madagascar. When they again got to Sumatra, however (in 1599), they were involved in a battle with the Sultan of Atjeh. Cornelius Houtman was killed, but Frederick was imprisoned. He took the opportunity to study Malay, mastering the language so well that on his return to Amsterdam in 1602 he compiled the first Malay dictionary (SEE ALSO MARTIN LLEWELLYN).

HSUAN-TSANG. c 600–664

Although China's Emperor forbade travel outside his country during Europe's Dark Ages, Hsuan-tsang was so strongly motivated by a desire to know more about his Buddhist religion that he undertook a long and dangerous journey, despite the ban. He set out in 629 for India, the home of Buddhism, and travelled across Central Asia to Bactria (Afghanistan) via the Tien Shan and Hindu Kush mountains, and from there east into Kashmir where he spent the next two years studying, before visiting monasteries along the Ganges River. From the river's mouth he travelled down the east coast of India, and made a long inland detour before returning to the coast. At Madras Hsuan-tsang crossed the west coast, which he followed north to the Indus. He followed this river into the Hindu Kush, and made his way back to China along the southern edge of the Taklamakan Desert. Hsuan-tsang was welcomed with great honour after his 16 years of travels; he translated the sacred books of Buddhism into Chinese from the Sanskrit, and a sect based on his teaching gained a great number of Buddhist followers in Japan.

HUC, Evariste Régis. 1813–1860

Huc was a Jesuit missionary who was sent by his order to Macao in 1839. He lived in southern China, and in 1844 set out on a journey that was to make him the first European for over 200 years to enter Tibet (the last having been Desideri). Accompanied by Joseph Gabet, Huc left Peking and crossed the Ordos Desert to Koko Nor, carrying on into the mountainous lands of Tibet towards the capital of Lhasa. The Chinese authorities, however, had forbidden Huc to preach in Tibet, and although he and Gabet were at first made welcome in Lhasa, they were eventually escorted from the citadel in March 1846. Huc's expedition returned to China via a treacherous and difficult southern route which entailed the crossing of every major river and tributary in the South-East Asian mainland, until they reached the Yangtse River (Ch'ang Chiang). From near present-day Nanch'ang they turned south for Macao, arriving towards the end of 1846. Two years later Huc retraced his steps to Nanch'ang, continued north-east to Hang-chou (south-east of Shanghai), and carried on to Peking. He returned to Europe in 1852.

HUDSON, Henry. c 1550–1611

English navigator who gave his name to the huge bay where he died so tragically. Hudson's earlier voyages were in search of a North-west Passage on behalf of the Dutch East India Company, and in 1607 he rounded the Shetland Islands, passed west of Iceland and sailed off Greenland before crossing to Spitzbergen. On his return trip he passed Bear Island and then discovered Jan Mayen before returning to the Shetlands. In 1608 he rounded the North Cape, and reached Novaya Zemlya before turning back.

Even Hudson's first visit to North America began as a North-east Passage trip; in 1609 he turned back after rounding North Cape, crossed the Atlantic, passed Newfoundland and Nova Scotia, and sailed on past Delaware Bay and Chesapeake Bay. Hudson then turned north again, and on rounding Long Island discovered the Hudson River, which he explored as far as present-day Albany before becoming convinced that it would not lead to the North-west Passage. The favourable reports he wrote brought

Hudson with Indians. (Mary Evans Picture Library)

Hudson abandoned by the mutineers. (Mary Evans Picture Library)

North America to the attention of the Dutch, who then began fur trading.

In 1610 Hudson, working for England, made his second voyage across the Atlantic, and after two fruitless ventures into Ungava Bay discovered the Hudson Strait and the enormous Hudson Bay. But the ship was ill-prepared for the duration of the voyage; conditions on board grew steadily worse and the winter of 1610–11 was particularly severe. As soon as the weather moderated, the crew mutinied and cast Hudson, his young son, and seven others adrift in a boat. The remainder returned to England under the command of Robert Bylot (who later sailed with William Baffin), and many believed that the expedition had indeed found the longed-for Passage. Of Hudson, his son and his companions, nothing was seen or heard again.

HUMBOLDT, Alexander von. 1769–1859

The German scientist and explorer who made major contributions to botany, and carried out extensive expeditions in South America. Humboldt was for a time a Prussian Government mining official, but in 1799 (accompanied by Aime Bonpland, a doctor and botanist) he set out for South America. Humboldt was initially interested in verifying Charles de la Condamine's account of a water link between the Orinoco and Amazon rivers, and he journeyed south from Caracas over the northern tropical grasslands to the Apure River, and so to the Orinoco. He went upriver, crossed to the upper reaches of the Negro, a major tributary of the Amazon, and followed it to its junction with the Casiquiare. This established la Condamine's report, for the Casiquiare is also an early tributary of the Orinoco. Humboldt returned down the Orinoco as far as Agnostura (now Ciudad Bolívar) before returning overland to the Caribbean Sea. He had been making observations and collecting samples and specimens throughout the journey, and although a large number were ruined by the heat and high humidity Humboldt was able, on reaching Cuba, to put together three almost identical collections. One remained in Cuba, the other two he sent to Europe – fortunately on separate ships, for one sank and that collection was lost.

Humboldt returned to South America in 1801, this time disembarking at Cartegena on Colombia's Caribbean coast, and followed the Magdalena River south into the Andes. This expedition was as scientific as his last, and Humboldt made a vast number of observations. South of Quito he watched Cotopaxi erupting, and further on, in central Ecuador, climbed up Mount Chimborazo. In north-west Peru he visited the ruins of the Inca city of Cajamarca, and then went down to the plains and on to Lima.

The first Europeans had come to South America simply in search of treasure, but la Condamine and Humboldt opened up new views of the continent, revealing it as a land with endless fascination for scientists of all persuasions. On his return to Europe in 1804, Humboldt published the results of his South American explorations in 30 volumes and went on to become the tutor to the Prussian Crown Prince, and to organize the first international scientific conference, held in 1828. The last 30 years of his life were largely devoted to a study of magnetism, and principally to the completion of his famous *Cosmos*, a history of science and a description of the universe.

HUME, Hamilton. 1797–1873

Discovered Lake Bathurst, south-west of Port Jackson (Sydney) in New South Wales, in 1818. The river system of south-eastern Australia aroused considerable speculation, the inland side of the Great Dividing Range containing numerous river sources. One strongly flowing river discovered early in the 1800s was the Murrumbidgee, and in 1824 Hume crossed the mountains and followed part of this river's course before heading south-west along the curve of the mountain range. He crossed the Murray River, also flowing west, and eventually arrived at Port Phillip Bay, the site of Melbourne. From the courses of the rivers he had seen, Hume concluded that all those on the western side of the mountain range must flow into a vast lake in the interior; an expedition with Charles Sturt into the interior north-west of Port Jackson in 1828 seemed to support his theory (SEE STURT).

HUNT, John. 1910–

The leader of the British Everest Expedition which resulted in the first ascent of the world's highest mountain in May 1953 by Edmund Hilary and Tensing Norgay.

HUNT, Wilson Price. c 1782–1842

John Jacob Astor, a New York merchant and trader, commissioned Hunt and Robert Stuart to establish a base (to be called Fort Astoria) at the mouth of the Columbia River on North America's west coast. In 1811 Hunt and Stuart left St Louis, and after a long journey up the Missouri River, headed west after meeting the Cheyenne River to pass south of the Bighorn Mountains. The Snake River led Hunt and Stuart through the

Salmon River Mountains, and they crossed the Blue Mountains to reach the Columbia River. At its mouth, however, they discovered that David Thompson had already claimed the Columbia region for Britain (though Astoria is still the name of the town at the river's mouth). Stuart set out to inform Astor of this development, and after leaving the Snake River he found a new pass through the Rockies. He was able to join up with the North Platte River, a Missouri tributary well to the south of the Cheyenne, and thus considerably shortened the outward journey from St Louis.

IBN-BATUTA, Sheik Muhammad ibn-'Abdullah.
1304–1369

An extraordinary Moslem traveller from Tangier who in 30 years covered about 75,000 miles (121,000 km) travelling in Africa, Arabia and Asia Minor, during which he visited every Moslem country except central Persia, Armenia and Georgia. Although ibn-Batuta did not discover any new lands, or make detailed scientific records, his social and historical observations of so many lands and peoples (he met some 60 kings, rulers, despots, etc) provide an invaluable and unique record of the time – his accounts were recorded in the *Rihlah*.

He was the first true explorer of Arabia, arriving in that area after an overland journey from Tangier in 1325, at the start of an expedition that was to last seven years. After covering much of Arabia and the Red Sea, and visiting East Africa, ibn-Batuta went to Baghdad and the upper regions of the Tigris. Another journey took him to China and the Far East, while in the years 1349–53 he travelled widely in northern Africa, discovering the Niger River near Djeuné, visiting Timbuktu and Kabara, and travelling through the Sahara region of Talak, to Tamanrasset, and through the Ahaggar Mountains before returning to the Atlas Mountains, and over them to Tangier.

IDRĪSĪ, ash-Sharif al'. 1100–c 1165

An Arabian geographer and scientist who wrote one of the most important mediaeval works of geography, known (translated) as *The Pleasure Excursion of One Who is Eager to Traverse the Regions of the World*. It is also known as *The Book of Roger (Kitāb Rujār)*, since Idrīsī was court geographer, friend and adviser to Roger II, the Norman King of Sicily. Idrīsī travelled extensively in his youth – from England to Asia Minor – but from 1145 lived and worked in Palermo. His book was initially compiled as the text to

Ibn-Batuta travelling in Egypt. (Mary Evans Picture Library)

accompany his silver planisphere which depicted a world map, and was completed in 1154.

INDICOPLEUSTES. (fl c AD 540)

A 6th-century Egyptian geographer and traveller, originally known as Cosmas, who as early as c 540 wrote that China could be reached by a sea voyage, going first east, then north (starting either at the Red Sea or the Persian Gulf) but that the overland route via Persia would be far shorter. He sailed round the shores of the Indian Ocean and traded between Ethiopia and India (Indicopleustes means 'the Indian navigator'). He became a monk and wrote a treatise *Christian Topography* (*Topographia Christiana*) which contains one of the earliest world maps – though it is based, like the treatise, on a very literal Testament depiction of the earth as a rectangular plane, above which is the sky, and then heaven.

JANZ, Willem. 1570–?

A Dutch mariner who helped Holland gain supremacy in the East Indies in the beginning of the 17th century. In 1605 Janz was sent to explore southern New Guinea, and arrived through the Strait of Malacca, sailing east to meet the New Guinea coast north of the Kepulauan islands. He followed the coast to just beyond 140° E, turned south, and in so doing missed discovering the Torres Strait (Torres arrived there from the west, within the next year). Janz sighted the western edge of Australia's Cape York Peninsula, and sailed along it until about 13° S, wrongly deciding that it was a southern extension of New Guinea.

JENKINSON, Anthony. ?–1611.

The Englishman who was chief factor of the Muskovy Company, which had been formed as a result of Richard Chancellor's accidental landing at Colmagro (Archangel). In 1557, a year after Chancellor died in a shipwreck, Jenkinson travelled via Colmagro to Moskva (Moscow), and Czar Ivan gave him permission to journey into unknown Muskovy (Russia). He went east as far as the Volga River and followed it to Astrakan and the Caspian Sea, from where he continued south-east, past the Aral Sea, to Bukhara, hoping to travel into China. However he was then turned back by the local Mongol ruler, and arrived back in England in 1559. In 1561 he began a three-year journey over the same ground to the Caspian Sea, this time sailing south to north of Baku before making his way overland to Qazvin in Persia. Jenkinson returned to Moskva with goods for trade, and was the first European to trade with Persia after the ousting of the Mongols by the Moslem Safarids.

JOHN OF MONTECORVINO. 1247–1328

A Franciscan friar who travelled to China in 1291, going overland through Persia to the mouth of the Persian Gulf, from where he went by sea round the coast of India to Madras, through the Strait of Malacca, round to the China Sea and up the coast to the Yellow Sea. John disembarked at the nearest point to Cambaluc (Peking) and arrived there in 1294. Through the magnanimity of Kublai Khan, John was welcomed at court, founded a church, and made a fair number of converts to Christianity.

JOLLIET, Louis. 1645–1700

French cartographer and explorer who was sent to explore the Mississippi River in North America in 1673, following the exploration of the Mississippi and Fox watershed by Jean Nicolet. Jolliet followed Nicolet's route along the Fox and Wisconsin to the Mississippi (accompanied by a Jesuit priest, Jacques Marquette), and sailed down the river to its junction with the Arkansas River – the first European to undertake such a long voyage on the river. Jolliet was almost into Spanish territory, but by that stage it was clear that the river must flow into the Gulf of Mexico; statements by local Indians backed up this deduction, so Jolliet returned to friendlier areas. He later travelled to Hudson Bay and charted the Labrador coast, and in 1697 was made royal hydrographer of New France.

KARLSEFNI, Thorfinn. (fl 1005)

The Viking who made the last real attempt (in 1005–6) to establish a Vinland colony. He followed the route of Ericsson and Thorwald to North America, but conflict with the Indians forced him to give up the fertile land.

Explorers and Their Discoveries
KELSEY, Henry. c 1670–1729

A Hudson's Bay Company employee who was probably the first European to explore and see the extent of Canada's vast central plains. Although the company usually waited for Indians to bring furs to them, Kelsey was ambitious, and in 1690 he left York Factory on a two-year journey to encourage more Indians to take fur skins to the company's depot. He went south-west from York Factory, crossed Lake Winnipeg, and circled west of the lake. Kelsey's was the first expedition into the North-west since the Groseilliers' – and was to be the last for over 60 years.

KENNEDY, Edmund. 1818–1848

An early explorer of eastern Australia, who in 1847 went on an expedition from Sydney to determine the direction of flow of the Barcoo River, which runs inland to Lake Eyre. The following year he led another expedition which sailed up the east coast to Rockingham Bay, the starting point for an exploration of Queensland. The expedition began to run short of food and Kennedy headed north towards Cape York to get help, but he was killed by Aborigines and only two of the explorers survived.

KINTUP. (fl 1879)

A 'pundit-explorer' (SEE NAIN SINGH) who in 1879 went from Darjeeling to Lhasa and further east, accompanied by a Mongolian lama. The security provided by such a companion was illusory, however, for the lama put a halt to Kintup's surveying by selling him into slavery and two years passed before he managed to escape and return to India. It was Kintup who, despite his misfortune, established that the Tsangpo and the Brahmaputra were the same river.

KISHEN SINGH. ?–1921

A 'pundit-explorer' employed by the British to help map Tibet (SEE NAIN SINGH). In 1869 he explored and measured areas of the Himalayas west of Dehra Dun – in this, and in all subsequent expeditions, Kishen Singh took measurements by counting his footsteps. Two years later, starting at Katmandu, he explored a vast expanse of the Himalayas stretching from Lhasa in the east, north round the Nam Tso lake, then west to Gartok, practically on the 80th meridian. Kishen Singh accompanied Nain Singh in

217

1873 on an expedition from Leh to Khotan (Ho-tien) and Yarkand (Soch'e), continuing in the next year on his own from Yarkand to Kashgar (K'ashih), and also south-west into the Pamirs. On his way back Kishen Singh ventured east into the Taklamakan Desert from Khotan, taking a more easterly route back to Leh. He undertook another long expedition (1878–82) from Darjeeling to Shigatse, east to Lhasa, north to the inhospitable Tsaidam depression (skirting its eastern edge), and continuing to Tunhwang on the south-west edge of the Gobi Desert. He returned through the region of present-day Cheng-tu and across the deep river courses of south-west China, back to the Tsangpo River and to Darjeeling.

KRAPF, Johann. 1810–1881

German missionary and associate of Johannes Rebmann — the first to venture inland in the Mombasa area. Krapf was the first to sight Mt Kenya (in 1849), and was instrumental in starting the search for the great African lakes. (SEE JOHANNES REBMANN).

KROPOTKIN, Peter. 1842–1921

A Russian who was widely recognized for his achievements in geography, zoology, sociology and history, but eventually gained widest fame as a leading figure and theorist in the anarchist movement. He was the son of a prince and from 1862 to 1867 served as an officer in the army in Siberia. During those years he also made extensive geographical observations, and these, together with his theory on the structure of mountain ranges, caused a considerable rearrangement of the images held of eastern Asia. Later in his life Kropotkin rejected fame, honour and his artistocracy in favour of the anarchist cause.

KUBLAI KHAN. c 1216–1294

The grandson of Genghis Khan, and Great Khan (emperor) 1260–94. Under Kublai Khan the Mongols conquered China, and he established his court at Cambaluc (from Khanbalik, or City of the Great Khan — now Peking). With the conquest of Burma and Korea, the Mongol Empire stretched from the Black Sea to the China Sea. In spite of his power, Kublai Khan was no despot and proved to be a broadminded, progressive Emperor. He encouraged the separate culture of the Chinese and even invited Christian missionaries to his Buddhist Empire. He also re-opened the old trading routes between the East and the West, and created the circumstances in which Marco Polo was able to make his travels.

LACERDA, Francisco de. ?–1798

Portuguese explorer who in 1787 travelled up the Cunene River (which marks the southern boundary of present-day Angola) to the western edge of the Bihé Plateau at about 15° S. In 1798 he explored the opposite, eastern side of the plateau, following the Zambezi to beyond the Quebrabasa Rapids and then travelling north, following the Luangwe River for some distance west of Lake Nyasa. He eventually headed westwards only to die near Lake Mweru without fulfilling his hopes of crossing the continent by land.

LA CONDAMINE, Charles Marie de. 1701–1774

The naturalist and mathematician who led the first true scientific expedition to South America. La Condamine was chosen in 1734 as the leader of one of two scientific missions to determine the true shape of the earth; one went to Lapland, while la Condamine was to discover the distance represented by a degree of longitude near the equator. He sailed in 1735 accompanied, among others, by the astronomer Louis Godin des Odonais, and landed at Cartegena on Colombia's Caribbean coast, from where they made their way to Manta on the coast of Ecuador. There they were joined by Pedro Vincente Maldonado, who guided them through little-known areas of Ecuador towards Quito.

La Condamine carried out many observations and discovered platinum ore and rubber trees, but then had to go all the way to Lima, an eight-month journey, to overcome the obstacles of officialdom and bureaucracy. The measurements and surveying that had to be carried out were arduous, and were not completed until 1743, the last being taken near Cuenca in Ecuador. La Condamine and Maldonado then set off down the Amazon on a raft, the first such voyage ever made by a scientist, and one that lasted until 1745. This expedition provided a spur to Humboldt's expedition of 1799.

LAING, Alexander Gordon. 1793–1826

Believed to be the first European to have been to Timbuktu. Laing's first

219

A small expedition winds through the vast Sahara. (Mary Evans Picture Library)

expedition into North Africa was in 1822 when he was with the British Army in Sierra Leone. He was sent inland north-east from Freetown to try to establish trade links and abolish the remaining remnants of the slave trade. In July 1825 he was sent to explore the Niger River and to visit Timbuktu. He set out from Tripoli for the Fezzan region and followed a caravan route across the Grand Erg Oriental to In Salah. Passing well to the west of the Ahaggar mountain region, Laing eventually turned south-west before the Adrar des Iforas hills and finally reached Timbuktu – but only after a fierce battle with a group of Tuareg nomads, during which he was badly wounded. Laing stayed in the citadel for about a month, but two days after leaving Timbuktu he was again attacked, and murdered.

LANCASTER, James. c 1554–1618

The pioneer of English trade in the East Indies. Lancaster served under Drake against the Spanish Armada, and in 1591 he sailed on Drake's ship, *Edward Bonaventure*, for the East Indies. In June 1592 he reached Penang Island just off the coast of Malaya, in the Straits of Malacca. This was the rich sea route between the Indian Ocean and the 'Spice Islands', and

Lancaster stayed to plunder likely ships that came his way. His attempts to establish legitimate trade were not quite so successful, but in 1601 he commanded the English East India Company's first fleet, and established the company's first trading post at Bantam, in Java. The fleet returned with a rich cargo of pepper in 1603, and Lancaster went on to become a director of the East India Company, in which capacity he sponsored a number of attempts to find the North-west Passage.

LANDER, Richard. 1804–1834

Accompanied Hugh Clapperton on his journey from the Gulf of Guinea to trace the Niger's course, but when Clapperton died at Sokoto (in 1825), Lander gave up the quest. In 1830 Lander and his brother John, commissioned by the British government, landed in the Gulf of Guinea at Badagri, and travelled inland to meet the Niger at Bussa. They explored upstream for some 100 miles (160 km), and then began the trip downstream – a hazardous journey by canoe. The Lander brothers successfully reached the delta mouth of the Niger, but were then captured by Ibo tribesmen who held them for a substantial ransom. This was paid, and they finally arrived at Fernando Po Island. In January 1834 Richard Lander returned to the Niger on a trading expedition, but was fatally wounded in another attack by tribesmen.

LA SALLE, Robert Cavelier, Sieur de. 1643–1687

The Frenchman who established his homeland's claim to Louisiana and the Mississippi Valley. La Salle emigrated to Canada with the intention of finding his fortune in the fur trade, but became preoccupied with the thought of discovering links in North America's waterways that would provide a route to the East Indies. In 1669 he travelled from Montreal to Lake Ontario, the Niagara Falls, and then found the Ohio River which he followed as far as present-day Louisville. In 1678, La Salle built *Le Griffon* which he intended to use on the Great Lakes to collect furs, but at Green Bay on Lake Michigan he sent his ship back, went ashore, headed south, and founded three settlements before returning to Montreal – his ship was not heard from again.

La Salle's ambition was to make a voyage down the Mississippi, and he began it in 1681, sailing on until he reached the Gulf of Mexico. He claimed the whole valley area for France, as Louisiana, and in his anxiety to raise a colony on the Gulf of Mexico coast rapidly returned upstream and headed back for France. In 1684 he returned directly to the Gulf of

Mexico by sea, but he missed the Mississippi Delta and was subsequently unable to find it. Bitterly disappointed, La Salle eventually went ashore much further west at Matagorda Bay (the site of Houston, Texas), and travelled inshore about 250 miles (400 km), hoping to reach Mexico. In 1687, however, his men rebelled and murdered him, reaching Mexico under the leadership of Henri Joutel.

LEICHHARDT, Ludwig. 1813–1848

A determined and energetic explorer of Australia, but a rather disorganized one. In 1884 Leichhardt set out from Moreton Bay (then the site of the Brisbane penal colony), initially crossing the Condamine River and then following the Great Dividing Range north along the length of eastern Australia to the Mitchell River on Cape York Peninsula. He skirted the Gulf of Carpentaria and crossed Arnhem Land to Port Essington on the Van Diemen Gulf, east of Melville Island. Leichhardt began another journey from Moreton Bay in 1846 with the intent of leading an expedition around three sides of Australia, finishing at Perth. But his qualities of leadership proved to be poor and the attempt was abandoned when the Tropic of Capricorn was reached. Leichhardt's last expedition started two years later when he began an east to west crossing of Australia. He crossed the mountains, travelled north-west across the headwaters of the Culgoa, Warrego and Barcoo Rivers, but then disappeared forever.

LE MAIRE, Jakob. 1585–1616

Discovered, with Willem Schouten, the Le Maire Strait between Tierra del Fuego and Isla de los Estados (Staten Island) – a much easier, quicker route than the 370 twisting miles (595 km) of the Magellan Strait (SEE SCHOUTEN).

LENZ, Oskar. 1848–1925

In two major African explorations Lenz reversed previous approaches, though he did not uncover any major new territory. In 1879 he began a journey that was more or less a reversal of Caillié's expedition, starting from Casablanca, crossing the Grand Atlas Mountains, and then heading across the Sahara to Timbuktu. Lenz spent three weeks there and then followed the Niger for some distance until he turned west to meet the

Adventurers from Europe on the Ogooué River, north of the Congo. (Mary Evans Picture Library)

Senegal River, which he followed to the Atlantic. His second expedition lasted from 1885 to 1887. He began at the mouth of the Congo and travelled upstream, then went up to the Lualaba before crossing to Lake Tanganyika, continuing from its southern tip to Lake Nyasa (Lake Malawi), and on to the Indian Ocean.

LEÓN.
SEE J PONCE de LEÓN.

LEONOV, Alexei. 1934–

Russian cosmonaut who in March 1965 became the first man to step out of a space capsule (*Voskhod II*) and 'walk' in space. Leonov's space-walk took place at an altitude of 110 miles (175 km) and lasted approximately 10 minutes, during which time he 'travelled' from over the Crimea to a point above western Siberia.

LEWIS, Meriweather. 1774–1809

With William Clark made the first overland expedition in North America to the Pacific coast – one of the longest transcontinental journeys ever undertaken, during which, in spite of the dangers posed by Indians, deserts, mountains, bears and rapids, only one person died. Spanish and French possessions in the late 18th century prevented the 13 United States from exploring many western areas of their continent, but when Louisiana was sold to the United States in 1803, President Jefferson wasted no time in commissioning exploration – specifically to see if there was a water route that led to the Pacific.

In May 1804 Lewis and Clark set out from St Louis (on the Mississippi, just south of its confluence with the Missouri) and followed the Missouri into the heart of the 'Badlands' country, due west of Lake Superior. They built a stronghold at Fort Mandan (now Mandan), and spent the winter there among the fairly friendly Mandan Sioux Indians. In the spring they set off again, aided by a French–Canadian interpreter and his Indian wife, who frequently acted as a guide. Lewis and Clark followed the Missouri up into the Rocky Mountains, passing through the Lemhi Pass into the Clearwater Mountains, where they arrived in autumn 1805. Then they went due west, intercepted the Snake River and followed it to the Columbia River, and so to the Pacific, arriving in November 1805. The two explorers then sailed into the Pacific for a short distance.

After wintering at the mouth of the Columbia, Lewis and Clark headed back in March 1806. They separated in June near the junction of the Bitterroot and Clark Fork rivers, Lewis looking for a more direct route through the mountains to Great Falls, and Clark retracing much of their outward journey, but crossing the mountains some way north of Lemhi Pass. Lewis found a quick route via the Blackfoot River, crossing the Lewis Range to the Sun River. After arriving at Great Falls in July, he explored the Marias River, then continued back down the Missouri and met Clark – who had gone east from Three Forks to the Yellowstone River and so to the Missouri. The two explorers arrived back in St Louis in September 1806 with a vast amount of invaluable information, thus inspiring another era of exploration and settlement.

LINSCHOTEN, Jan Huyghen van. 1563–1611

Dutch traveller and explorer whose knowledge of the East led directly to Dutch supremacy in trade with the Spice Islands and surrounding areas. In 1583 van Linschoten sailed via the Cape of Good Hope to Goa in India, where he worked for the Portuguese and so gained first-hand knowledge of trading methods and of important sea routes. He returned to Holland in 1589 and wrote *Itinerario*, an account of the years he spent in Goa which included maps and other shipping information. It was this book that aroused Dutch interest in the East, providing the knowledge that enabled them to begin trading voyages.

Later, van Linschoten became preoccupied with finding a shorter route to the East, and in 1594 he sailed with Willem Barents in search of the North-east Passage (SEE BARENTS). After Barents turned back from Novaya Zemlya, van Linschoten sailed into the Kara Sea (Karskoye More) before he too was forced back by bad weather. He was also on Barents' 1595 expedition with seven ships, but ice again stopped the voyage.

LIVINGSTONE, David. 1813–1873

The extraordinary Scottish explorer whose personal courage and endurance, combined with religious zeal and firmly fixed ideas on Christianity and civilization, made him the harbinger of both the good and the ill fortunes that were to fall on Central and Southern Africa over the next 100 years and more. He was born in Blantyre, Scotland, one of seven children brought up in poverty and piety – the latter, together with an unreal dedication to work, being further enforced by unyielding parental discipline. That he was unusual is amply illustrated by his use of part of his first week's wages (when he was sent to work, aged ten, in a cotton mill) to buy a Latin grammar book. Livingstone became determined on missionary work at an early age and initially hoped to go to China for the London Missionary Society, but the Opium War ended that ambition. He then met Robert Moffat who was a missionary in Southern Africa, and very quickly decided to work there; in 1840 he was ordained, and arrived in Cape Town in March the following year.

Livingstone went almost immediately to Moffat's mission at Kuruman in the northern Karoo and threw himself into missionary work, rapidly becoming equally absorbed with exploration. Within a year of his arrival in Africa, he had already been further north than anyone else, pushing on into the barren Kalahari in search of converts and of knowledge about the country. His abilities as a linguist proved invaluable among the numerous native dialects, and in 1843 he founded his own mission at Kolobeng, some 320 miles (515 km) north-east of Kuruman, which he used as a base for a number of expeditions into areas of the Transvaal highveld. In 1844 Livingstone's personal endurance and strength were dramatically tested when, on a journey to Mabotsa, he was attacked by a lion. Before he was saved by his companions, he suffered permanent injuries to his left arm.

In 1845 he was married (to Moffat's daughter), but though he was to

Livingstone narrowly escapes being killed by a lion. The missionary had shot and wounded the lion, but it mauled him badly, as well as two of his companions, before falling dead, leaving eleven teeth wounds in Livingstone's arm. (Mary Evans Picture Library)

father four children, his marriage seemed to take a definite third place behind missionary work and exploration. It was in 1849 that Livingstone first achieved the public recognition on which the rest of his life was to depend. He set off from Kolobeng that year accompanied by two other Europeans, guides and porters, and travelled north, discovering Lake Ngami, a large pan in the northern Kalahari. This brought him an award from the British Royal Geographical Society, and prompted another journey the next year when he attempted to reach Linyanti (roughly between Lake Ngami and the Victoria Falls). Passing east of it, Livingstone's expedition carried on as far as the Zambezi before turning back, and visited Linyanti on the return leg. He made his way back to Cape Town, sent his wife and children to the comforts and safety of England, and returned to Kolobeng, from where he set out on a four-year expedition exploring the Zambezi River. North of Linyanti he followed the river upstream, crossed the Congo watershed and eventually turned west more or less on the 10th parallel. Consequently Livingstone came across the Cuanza River, which led him to Luanda on the Atlantic coast. Retracing his steps south along the Zambezi, he carried on past the region he already knew, and not long after made his most famous discovery – the majestic Victoria Falls. The long, difficult and arduous expedition continued along the river, past Tete, and eventually arrived near the mouth at Quelimane on the Indian Ocean coast, in 1856.

This great crossing of Africa and the exploration of the awesome river had caught the imagination of hundreds of thousands, and on his return to England Livingstone found himself to be a national hero; the book he wrote describing the expedition sold great numbers, and for the first time he was able to provide his family with some degree of comfort. But in March 1858 he left again for Africa, as the British Consul at Quelimane. From there, he explored the lower region of the Zambezi and the Shire River, and discovered Lake Shirwa and Lake Nyasa (Lake Malawi). Livingstone was frequently accompanied by other European explorers, but their attempts to navigate the Rovuma River in a paddle steamer from the Indian Ocean to Lake Nyasa were unsuccessful, and little was gained from trying to navigate the Zambezi or Shire rivers either; eventually the British Government recalled the expedition in 1863. The following year, Livingstone took the little paddle-steamer 2,500 miles (4,000 km) across the Indian Ocean to Bombay, where he sold it for a good price, and returned to England.

In 1864 Baker had discovered Lake Albert, and shown that the area of the Nile source was a good deal more complex than Speke had indicated. The Royal Geographical Society had little hesitation in choosing Livingstone to complete the mapping of the vital area, and 1866 consequently found the missionary back at the Rovuma River. From there he rounded the southern end of Lake Nyasa and travelled north-west to cross the Luangwa River, heading for Lake Tanganyika. West of the southern tip of that lake, Livingstone discovered Lake Mweru and Lake Bangweulu, and then made his way to central Lake Tanganyika, establishing a base at Ujiji. Although he was by then considerably weakened by the numerous afflictions and hardships imposed by travel in Central Africa, he set out again in 1869 in search of a river reported in the west. This turned out to be the Lualaba River, which he met at Nyangwe; a brief exploration showed that it did not belong to the Nile, but to the Congo river system. Livingstone returned to Ujiji, and it was there that Stanley, sent from America by the *New York Herald*, found him in November 1871.

Although Livingstone was very ill, he accompanied Stanley on a search of the northern part of Lake Tanganyika, but when Stanley set off back to the east coast, the ailing missionary went only as far as Tabora, scene of Burton and Speke's disagreement. With the source of the Nile still not positively established, Livingstone refused to leave Africa, and he returned to Lake Tanganyika. He believed that the river must have its earliest beginning in the region of Lake Bangweulu, and slowly made his way back to that region. But Livingstone was mortally ill, and on 1 May 1873 he died, near the source of the Luapula River – one of the most distant

227

sources of the Congo River, but a long way from the true source of the Nile. So highly was he regarded by those who had lived with him in Africa that his servants buried his heart and other internal organs, to 'embalm' them in Africa, and carried his body on a nine-month journey to the coast of East Africa. From there it was taken to England, and buried in Westminster Abbey on 18 April 1874.

LLEWELLYN, Martin. ?–1634

Cartographer who compiled the first English atlas of any segment of the globe, probably in 1598. His atlas, containing the earliest known charts of the East, lay undiscovered in Oxford for nearly 350 years, and covers the Cape of Good Hope as well as the East Indies, Japan, the Philippines and the Marianas.

The charts contain the names given to various islands by the Dutch expedition under Cornelius de Houtman, so it is likely that Llewellyn sailed with the Dutch ships, and was one of the 80 survivors of the expedition. He was Steward of St Bartholomew's Hospital from 1599 until his death, years which were apparently characterized by constant debt and the 'annual succession of children born to him'.

LOBO, Jerônimo. 1593–1678

A missionary who saw the source of the Blue Nile in about 1628, some 15 years after Pedro Paez. Lobo travelled to Gondar on Lake Tana from Assab, on Ethiopia's Red Sea Coast, made expeditions west and south of the lake, and went on a longer journey along the river from Lake Tana, past the Tisisat Falls, and along the river's westward bend.

LONG, Washington de. 1844–1881

Unwittingly contributed to the knowledge of the Arctic, while attempting an east-to-west navigation of the North-east Passage. De Long took part in an expedition which sailed around Greenland in 1873, and this inspired his next journey. He arrived at the Bering Strait from North America, but his ship, the *Jeanette*, became ice-bound in September 1879, soon after entering the Arctic Ocean. De Long was heading for Wrangel Island (Vrangelya), which he believed to be a substantial land mass. Although caught firmly in the ice, the members of de Long's expedition soon realized they were drifting westwards, steadily nearer to the North Pole. The ice pressure eventually began to break the sides of the ship and in June 1881, at about 77° N and 155° E, north of the New Siberian Islands, three groups left the now disintegrating wreck and made off across the ice, each group dragging a small boat. When they reached open water they took to the boats. One sank very soon with the loss of all aboard, while the other two became separated, landing on opposite sides of the Lena River delta. The group on the west side was rescued, but de Long and the men with him on the east side died of exposure (his journal was found a year later). Meanwhile the wreck of the *Jeanette*, still caught in the ice, continued to drift westwards. Some of the wreckage came ashore on Greenland three years later; this gave an insight into the behaviour of the ice packs, and inspired Nansen's first attempt to reach the Pole by drifting with the ice.

LYON, George. 1795–1832

Took part in a British Government expedition led by Joseph Ritchie, with the intention of crossing the Sahara Desert. The group left Tripoli in 1818, but Ritchie died at Marzūq after crossing the Fezzan. Although Lyon attempted to continue the journey, heading south-west from Marzūq to cross the Edeyin Marzūq, the expedition was soon abandoned entirely.

MACKENZIE, Alexander. c 1764–1820

Scottish fur trader and explorer whose combined journeys constituted the first crossing of the North American continent (north of Mexico), and who traced the course of the 1,100-mile (1,750-km) Canadian river that carries his name. Mackenzie set off on his first expedition in 1789 on behalf of the North-west Company, a consortium of independent traders formed in opposition to the giant Hudson's Bay Company. Peter Pond, another independent trader operating at Lake Athabasca, had earlier propounded theories of a waterway to the Pacific, and it was in search of this that Mackenzie left the Fort Chipewyan trading post at the west end of Lake Athabasca. He travelled north along the Slave River to the Great Slave Lake, and took its western exit, the Mackenzie River. The northerly direction in which the river soon began to flow made it clear to Mackenzie that he was more likely to reach the Arctic Ocean than the Pacific, but he followed the river all the way to its mouth in the bay which is also named after him.

In 1792 he began another expedition in search of the Pacific, this time heading directly west from Lake Athabasca along the Peace River. At the junction of the Finlay and Parsnip rivers (Finlay Forks), Mackenzie turned south along the Parsnip and discovered the upper reaches of another, larger river which he followed, believing it to be the Columbia River. However the Columbia was still further south, and Mackenzie was really following the unnavigable Fraser River. He abandoned the Fraser when he realized its nature, briefly headed north again, and eventually turned west, encountering the Dean River and following it to the Pacific coast opposite Bella Bella on the shores of Queen Charlotte Sound.

MAGELLAN, Ferdinand. c 1480–1521

One of the most famous of explorers, whose voyage was a major step in European knowledge of the world – and simultaneously debunked a great deal of superstition and mythology. Magellan went to sea in 1505 when he joined Francisco de Almeida's fleet, which was being sent by King Manuel to oppose Moslem power in the East and in the Indian Ocean. He was

involved in a number of skirmishes with Arabian and Indian ships, and took part in the capture of Malacca which finally established Portuguese supremacy in 1511.

Later, however, Magellan fell out with King Manuel, and in 1517 he swore allegiance to Spain. By this stage he had developed his concept of sailing round the world, dispelling scepticism and caution with the tempting hypothesis that, since the Papal Bull granted Spain all territories west of a certain line, if he could reach the Spice Islands of the East by continually sailing westward, those islands would consequently belong to Spain. Royal assent to his voyage was duly given, and in September 1519 Magellan's fleet of five ships set sail. In December they arrived in Rio de Janeiro Bay, and continued down the South American coast. The wide estuary of the Rio de la Plata cost Magellan 23 days, for he thought it might be the route past

Ferdinand Magellan. (The National Maritime Museum, London)

230

The Old World's impression of New World customs – from a 16th-century woodcut.

the continent and explored it thoroughly before sailing south again. At the end of March 1520 the five ships anchored in San Julian Bay for the southern hemisphere winter.

Strict food rationing, cold winter storms, unrelieved routine and monotonous scenery brought the crews to the brink of mutiny, but Magellan quelled it in time, and in October the ships were again under sail. One was very soon shipwrecked, but Magellan shortly saw the wide break in the land that was the opening of the strait between South America and Tierra del Fuego. One of the ships deserted and returned to Spain while the remaining three began the long, slow journey through the winding strait – a 370 mile (595 km) passage which ranges in width from $2\frac{1}{2}$ miles (4 km) to 15 miles (24 km). At last, on 28 November 1520, the ships emerged into a clear, calm ocean, which Magellan named the Pacific.

In many ways, however, the hardships of the voyage had only just begun, for the three ships sailed day after day without a glimpse of land. Through sheer misfortune their course took them beyond sight of any of the thousands of Pacific islands, and when at last they did land at Guam (in the Ladrones, or Marianas Islands) they had been 99 days without fresh water or fresh food, and many of the crew had died. After gathering fresh provisions, the expedition continued to the Philippines. Here, even greater disaster struck, for Magellan was killed during a skirmish between the local natives, on Mactan, a small island adjacent to Cebu.

So severely were their numbers reduced by then that the Spaniards burnt one of the ships, the *Concepcion*, and sailed in two ships to Mindanoa,

231

Borneo and the Moluccas. One ship again set off across the Pacific in an attempt to retrace its route to Spain, while Sebastian del Cano took the *Victoria* on across the Indian Ocean and round the Cape of Good Hope, this ship thus becoming the first to sail round the world, and del Cano the first navigator to do so. The *Victoria* reached Spain on 6 September 1522, almost three years after sailing out. A new route to the East was found, the earth was proved to be round, and another era in exploration began.

MANNING, Thomas. 1772–1840

The first Englishman ever to enter the 'forbidden city' of Lhasa. On a private visit in 1811, Manning was also the first to see Tibet's supreme ruler, the Dalai Lama. His presence, there, however, was not much appreciated by the Chinese (who had 'influenced' Tibetan affairs since they seized the country in 1791), and after four months he was forced to leave. He retraced his steps through Bhutan back to Calcutta – the last European to see Lhasa for quite some time.

MARSDEN, Samuel. 1765–1838

The chaplain to the colony of New South Wales, who in 1814 founded the first mission in New Zealand, at the Bay of Islands on North Island. Marsden went to New Zealand primarily to convert the Maoris, but made three expeditions between 1814 and 1820. He explored the east coast in the far north from Doubtless Bay to Firth of Thames in Hauraki Gulf, as well as much of the inland area from Wangaroa Harbour south to the beginning of the Bay of Plenty, discovering the narrow strip of land between Hauraki Gulf and Manukau Harbour on the west coast.

MAWSON, Douglas. 1882–1958

Went with Ernest Shackleton in 1907–8 to the Antarctic and located the South Magnetic Pole (SEE SHACKLETON). In 1911 Mawson led an expedition to the Antarctic in the *Aurora*, and established a base at Commonwealth Bay. In 1912–13 he went inland with sledge parties, heading east and naming King George V Land. Two of his companions, Ninnis and Mertz, died on this journey. Frank Wild was also on the expedition, leading sledging parties from the Shackleton Ice Shelf and naming Queen Mary Land. The *Aurora* picked up Mawson from the continent in 1914. In 1929, he returned to Antarctica in the *Discovery*,

Samuel Marsden lands at the Bay of Islands, New Zealand. (Mary Evans Picture Library)

leading an expedition which concentrated on oceanographic research, and made intensive studies of the coastal areas.

McCLINTOCK, Leopold. 1819–1907

Took part in expeditions with John and J C Ross searching for Sir John Franklin and the North-west Passage. After the official searches had been called off, he was commissioned by Lady Franklin to lead another expedition which established conclusively the fate of Sir John. (SEE JOHN FRANKLIN 1848–9, 1850–1, 1857–9.)

McCLURE, Robert. 1807–1873

Took part in two searches for Sir John Franklin. On his second trip, undertaken with Richard Collinson, McClure established two exits from Melville Sound, McClure Strait and Prince of Wales Strait, thus

233

McClintock interviews Eskimos at Cape Victoria to find out what happened to Franklin.
(Mary Evans Picture Library)

identifying the last part of the North-west Passage. (SEE JOHN FRANKLIN 1848–9, 1850–1.)

MENDAÑA, Álvaro de. 1541–1595

In the second half of the 16th century most of the world had been criss-crossed, but for mariners there still remained the lure of the missing southern continent – Terra Australis, or Terra Incognita. Mendaña was one who finally set out in search of it, leaving Peru in 1567 with the secondary aims of settling the land, once found, and of converting its inhabitants to Catholicism. However, he sailed almost due west, and so became the discoverer of the Solomon Islands. He explored these islands, then headed due north to beyond the Tropic of Cancer, before turning east on a course which led him to the Santa Barbara Islands off present-day Los Angeles, after which he followed the coastline back to Callao in Peru, near Lima.

Many years later, in 1595, Mendaña once more set out on a voyage, deciding that he would settle the islands he discovered. But this time he was unable to find the Solomons, for he had incorrectly plotted them in 1567. However, he did discover the Marquesas Islands, and got as near to

234

the Solomons as the Santa Cruz Islands, before he died. His pilot, Pedro de Quiros, continued the voyage to the Philippines, and later went on to make his own discoveries (SEE QUIROS). The Solomons continued to prove elusive, and were not re-discovered until Bruni d'Entrecasteaux's voyage some 200 years later.

MERCATOR, Gerardus, 1512–1594

The Latinized name of Gerhard Kremer, Flemish geographer, cartographer and mathematician who devised the revolutionary method of map projection, using straight lines of longitude and latitude bisecting at right angles, which is still the basis of the majority of maps used today. Two years before he perfected this projection he published a world map which was then the most accurate and comprehensive. He, and later his son Rumold, continued to improve and add to it through various editions.

Mercator believed strongly in the existence of a vast southern continent, considering it to be necessary to 'counter-balance' the weight of Europe and Asia. Consequently Terra Australis covered a large part of the southern

Gerardus Mercator. (The National Maritime Museum, London)

hemisphere on his maps – virtually the whole unexplored area of the Pacific Ocean, up to about 20° S, and in the Atlantic to about 40° S. Mercator portrayed Tierra del Fuego as a promontory of this supposed continent, but although the Torres Strait was not then discovered (as far as is known, Torres was the first to sail it in 1606) Mercator distinctly separated New Guinea from Australia.

MESSERSCHMIDT. ?–1735

A Prussian naturalist who took advantage of Czar Peter I's decrees permitting a more scientific exploration of Siberia. Messerschmidt left St

Petersburg (Leningrad) in 1719, and went by way of Moscow, Tobolsk and Tomsk to the Ob, Yenisei and Amur rivers, accompanied for part of his journey by a Swede named Strahlenberg. He spent eight years in Russia, mostly beyond the Ural Mountains, reaching as far north as Turukhansk on the Yenisei, as far south as Irkutsk on Lake Baykal, and as far east as the upper course of the Amur River. In spite of the great amount of useful information he had gathered, his return in 1727 to St Petersburg aroused little interest, and he fared no better in his own Danzig. Messerschmidt went back to Russia, and was virtually penniless when he died.

MIDDLETON, Henry. ?–1613

Led the second fleet of ships sent by the English East India Company to trade with the East Indies, in 1604. In the time since Lancaster's fleet had been there, however, the Dutch had drawn up their own united and powerful East India Company, and Middleton came up against considerable opposition.

MITCHELL, Thomas. 1792–1855

In four periods from 1831 to 1845 made an intensive study of the river systems of eastern Australia, and determined the relationships of the main rivers which drain from the western slopes of the southern region of the Great Dividing Range. Mitchell also discovered the northern course of the Barcoo River, which becomes Cooper's Creek and flows into Lake Eyre.

MOFFAT, Robert. 1795–1883

Missionary who spent over 50 years among the Batswana people in the southern Kalahari region of Southern Africa. In travelling between his missionary area and the 'Europeanized' area of Cape Town, Moffat took three major longitudinal routes across the escarpment and the highveld, and he also carried out a number of journeys into present-day Transvaal, and up into Zimbabwe. Livingstone decided to go to Africa after he met Moffat in England, and married Moffat's daughter.

MOORCROFT, William. ?–1825

Made his first expedition to Tibet in 1812 (SEE H J HEARSEY). Moorcroft returned in 1819 accompanied by a geologist, and explored in depth the mountainous country between Lahore and Leh. Eventually he began to make his way westwards, initially into the plains north-west of Lahore, and followed the Kabul River through the Hindu Kush, whose northern slopes he also explored. Moorcroft travelled to Bukhara and turned south, but somewhere between the Amu Darya and Murgab rivers he was killed by Afghan tribesmen.

NACHTIGAL, Gustav. 1834–1885

German explorer of Africa who was the first to be able to present a cohesive picture of the dominant features of Northern Africa. In 1868 he left on an expedition ordered by the King of Prussia which was to last six years and be one of the most significant of all African explorations. Nachtigal travelled south from Tripoli across the Fezzan to Marzūq, and continued south on a caravan route, branching off eastwards to explore the Tibesti Mountains. North of Lake Chad he again explored to the east, south of the Tibesti, and after he had rounded Lake Chad's western side he explored the Chari River from Kousseri (Fort Lamy) to about 10° N. After returning to Kousseri he headed east, and in the region of Abéché went on a long diversion into Central Africa, almost on the 20th meridian and reaching about 6° N, before returning to continue eastwards.

Nachtigal became the first person to have crossed the south-east Sahara when he reached the White Nile in the Kordofan region, south of Khartoum. He later served as German consul in Tunis, and was sent by Bismarck to Western Africa on a trade mission, with the real intent of establishing German protectorates over territories which now form Togo and Cameroun.

NAIN SINGH. (fl 1870)

When Tibet was closed to Europeans by China, British map-makers came up with the idea of training Indians in surveying, since they could more easily adopt disguises as merchants or pilgrims. They came to be called 'pundit-explorers', and Nain Singh was the most experienced and accomplished of them. In just over ten years he covered more than 3,000 miles (4,800 km), measuring all his distances in footsteps as he walked. He was sometimes accompanied by Kishen Singh, Main Singh or Kalian Singh, and began his first expedition in 1865, when he went from Bareilly to Katmandu, crossed the Himalayas and travelled to Shigatse, tracing the course of the Tsangpo (Matsang, the upper part of the Brahmaputra River) and mapping the Nyenchentanglha Mountains north of the Himalayas.

Nain Singh went all the way back to Lake Manasarowar before re-crossing the Himalayas to Dehra Dun and returning to Bareilly. The next expedition took him to the area west of Gartok, along the Indus to Leh, north to Khotan (Ho-tien) on the edge of the Taklamakan Desert, and to Yarkand (Soch'e). His final long journey was from Leh across the Plateau of Tibet, north of the Aling Kangri Mountains (once called the Nain Singh Range), and eventually south to Lhasa and the Brahmaputra.

NANSEN, Fridtjof. 1861–1930

Norwegian scientist who gained fame as a polar explorer, a politician, and a humanitarian. Nansen made his first journey in Arctic regions in 1882 when he went to collect zoological specimens; the expedition went as far as Spitzbergen and on the return passed well to the west of Iceland, almost skirting the Greenland coast. In 1888, accompanied by Otto Sverdrup, he made the Greenland expedition which revealed the true nature of the land and its enormous ice-cap, which has depressed the ground surface in the interior to more than 1,000 feet (300 m) below sea level.

Inevitably Nansen learnt of the tragic voyage of Washington de Long,

Fridtjof Nansen and Frederic Johansen. (Mary Evans Picture Library)

how his ship was caught in the ice near the Bering Strait, and how parts of its wreckage were eventually brought ashore on Greenland. Nansen theorized that it should be possible to get caught in the ice deliberately, and use its drift to reach the North Pole. Consequently, in 1893, he and Sverdrup sailed from Oslo in the *Fram* and after rounding North Cape hugged the Russian shore as far as the New Siberian Islands, where they turned north. Ice gripped the *Fram* at 140° E, almost on 80° N, and the westward drift began; but the northward drift was much less than had been hoped for, and north of Severnaya Zemlya, in 1895, Nansen realized he would miss the Pole unless he tried for it on foot, using dog sledges. With Frederic Johansen, he left the ship in a bid to reach his goal, but at 86°14' N they had to turn back. Heading south-west they reached Franz Joseph Land and although they were ill-prepared, managed to survive the hardship of a winter north of the 80th parallel.

In 1896 a British expedition called at the islands and the two Norwegians were rescued. It was not until August that year that the *Fram*, still commanded by Sverdrup, was released by the ice pack north of Spitzbergen, and was able to sail back to Norway. Although his main mission had failed, Nansen learnt a great deal about the Arctic and achieved considerable fame. (In 1922 he won the Nobel Peace Prize, chiefly for his League of Nations work for the relief of refugees and prisoners of war.)

NARES, George. 1831–1915

The commander of HMS *Challenger* on its $3\frac{1}{2}$ year (1872–6) 69,000 mile (111,000 km) voyage round the earth carrying out scientific observations, chiefly connected with oceanography. (SEE CHARLES THOMSON.)

NARVÁEZ, Panfilo de. c 1478–1528

A Spaniard who heard of the discovery of Florida by Juan Ponce de León and left Europe hoping to find gold and to colonize the 'island' (as Ponce de León reported it to be). Narváez reached Tampa Bay in 1527, having come via Hispaniola and Cuba, and then travelled inland northwards along the peninsula. But there was no sign of the expected riches, and in fact very little about the land appealed to Narváez. He returned to the coast at the western end of Apalachee Bay only to find that his ships had abandoned him. The once-keen colonists immediately began to build five boats from available material and in 1528 attempted to cross the Gulf of Mexico to the Spanish colonies. Narváez was caught in a storm off the

Mississippi delta; his boat was blown out into the Gulf, and he was not seen again. Only one crew survived the whole expedition – most of those that reached shore safely were used as slaves by Indians and died on the mainland. But Alvar de Vaca, Narváez's treasurer on the voyage, travelled extensively, if involuntarily, with a group of Indians and eventually escaped to Mexico City (SEE VACA).

NEWBERRY, John. ?–c 1585

Became the first Englishman to cross Persia when in 1581 he attempted, on behalf of the Levant Company, to re-open the ancient caravan route between the Mediterranean and the Persian Gulf. Newberry arrived at the head of the Gulf via Baghdad and Basra, and sailed down to Hormuz and Bandar Abbas. He then returned overland across Persia to Isfahan, Qazvin and Tabriz. The knowledge he gained on this journey led to his being chosen to guide the 1583 expedition which was commissioned to look for an alternative route to India, an undertaking which proved to be filled with incident (SEE RALPH FITCH). After Newberry left the Mogul court at Fatephur Sikri in 1585 to return to England, he was never seen nor heard from again.

NICOLET, Jean. 1598–1642

French protégé of Champlain, and discoverer of Lake Michigan. In 1634 Nicolet explored the northern edges of Georgian Bay and Lake Huron, and then found Lake Michigan. At Green Bay he discovered the Fox River and briefly explored the watershed between the Fox and Mississippi rivers. He went part of the way down the Wisconsin towards the Mississippi, and the descriptions Nicolet heard from Indians of the size of the river led to Louis Joliet's Mississippi voyage in 1673.

NIEBUHR, Carsten. 1733–1815

The surveyor on a Danish scientific expedition to Arabia in 1761. Although the expedition was fortunate in coinciding with a temporary lull in Islamic fanaticism, it was dealt severe blows by circumstance, and Niebuhr was the only scientist (out of five) to survive the six-year journey. The group visited the Nile delta, Mount Sinai, Suez and Jedda, before going overland to Mocha (al Mukhā) in south-west Arabia; they then concentrated on the Yemen area. In May 1763 the expedition's philologist died, and the naturalist died two months later. The three remaining scientists later went to Bombay, and there the scientist who was also the party's artist died, followed not long after by the surgeon. After 14 months alone in India, Niebuhr returned to Europe via Muscat, Persia and Cyprus, arriving back in Copenhagen in November 1767.

NOORT, Oliver van. (fl 1599)

The first Dutchman to circumnavigate the world (1598–1601) when he led a Dutch fleet to the Orient by the western route through the Magellan Strait, returning via the Cape of Good Hope.

NORDENSKJÖLD, Nils. 1832–1901

Geologist, geographer and explorer who became the first to navigate the whole North-east Passage from Europe to the Pacific. His first expeditions were to Spitzbergen, and he visited the islands five times. In 1870 he led an expedition to study Greenland's ice-cap, and five years later made his first attempt on the North-east Passage. He began in Goteberg, but only got as far as Dickson, on the edge of the Kara Sea. Another attempt in 1876 followed an identical pattern, the voyage being halted by ice and the approaching winter.

In 1878–9 Nordenskjöld successfully navigated the Passage in the steam/sailing vessel *Vega*; even more important than the assistance of steam was his decision to begin the voyage from Tromsø, which gained him valuable summer time. He sailed from Tromsø near the end of July 1878 and reached the half-way mark (Cape Chelyushkin, about 105° E) a month later. Even then the *Vega* became stuck in the ice near the Bering Strait in September 1878, and it only broke free ten months later. After calling at Port Clarence, Alaska, Nordenskjöld returned to Europe via Canton (Kwangchow), Ceylon, and the Suez Canal.

ODORIC of Pordenone. c 1274–1331

Franciscan friar, beatified in 1766, whose account of China was almost as early and as popular as Marco Polo's. Odoric began a 12-year expedition in 1318, his intention being to convert the Orient to Christianity – an ambitious plan, but he did manage to baptize over 20,000 people. He travelled through the Black Sea to Persia, sailed from the Persian Gulf around India to the Malacca Strait, Sumatra and Java, and eventually reached the China Sea and Canton (Kwangchow). Shortly after he left his ship and went overland to Peking, where he stayed for three years. Odoric took a tortuous route home – through Lhasa and Tibet, skirting the northern edge of the Himalayas, through the Hindu Kush and then south round the Caspian Sea. When he reached Padua another friar recorded in Latin Odoric's account of his journeys, including a graphic description of Canton, then regarded as the most wonderful city in the world. Odoric died not long after he had completed his recitation.

OGDEN, Peter Skene. 1794–1854

American fur trader who travelled widely in the western part of North America, and did much to open the north-west area to settlers. In 1824–5 he explored the Blue Mountains, the Snake River and the Bitterroot Mountains, and Great Salt Lake. Leaving Fort Vancouver (on Oregon's Columbia River) in 1826, Ogden travelled up a tributary, the Deschutes River, to Malheur Lake in the Harney Basin, and then discovered the Klamath River (which crosses the Oregon–California border). A year later, going south from Malheur Lake, Ogden discovered the Humboldt River (as it is now called – Ogden dubbed it the Unknown River). In 1829–30 he travelled south to Colorado, and thus became the first to travel the length of the West Country from north to south. He was also the first to explore the eastern slopes of the Sierra Nevada, and in 1829 discovered the Carson and Owens Lakes. Ogden had a reputation for ruthlessness, was apparently as tough as they come, and was twice married to Red Indian women, in those days a most unconventional action.

ORELLANA, Francisco de. c 1500–1550

The Spaniard who was the first European to travel the full length of the Amazon River in South America. In 1540 Orellana journeyed with Gonzalo Pizarro (brother of Francisco Pizarro) from Cusco in southern Peru to Quito, high in the Andes in Ecuador, in search of rich quantities of cinnamon said to be found east of Quito. They went down the east side of the Andes and followed the course of the Coca River towards the Napo River. When the expedition ran short of supplies, Pizarro sent Orellana down the Coca River to search for food. He failed to return, and after Pizarro and his group had searched for him down the Coca, they returned to Quito, believing that he had deserted the expedition.

Orellana, however, had been swept down to the Napo, and since to return was impossible he had continued on until the Napo flowed into the Amazon – and on and on till the Amazon flowed into the Atlantic Ocean, whereupon he sailed to the Caribbean, hugging the coast until beyond Trinidad. The dramatic and adventurous voyage was recorded by a Dominican friar who travelled with Orellana, Gaspar de Carvajal, and the epic captured the interest of Europe. Of particular popularity was de Carvajal's account of an encounter with a tribe of warrior women who had reminded him of the legendary Amazons. So the great river's name was changed from Rio Santa Maria de la Mar Dulce to Amazonas.

ORTELIUS, Abraham. 1527–1598

Antwerp cartographer who in 1570 published *Theatrum Orbis Terrarum* which is regarded as the first modern-style atlas, being a uniform collection with all its 70 maps having been specially drawn. A number of editions were published and by 1601 the atlas contained 121 maps. Ortelius, like Mercator, made Tierra del Fuego part of a massive southern continent, but in North America he showed a large inlet which closely resembled Hudson Bay in shape and position, though some 40 years were to pass before Hudson's reported discovery.

ORVILLE, Albert d'. 1621–1662

The Jesuit who accompanied Johann Grueber on an expedition from China to Tibet and India. They were the first Europeans to enter Lhasa for 300 years, but Orville died not long after, in Agra (SEE GRUEBER).

OVERWEG, Adolf. 1822–1852

German geologist and astronomer who was on James Richardson's African expedition of 1850. Overweg was the first European to explore and map the complete perimeter of Lake Chad, but he died before the expedition headed for Timbuktu. With Richardson already dead, only Heinrich Barth could continue the planned journey. (SEE RICHARDSON; BARTH.)

PAEZ, Pedro. 1564–1622

Spanish Jesuit, known as the second apostle of Ethiopia, who was the first

European to see the source of the Blue Nile. In 1613, when he was a missionary at the court of the King of Ethiopia, Paez travelled from Massawa to Gondar, and then went south along the west shore of Lake Tana, from which the Blue Nile flows. South of the lake he saw the Springs of Geesh, which flow into Lake Tana. Paez's journey to Ethiopia was hazardous and long-delayed; travelling from Goa in 1589 he was captured by Turkish pirates and held in slavery for seven years. He was then returned to Goa, and only reached his destination in 1603, 17 years after setting out.

PARK, Mungo. 1771–1806

Scottish surgeon who began his travels as medical officer on a ship trading to the East Indies. After Park had published a study of plant and animal life in Sumatra, the African Association backed him in an expedition to trace the Niger's course. In 1795 he set out from the mouth of the Gambia and near Nioro saw where Houghton had died after being captured by Tuaregs. Then Park himself fell captive to Moslem tribesmen and four months passed before he was able to escape, taking with him little more than a horse and a compass. Travelling south-east, he came to Ségou on the Niger, and noted that the river was flowing eastwards (early maps frequently combined or confused the Niger and the Gambia and even the Senegal

Mungo Park. (The National Maritime Museum, London)

Rivers). Park followed the river downstream for some 80 miles (130 km), but he was ill-equipped for further exploration and so returned upstream as far as Bamako, when he turned due west. Very shortly afterwards, at Kamalia, he was struck by fever and lay dangerously ill for seven months. With the aid of a slave trader, Park eventually reached Pisania (Kuntaur) in June 1797, and took a ship back to Britain.

Park soon achieved fame with his book *Travels in the Interior Districts of Africa*, but returned to Scotland and the life of a medical practitioner. He was then asked by the British Government to lead another expedition to

244

the Niger, and in 1805 arrived at the Gambia with 40 Europeans who were to accompany him on the expedition. Not all of them wanted, or were able to play a full part, however, and when Park arrived at Bamaka in August 1805, he was accompanied by only 11 survivors. Shortly after Ségou, at Sansanding, the group built a boat and began the downstream journey. None of them reached the mouth of the river. Three years passed before the fate of Park and his companions was discovered – they had been attacked by Africans and while fleeing had all been drowned in the Bussa rapids, some 1,000 miles (1,600 km) downstream from Sansanding.

PARRY, William. 1790–1855

English Rear-Admiral who spent many years seeking the North-west Passage and exploring the Arctic regions. He was a member of John Ross' 1818 voyage which explored Baffin Bay (SEE JOHN ROSS), but although Parry was convinced (correctly) that Lancaster Sound would prove to be the start of the North-west Passage, he was unable to convince Ross. Parry returned on his own expedition the next year – the first of three to the region. He sailed furthest on his first expedition – passing through Lancaster Sound, negotiating Barrow Strait past Somerset Island and entering Viscount Melville Sound before being forced to turn back. He returned in 1821, but this time made a more southerly attempt, sailing up the Hudson Strait into Foxe Basin and almost rounding the Melville Peninsula into the narrow Fury and Hecla Strait.

Parry was not only determined and methodical, but earned a high reputation for doing everything possible to reduce the unpleasantness of Arctic winters for his crews; he also took the then revolutionary step towards achieving maximum results by combining land and sea exploration. His last visit to north-east Canada was in 1824, but this time he turned south before Somerset Island into the Gulf of Boothia, which did not lead anywhere. Parry made an attempt on the North Pole in 1827, sailing past Spitzbergen and then following the line 20° E. He got nowhere near the Pole, but reached a latitude equal to that of Greenland's northern tip, further north than anyone else had been before.

PATERSON, William. 1755–1810

Made four journeys of exploration in Southern Africa; in 1777 he accompanied Robert Gordon for part of the way on an expedition along the southern coast, as far as the end of the Swartberg range. A Dutch settler named van Reenen joined Paterson the following year on a journey from the Swartberg up the western edge of the escarpment, crossing the Groote (Orange) River some 80 miles (130 km) inland. Later that year the Scot and the Dutchman returned to the southern coast and followed it eastwards to beyond the Great Fish River, about half-way to the Great Kei. In 1779 Paterson again travelled with Gordon, going north from Cape Town through Namaqualand to the mouth of the Orange River and following its course inland.

PAULINUS, Suetonius. (fl AD 42)

The Romans seem to have had little interest in exploration for curiosity's sake, but Paulinus led one expedition that apparently had no other major motive. In AD 42 he crossed the Atlas mountains (between the Grand Atlas and the Saharan Atlas) into the Sahara, and faced Africa's vast unknown interior. Paulinus received great acclaim for his ventures, but they did not inspire many imitators.

PEARY, Robert Edwin. 1856–1920

The American who was the first man to reach the North Pole. Peary made a number of expeditions to Greenland which were initially concerned with continuing the observations of the ice-cap begun by Nansen; in 1886, for instance, Peary travelled from Disko Bay to the interior, and reached an altitude of 7,500 feet (2,300 m). He made two expeditions to Hayes Peninsula (near the site of present-day Thule), in 1891 and 1893, being accompanied (as on all expeditions since 1891) by Matthew Henson. On the second expedition Peary crossed from Hayes Peninsula to Independence Fjord on the east coast. A long expedition took place between 1895 and 1902, during which Peary explored Ellesmere Island, and in 1900 he rounded the northernmost tip of Greenland, the main eastward-jutting promontory thereafter being named Peary Land. The first attempt on the North Pole was made in 1905–6, but weather conditions caused it to be abandoned at 87°6' N. Peary's second expedition reached the North Pole on 6 April 1909. His success was somewhat spoilt by the claim made by Dr Frederick Cook (who accompanied Peary on his 1891 expedition – as had Peary's wife) that he had already reached the Pole in 1908, though this claim found few authoritative supporters.

PÉROUSE, Jean de la. 1741–1788

Sailed from Europe in 1785 to assess prospects for the whaling and fur industries in the North Pacific, and to find the elusive Solomon Islands. Pérouse called at Easter Island after rounding Cape Horn, and then crossed the Pacific to the Sandwich Islands (Hawaii). From there he sailed to North America, meeting the coast in the far north and then sailing down almost to Monterey Bay before again crossing the Pacific to Macao.

Pérouse visited Luzon in the Philippines and sailed north along the Asian coast, turned back when he reached the narrowest point between Sakhalin and Russia, and entered the southern Sea of Okhotsk through the La Pérouse Strait, north of Japan. He continued north to Kamchatka and eventually returned to the central Pacific, calling at Samoa and the Friendly Islands before sailing on to Australia, arriving at Port Jackson in 1788. He then set out to find the Solomons, but that was the last that was seen of him and his men. Bruni d'Entrecasteaux went on a search for Pérouse but found no trace of him; he did, however, rediscover the Solomons.

PHILBY, Harry St John. 1885–1960

Englishman who gained prestige as a leading Arabist, adopted the Islamic faith, became an adviser to King Ibu Sa'ūd of Saudi Arabia, and was one of the very few Europeans to cross the notorious 'Empty Quarter' before motor vehicles made it rather less formidable. Philby made his first crossing of Arabia in 1917, from the east coast (opposite the Qatar Peninsula) via Riyadh to Jedda. In numerous long journeys, he covered vast areas of Arabia and made the crossing of the Empty Quarter (Rub'al Khālī) in 1931–2; this was the second crossing of that desert, Bertram Thomas having made the first the year before.

PICARD, Jean. 1620–1682

French astronomer who was the first to measure accurately the distance between two degrees of longitude (or 'the length of a degree of a meridian') at a particular degree of latitude, thus being able to compute the true size of the earth.

PICCARD, Jacques. 1922–

One of a large famous Swiss family of scientists, explorers and scholars. Auguste Piccard, Jacques Piccard's father, was a pioneer of balloon aviation and established their use in numerous scientific undertakings. He was also a forerunner of deep-sea exploration and designed the bathyscape *Trieste* in which Jacques Piccard and Donald Walsh reached a depth of 35,800 feet (10,900 m) in 1960. In July and August 1969 Jacques Piccard commanded a specially constructed medium-depth underwater craft, the *Ben Franklin*, in which a crew of five drifted underwater on the Gulf Stream from the Strait of Florida off Palm Beach to well to the east of Cape Cod. Apart from revealing valuable information about the Gulf Stream, the experiment also investigated human reaction to prolonged confinement in cramped conditions on behalf of the National Aeronautics and Space Administration (NASA).

PIKE, Zebulon Montgomery. 1779–1813

An army officer in the United States of America who travelled up the Mississippi from St Louis in 1805 to discourage the British presence in North America from attempting a southward drift. His expedition was also instructed to discover the exact source of the Mississippi; this Pike wrongly identified as Leech Lake, there being three other more northern lakes on a longer fork above Grand Rapids in Northern Minnesota.

His superiors were not aware of this, however, and in 1806 sent him to explore the upper regions of the Arkansas and Red Rivers. Zebulon Pike was not much more accurate on this trip, and mistook the Rio Grande's headwaters for those of the Red River. He followed its course and that led him into Spanish territory, where he was arrested and had his notes confiscated. When he was allowed to return to the United States, Pike relied on his memory to write a detailed report, and while he paved the way for many explorers and traders, he was also responsible for a misunderstanding that was not put right for over 30 years. He commented very unfavourably on the Arkansas River area as farming land, giving rise to the belief that it was virtually a desert; the plains were settled only after John Frémont reported the real nature of the country after his 1842 expedition.

PINTO, Fernão Mendes. c 1509–1583

A flamboyant Portuguese who spent from 1537 to 1552 in Eastern Asia, travelling from India to the Malay Peninsula to Peking, and who was probably the first European to visit Japan. As colourful as his exploits no doubt were, his book describing his travels, called *Peregrinacam* (*Peregrination*), stretched the imagination of its readers so much that he was given the nickname 'Prince of Liars'. He had, he claimed, been imprisoned 13 times, served 17 masters as a slave and been convicted in China of robbing royal tombs, for which both his thumbs were cut off.

PINZÓN, Martin. c 1441–c 1493

One of a Spanish family of ship owners and navigators, and part owner of the ships *Pinta* and *Niña*. Pinzón helped Colombus get royal patronage, and sailed with him in 1492 as commander of the *Pinta*, considerably influencing the navigation of the crossing (SEE COLUMBUS). There is some reason to believe that Pinzón's loyalty to Columbus was not without limits – near Cuba he disappeared with the *Pinta*, probably looking for gold and spices, although he blamed the weather for the separation. On the return voyage he again suddenly abandoned Columbus and tried, vainly, to be the first to reach Europe and announce the discoveries.

PINZÓN, Vicente. c 1460–1523

One of Spain's most successful explorers, brother of Martin Pinzón and part-owner of the *Pinta* and *Niña*. He commanded the *Niña* on Columbus' voyage (SEE COLUMBUS; MARTIN PINZÓN). Vicente Pinzón was also the discoverer of the mouths of the Amazon; in a voyage in 1500 he made a landfall at present-day Recife, and then sailed northwards along the coast, following it around Cabo de São Roque, and eventually coming to the mouth of the Amazon. Pinzón called it the Rio Santa Maria de la Mar Dulce (Orellana was to be indirectly responsible for its shorter name), and he then sailed on round the northern coast of the continent, past Isla de Margarita, possibly going as far as Costa Rica. In 1508 he was commissioned by the Spanish Crown to look for a short route to the Spice Islands, and he sailed with Juan Diaz de Solis. They went to Central America and perhaps discovered Honduras and Yucatan. He and de Solis disagreed over a number of points, however, and Pinzón returned to Spain in 1509.

PIZARRO, Francisco. c 1475–1541

The Spanish Conquistador known as the conqueror of the Incas, though 'destroyer' would be as fitting. His arrival in South America was the last of a series of disasters that befell the Incas and caused the collapse of their remarkable society.

Pizarro's early years had much in common with those of Cortes, to whom he was distantly related – a tough, peasant existence of poverty and privation, compounded in Pizarro's case by being illegitimate. Hoping to find fortune in the exciting New World, he sailed for the West Indies in 1502, took part in an expedition to Colombia eight years later, and in 1513 was with Balboa in Darien when the Spaniards first saw the Pacific. A few years later Cortes discovered the true wealth of the Aztecs, and not long after Pascual de Andagoya brought word from the southern continent of a tribe of Indians in the wealthy kingdom of Biru. Pizarro was quick off the mark, but it was not at all a straightforward venture, and by 1524 the furthest south he had sailed was about 5° N, while he had seen no evidence of any rich kingdom. The Governor of Panama tried to stop the voyages on the basis of their being too dangerous and costly, but Pizarro was confidently defiant and had a number of loyal followers.

His persistence paid off. In 1526 he reached the port of Tumbes (on the Peru–Ecuador border), and there Pizarro heard definite accounts about the very wealthy civilization. All along Pizarro had been acting in partnership with Diego de Almagro, and Almagro now went back to Panama to try to arrange extra support for the expedition. Help on the scale that was needed to conquer a large empire was not something that could easily be found in Panama, and a ship sailed to bring Pizarro back to the isthmus. Torn between avaricious curiosity and a sense of priorities, the Conquistador first took the ship further south to the mouth of the Santa Pau, near present-day Chimbote. Eventually, back in Spain (in 1528), Pizarro managed to get most of the financial aid he needed from sympathetic royalty, and he was also given the governorship of any lands that he conquered. This show of favour caused immediate animosity between Pizarro and Almagro, since the two of them (and, initially, also Hernando de Luque) had been equal partners. Under an uneasy truce with his fellow Spaniard, Pizarro sailed for Peru in 1531, with one ship, 180 men and 37 horses, and more ships due to follow.

In the meantime, however, the Aztec Empire had already been mortally wounded – Pizarro's Spanish cut-throats would simply spill the last blood. Just as happened with the Aztecs, the Incas were struck down in their tens of thousands by the imported European and African diseases of influenza, scarlet fever, measles and smallpox. The 11th Inca, Huayna Capac, died in Quito as the diseases swept south; his successor died before his coronation, and amid the chaos and fear, opposing Inca factions took sides. Civil war further weakened the society and it was a bewildered kingdom that Atahuallpa attempted to unite after his victory over Huascar, the rightful heir to the Inca throne.

Into this chaos came Pizarro, establishing San Miguel (near Sullana in north-western Peru) as his base. The Spaniard then learnt that Atahuallpa and an escort of some 5,000 were in Cajamarca, not far to the south-east in the Andes. Pizarro marched to Cajamarca, arriving in November 1532 whereupon Atahuallpa withdrew to a strategic position outside the town. An uneasy meeting was arranged, ostensibly under peaceful conditions, but after Atahuallpa immediately and vigorously refused to obey Spanish authority or to convert himself and all the Inca people to Christianity, Pizzaro threw him into captivity and the Spaniards massacred the unprepared Indians. Pizzaro eventually agreed to release Atahuallpa on payment by the Incas of enough gold and treasure to fill a room 22 feet (7 m) long, 17 feet (5 m) wide, and as high as their captive leader could reach. This took some time to collect, but when the huge fortune had been handed over, Pizarro once again broke his word, and had Atahuallpa summarily tried and garotted.

These atrocities encouraged the Spaniards to greater havoc, and Pizarro continued the path of destruction to Cusco, where the invaders carried out uncontrolled and savage plunder, rape and murder. Pizarro eventually restored a degree of normality to the former kingdom, founded the city of Lima, and appointed an Inca to rule the Incas on behalf of the Spanish King, under Pizarro's control. By 1537 however, the Incas realized that they had nothing more to lose. They rose in revolt, and from their familiarity with the high terrain achieved considerable success over the Spaniards; Cusco was besieged and Spanish reinforcements from Lima were attacked and forced back. The besieged Spaniards were only saved by the eleventh hour arrival of Almagro, but Pizarro's relief was short-lived. Almagro saw an opportunity to gain redress for his treatment and took possession of Cusco. It was not until the following year that Almagro was defeated by Pizarro, whose half-brother, Hernando Pizzaro, had him executed. Even in death, however, Almagro was to plague the destroyer of the Incas: in June 1541 Pizarro was killed by faithful supporters of his one-time partner.

PIZARRO, Gonzalo c 1506–1548

One of Francisco Pizarro's five half-brothers who went to South America in his wake. Gonzalo accompanied Francisco de Orellana on a search for cinnamon east of Quito, a journey which resulted in Orellana making the first journey down the Amazon. (SEE ORELLANA.)

POLO, Maffeo and Niccolo. (fl 1260)

Venetian brothers who were the first Europeans to reach Cathay (China). The brothers originally set out for Constantinople, but followed the overland Silk Route and turned their modest journey into a 14-year expedition (1255–69), the climax of which was meeting Kublai Khan at Cambaluc (Peking). Kublai Khan took a far broader view of life than his predecessors, and the Polo brothers – the first Europeans the Khan had ever seen – were persuaded to return to Cambaluc. This they did in 1271, taking with them Niccolo's son Marco. On this occasion they stayed 16 years, and served in the Khan's court. (SEE MARCO POLO.)

POLO, Marco. c 1254–c 1324

Probably surpasses Christopher Columbus in popular fame as an explorer and discoverer – fittingly, for Marco Polo was not only an intrepid adventurer but an excellent observer of people and places who went to see, experience, and record, and not to plunder and conquer. He was the son of Niccolo Polo (SEE ABOVE) and accompanied his father and uncle on their second expedition in 1271, travelling via Jerusalem, Persia, the northern Hindu Kush, through the Pamirs and then skirting the Taklamakan and Gobi Deserts to Cambaluc (Peking), arriving in 1275. They were taken to meet Kublai Khan in his summer palace at Chandu (the Xanadu of Coleridge's famous poem), which lay north-west of Cambaluc. Marco Polo mastered languages fluently and Kublai Khan, impressed by the honesty and intelligence of the Venetians, retained them as advisers and sent Marco Polo on extensive diplomatic journeys to many parts of the East; he was also Governor of Yangchow for three years.

In 1292 Kublai Khan consented to the Polos returning to Europe, and made them escorts of a Mongol princess to the Ilkhan of Persia. They returned to Europe by sea – via the Malay Peninsula, the Strait of Malacca, Ceylon and the Persian Gulf, overland to Constantinople and again by sea to Venice, where they arrived in 1295.

Three years later Marco Polo was captured in a sea battle between Venice and Genoa. Sharing his imprisonment was the writer Rusticello, and he took down Polo's remembrances of the East, of Cathay and the elaborate splendour of Chandu. Parts of the book were greeted with disbelief and scepticism – which was only to be expected, so vast a difference was there between 13th century Europe and the Mongol Empire.

Marco Polo in the court of Kublai Khan. (Mary Evans Picture Library)

That apart, the account had an extraordinary effect on the people of all Europe, blowing away the oppressive dust of the Dark Ages and loosening the hitherto unyielding grip of Christian dogma. Marco Polo opened European minds to the fact that other people, ostensibly heathens, lived in a rich and often more awesome world, the product of a civilization far older than their own.

There are some puzzling omissions from Polo's account (it was so popular that 138 manuscripts survived, and by 1500 it had been translated into four languages): it never mentions the Great Wall of China, nor the vastly different Chinese languages – and nothing is said about tea. But as Marco Polo reportedly said on his deathbed, in answer to accusations of exaggeration, 'I did not write half of what I saw'.

PONCE de LEÓN, Juan. c 1460–1521

A Spanish Conquistador who first went to the West Indies on Columbus' second voyage. In 1513 Ponce de León sailed in command of his own vessel westward from the Bahamas – reportedly in search of a fountain whose waters would ensure lasting youth – and on Easter Sunday ('Pascua Florida') sighted what he took to be a very large island. He named it Florida and then sailed north off the peninsula's coast as far as Okefenokee Swamp, before turning south again. He rounded the southern tip and sailed up the west side as far as Tampa Bay before turning south for Cuba.

POND, Peter. 1740–1807

When the Hudson's Bay Company established a near monopoly on fur trading in Canada, many independent traders (whom the Company called 'Pedlars') set up trading posts in the interior well to the west of Hudson Bay, and so intercepted trade on its way to the Company. Pond was one of these traders and in 1778 he tried to find new sources on behalf of a group of merchants. He set off from Lake Winnipegosis (just west of Lake Winnipeg) and travelled north-west, arriving at the western end of Lake Athabasca. The trading post that he set up there saved the Indians from making a much longer journey, and consequently prospered. It was Pond's conviction that there was a water route to the Pacific that instigated Alexander Mackenzie's expeditions.

POTTINGER, Henry. 1789–1856

(SEE CHARLES CHRISTIE.) Pottinger travelled from Bombay with Christie in 1810. Disguised as horse dealers, they went to Nushki, south-west of present-day Quetta. There they separated, Pottinger travelling through Baluchistan to Kernan, then west to join the Bushire–Isfahan route, and so on to Isfahan where he met up with Christie. After travelling with Christie to Qazvin, Pottinger went to Baghdad and down the Euphrates to Basra and the Persian Gulf. He later became the first British Governor of Hong Kong.

POYARKOV, Vasily Danilovich. (fl 1645)

A Cossack explorer of Eastern Siberia, from 1643 to 1646. Poyarkov began his expedition at Yakutsk (on 130° E) and travelled east and south along the Aldan River (a Lena tributary), continuing south across a vast area until he met the Amur River at Blagoveshcensk (50° N, 130° E). He followed the Amur to its mouth, and returned to Yakutsk via the Sea of Okhotsk and overland from near Okhotsk itself.

PRIESTLEY, Raymond. 1886–1974

Antarctic explorer, 1907–1912. (SEE ERNEST SHACKLETON, and ROBERT SCOTT.)

PRZHEVALSKY, Nikolay Mikhaylovich. 1839–1888

Russian explorer whose extensive and detailed explorations, surveys of routes and collections and observations of fauna and flora added enormously to European knowledge of Central Asia at a time when visitors from countries further west were positively discouraged – especially in Tibet, where even Przhevalsky encountered opposition that prevented him reaching Lhasa, one of his major goals. In 1869 Przhevalsky travelled to Irkutsk and the following year went from near Lake Baikal across the eastern end of the Gobi Desert to Kalgan, 100 miles (160 km) north-west of Peking. After exploring parts of north-east Mongolia, he followed Huc's route to Koko Nor (Ch'iang Hai, a great lake south of the Nan Shan mountains) and to the edge of the Plateau of Tibet, where the onset of winter prevented him from going any further.

Przhevalsky began a second long journey in 1876, going south from Dzungaria through the eastern end of the Tien Shan mountains into the sands of the Taklamakan Desert. He discovered the shifting, varying lake, Lop Nor, and in an attempt to reach Lhasa, discovered and was stopped by the Astin Tagh mountains. On his third expedition (1879), Przhevalsky used a more easterly route between the Astin Tagh and the Nan Shan ranges, went round the Tsaidam depression to Koko Nor and explored south of the lake to the headwaters of the Hwang Ho. Then he travelled south-west and came as close as he ever would to Lhasa, being turned back by Tibetan officials 170 miles (275 km) from the city.

Przhevalsky began his next journey in 1883; from Urga he crossed the Gobi Desert and returned to Koko Nor and the river sources south-west of the lake. He then travelled along the southern edge of the Tsaidam but once more found that his way into Tibet was barred by the Chinese. The explorer then wound his way over the Astin Tagh and followed the edge of the Taklamakan to Khotan, where he struck out northwards across the

255

shifting sands, finally reaching Issyk-Kul, a large lake north of the Tien Shan range. It was on his second visit to the lake, in 1888, that Przhevalsky died, and the lake-side village was subsequently named Przheval'sk. The Russian is also credited with the discovery of a wild Asian camel and a breed of wild horses, known as Przewalski's horse.

PTOLEMY (Claudius Ptolemaeus). AD 90–168

Greek geographer, astronomer and mathematician whose eight-volume work *Geography* recorded the sum of European knowledge of the world at that time. Volume I discussed basic principles of geography; six volumes followed, listing 8,000 place names and their latitude and longitude – these were frequently inaccurate, being taken from old maps and descriptions by travellers. The last volume was the most important, dealing mainly with map drawing and with mathematical geography.

Ptolemy's own world map was the surest representation possible yet it contained fundamental errors, some of which Herodotus had not made 600 years earlier (such as joining South-east Asia to Southern Africa, enclosing the Indian Ocean). Other incorrect assumptions by Ptolemy concerned the size of the world, and the proportionate sizes of the various land masses. He represented the globe considerably smaller than it is, and also made Europe and the Mediterranean far larger. These two errors played a major part in Columbus' miscalculations of the distance of the East Indies from Europe by sea.

PYTHEAS. c 325 BC

Greek navigator, astronomer and geographer who lived in Massalia (Marseille) and was the first Greek to visit and describe the British Isles and Europe's Atlantic coast. His major voyage was apparently in search of Thule, which was probably Iceland. He described it as being six day's sailing from northern Britain, claiming that it doubtless extended as far as the Arctic circle. On his way he apparently called at Belerium (Cornwall), then famous for its tin mines, and possibly covered large areas of Britain on foot – he estimated, very accurately, Britain's island circumference as 4,000 miles (6,450 km). Pytheas also noted anthropological information, observed that tides are affected by the moon, and determined that the Pole Star is not above the true Pole. But he was too far ahead of his time, and many of his pronouncements were dismissed as fantasy.

QUESADA, Gonzalo Jiménez de. c 1497–c 1579

A Spaniard who was the first to go in search of El Dorado (the gilded one), a mythical monarch of a 'city of gold' who was said to cover his body with gold dust every day. Quesada landed in Colombia near Barranquilla and travelled south up the Magdalena River basin (his supply ships managed to battle some way upstream) to the plains of Bogotá. He founded Sante Fé, which later became Santa Fé de Bogotá and is now Colombia's capital, Bogotá. Quesada soon gave up searching for El Dorado and instead attacked, defeated and plundered the last remaining Indians who had some wealth, the Chibchas. Many years later (1569–71) he travelled east into Venezuela, and explored part of the upper Orinoco River.

QUIROS, Pedro de. 1565–1615

The pilot who sailed with Álvaro de Mendaña in the Pacific, and who continued the voyage to the Philippines after the leader's death in the Santa Cruz Islands (SEE MENDAÑA). Quiros had acquired a taste for voyages of exploration and was also intrigued by the mystery of a possible southern continent. In 1605 he sailed with three ships from Callao in Peru, initially taking a more southerly route than Mendaña had in 1595. By 135° W he had veered further north again, but although he then turned south once more and reached the New Hebrides, his exploration had come to an end, for he was a poor leader and unable to unite his expedition. From Espiritu Santo Island, in 1606, Quiros returned to America practically along the 40th parallel and followed the coast of North America until he put in at Acapulco in Mexico. His voyage was to produce something of value, however, for the captain of one of the ships he parted from at Espiritu Santo went on to make a significant discovery (SEE LUIS DE TORRES).

RADISSON, Pierre Esprit. c 1636–1710

French explorer and fur-trader in Canada. Radisson arrived in 'New France' in 1651. The following year he was captured by Iroquois Indians, who adopted him into the tribe. In spite of many opportunities to escape, Radisson remained with the Indians until 1654 when he returned to France. In the same year he sailed back to Canada with Médart Groseilliers, his brother-in-law, with whom he explored large areas, providing cartographers with enough information to enable them to locate the Great Lakes accurately (SEE GROSEILLIERS). Radisson worked for both the English and the French, and in 1668 established his own trading mission which was also directed towards finding the North-west Passage. In 1671 he founded Moose Factory, a trading post south of James Bay (on the south of Hudson Bay).

RAE, John. 1813–1893

Scottish explorer who in the course of searches for Franklin's expedition mapped some 1,400 miles (2,250 km) of Canada's Arctic coastline. It was Rae who, in 1853, heard from an Eskimo the first account of the fate of Franklin and his men. (SEE JOHN FRANKLIN, 1847–9, 1851, 1853.)

RALEIGH, Walter. c 1552–1618

The romantic and popular Elizabethan who went to considerable lengths to be noticed by the Queen, and eventually became one of her favourites. Raleigh was a half-brother of Humphrey Gilbert and, sharing Gilbert's enthusiasm for settling the New World, organized a number of voyages. The first, in 1584, mainly reconnoitred the vicinity north of Cape Hatteras. Queen Elizabeth named the area Virginia and knighted Raleigh, who sent out a group of settlers under Richard Grenville. They explored inland up the Roanoke River and Pimlico Sound, and Grenville left some settlers on Roanoke Island. However, their plans were soon disrupted by Indians, and they left on Drake's ships in 1856.

Raleigh despatched a third expedition the next year under John White, who had been on the previous voyage. White returned to England for further provisions, but when he once again reached Roanoke Island he could find no trace of the settlers, and they were never seen or heard of again. In 1595 Raleigh caught 'El Dorado fever' and went in search of the mythical king and his measurelessly rich kingdom – hoping to regain the Queen's favour after the loss of his North American settlement. Raleigh sailed with his nephew John Gilbert and with Lawrence Keymis, and headed for the Orinoco River (in Venezuela) in whose basin he expected to find fortune. They sailed up the delta's main channel and continued up the river as far as its junction with the Caroní River, at Ciudad Guayana. Raleigh sent Keymis back with optimistic but groundless reports, and continued his exploration of river mouths on South America's north and north-east coast; but there was no El Dorado, and even moderately rich Indian tribes had long since been deprived of their wealth by the Spanish.

Raleigh takes Trinidad from the Spanish. (Mary Evans Picture Library)

In 1603 Queen Elizabeth died and James VI of Scotland became James I of England as well. Raleigh had strongly opposed this assumption, and James retaliated by imprisoning him in the Tower of London; there he stayed, until the King himself began to fantasize about El Dorado and promised Raleigh a full pardon if he found the treasures. In 1616, the year he was released from the Tower, Raleigh set out once again for South America, this time with his son and Keymis. The expedition was disastrous – Raleigh caught fever in Trinidad and stayed there, while Keymis, disobeying King James' instructions not to 'annoy' Spaniards, attacked the Spanish town of San Thomé. Raleigh's son was killed in the battle and Keymis killed himself. Foolishly, or perhaps fatalistically, Raleigh went back to England. The treason charge was reimposed and augmented, and he was beheaded in October 1618.

REBMANN, Johannes. 1820–1876

A German missionary and explorer who, with his associate Johann Krapf, made the first expedition by Europeans into the interior of Africa from its

Indian Ocean coast. In 1848 Rebmann was the first European to see Mount Kilimanjaro, at 19,340 feet (5,895 m) Africa's highest mountain. (Krapf was the first to see Mount Kenya.) Their discoveries and their accounts of what they had been told about Africa's interior were at first disbelieved, but the rumours of vast lakes opened the way for Burton, Speke, and the rush to find the source of the Nile.

RICHARDSON, James. 1806–1851

Led a British scientific and commercial expedition with Barth and Overweg into the Sahara in 1850. The explorers went south from Tripoli across the Fezzan to Marzūq, on to Ghāt, and crossed the Sahara to Agadez. There the party split up, making three different approaches to Lake Chad; Richardson headed south-east, but he became ill and died before he could reach Kukawa on Lake Chad. (Overweg also died on this expedition, and Barth completed it on his own.)

RICHARDSON, John. 1787–1865

Scottish naval surgeon and naturalist who made accurate surveys of a greater extent of Canada's Arctic coast than any other explorer. Richardson served in the Royal Navy for 48 years, was surgeon and naturalist in Franklin's 1819 expedition, surveyed the coastal stretch between the Mackenzie and Coppermine Rivers when he was second-in-command of Franklin's 1824 expedition, and led the first search for Franklin in 1847. (SEE JOHN FRANKLIN, 1819–22, 1824–7, 1847–9.)

RITCHIE, Joseph. ?–1818

Appointed to lead a British Government expedition to cross the Sahara in 1818. Ritchie left Tripoli with George Lyon and crossed the Fezzan south to Marzūq, but there he died. Lyon was forced to abandon the venture shortly thereafter.

ROGGEVEEN, Jakob. 1659–1729

Dutch Admiral, Pacific explorer and discoverer of Easter Island. In 1721 he sailed round Cape Horn into the Pacific, one of the few Dutchmen to ply those waters by that date. Varying weather caused Roggeveen to make a rather erratic north-westerly course, and he eventually came upon Easter Island. However, the Admiral was obsessed by the thought of the missing southern continent, and spared little time investigating the intriguing mysteries of the island before continuing his voyage. Roggeveen's approach lacked the determination that Cook was to show and he closely followed prevailing winds, as had numerous mariners before him – and they had not seen any continent. Inevitably, he found nothing more of interest on his voyage. He had the misfortune to be arrested by the Dutch East India Company for infringing their monopoly in the East, although he was eventually compensated for his ships, which the Company had confiscated. He believed avidly in the southern continent for the rest of his life.

ROHLFS, Friedrich Gerhard. 1831–1896

A one-time member of the French Foreign Legion, and an adventurer rather than an explorer. He was the first European to cross Africa from the Mediterranean to the Gulf of Guinea (1865). Rohlfs was one of the most widely travelled of all the North African explorers – he saw much of the country while serving in the Legion, and between 1862 and 1881 covered vast expanses of Africa, from Tangier to Lagos, from the Niger to Ethiopia, the Libyan Desert and the Mediterranean coast.

RONDON, Candido. 1865–1958

A Brazilian explorer after whom Rondonopolis and Rondonia in Brazil (more or less at either end of the Sierra dos Parecis in south-west Brazil) are named. The source of a river was discovered in the Sierra dos Parecis in 1909, and it was named Rio Duvido (River of Doubt) since its course was unknown. When Rondon learnt that Theodore Roosevelt was planning a South American expedition with his son Kermit, Rondon suggested that they should explore the course of the Duvido together. In 1913 the group travelled up the Paraguay River, went overland to the Teles Pires River, and crossed the Serra do Tombador to the headwaters of the Rio Duvido. They built seven dug-out canoes and then set off downstream. Under the toughest conditions, it took them three weeks to cover some 70 miles (112 km), during which four canoes were destroyed. Eventually they established that the river ran into the Aripuana – they followed it into the Madeira and eventually into the Amazon, which they sailed down to the sea. After this expedition the Rio Duvido was named the Theodore Roosevelt.

ROOSEVELT, Theodore. 1858–1919

Twenty-sixth President of the USA (1901–1909), and an enthusiastic explorer. (SEE RONDON for his 1913 Amazon exploration.)

ROSS, James Clark. 1800–1862

James Clark Ross. (Mary Evans Picture Library)

Nephew of John Ross, and a pioneer of polar exploration. James Ross was with his uncle and William Parry on the 1818 voyage to Baffin Bay which was sent to look for a North-west Passage, and sailed again on a scientific voyage with John Ross in 1829, spending four winters in the Canadian Arctic. (SEE JOHN ROSS, 1818–19, 1829–33.) In 1839 James Ross commanded an Antarctic expedition with the ships *Erebus* and *Terror*, F R M Crozier being second-in-command. From Hobart, Tasmania, they sailed south-east to the Auckland Islands, and then south and managed to penetrate an ice-barrier to reach open sea. This was the first major voyage of discovery to the Antarctic, during which Ross discovered the Ross Sea and the Ross Ice Shelf, a permanently frozen sea-ice 'bay' into the mainland. Cape Crozier's active volcano and another prominent mountain nearby were named Erebus and Terror by Ross, after his ships. The expedition also discovered and landed on Possession Island, Franklin Island, and Victoria Land.

In 1841 J C Ross and Crozier sailed south-east from New Zealand, crossed 60° S on approximately 148° W, and underwent a tortuous struggle south-west to the Ross Sea, where they were able to reach almost 78°10′ S – the furthest south anyone had ever been. In the summer of 1842 (December), Ross sailed from the Falklands in an attempt to reach even further south, but he was stopped by ice in the eastern Weddell Sea, at 71°30′. In spite of these significant achievements, it was the Arctic that captured Europe's attention – largely because of the drama of Franklin's disappearance – and some 60 years were to elapse before Scott and

Shackleton brought much public attention to the South Pole.

James Ross went back to the Canadian Arctic in 1848–9, when he led one of the first search expeditions for Franklin.

ROSS, John. 1777–1856

A change in climatic trends in 1817 resulted in far less Arctic Ocean ice than usual and this spurred British interest in far-northern latitudes, an interest that had been dormant for some 200 years after Hudson's death. At the same time as Buchan and Franklin were despatched to attempt to reach the North Pole, John Ross was commissioned with William Parry to look for the North-west Passage. They sailed in 1818, accompanied by Ross' nephew, James Clark Ross. Having explored most of the boundaries of Baffin Bay, Ross came to the mouth of Lancaster Sound but would not enter it, despite Parry's justified entreaties (SEE PARRY). Ross returned with his nephew in 1829, this time entering Lancaster Sound and sailing into the Gulf of Boothia. This expedition lasted till 1833, and four winters were spent well north of the Arctic Circle. The younger Ross explored the Boothia Peninsula and King William Island and assisted in other

John Ross, formally if unsuitably dressed, meets Eskimos. (Mary Evans Picture Library)

Ross' ships caught in Arctic ice. (Mary Evans Picture Library)

observations that enabled John Ross to determine the position of the North Magnetic Pole.

SAAVEDRA, Álvaro de. ?–1529

First Spaniard to attempt an eastward crossing of the Pacific. After Magellan's circumnavigation, Spain sent out a seven-ship expedition in 1525 to emulate the voyage. The fleet met with a great deal of misfortune, and one ship that sank among the Moluccas left its survivors stranded. Word of their predicament reached Cortes in Mexico in 1527 and he sent Saavedra across the Pacific to their aid. Saavedra rescued the survivors, and turned to head back across the Pacific. Prevailing head winds forced the first attempt to be abandoned, and Saavedra died at the start of his second attempt. The Spanish did not accomplish an eastward crossing of the Pacific until 1565.

SACROBOSCO.
SEE JOHN HOLYWOOD.

SAINT BRENDAN.
SEE BRENDAN.

SCHOUTEN, Willem. c 1567–1625

The first to sail through the 600-mile-wide (965 km) Drake Passage between South America and Antarctica, in 1615. Schouten was accompanied by Jakob le Maire, who discovered the Le Maire Strait between Tierra del Fuego and Isla de los Estados (also called Staten Island). The explorers sailed around the large southernmost islands, the Islas Wollaston, and named the prominent extremity Cape Horn. Schouten and Le Maire sailed north, discovered the Juan Fernandez Islands, and crossing the Pacific discovered islands in the Tuamotu group (140° W), and, further west, the Friendly (Tonga) Islands. They continued to the Moluccas, passing north of New Guinea, but there the Dutch East India Company impounded their ships in retaliation for infringing the Company's monopoly.

SCHWEINFURT, Georg August. 1836–1925

A German botanist who went on a Nile expedition in 1869. Just south of the 10th parallel, he left the Nile to explore the Bahr-el Ghazal watershed and continued south, discovering the Uele River. Schweinfurt was therefore the first to explore both Nile and Congo systems in one expedition, though he was not then aware that the Uele flowed into the Ubangi, a major Congo tributary.

SCOTT, Robert Falcon. 1868–1912

Commissioned by the Royal Geographical Society to lead an Antarctic expedition, which sailed in 1901. Scott was accompanied by Ernest Shackleton, Frank Wild and Edward Wilson, and the expedition provided the first knowledge of the continent's plateau. Their base was at McMurdo Sound, and from it Scott established a new 'southernmost' record in 1902, travelling to 82°17′ S on the Ross Ice Shelf. In the summer of 1903–4, he made a 300-mile (485-km) exploration west into Victoria Land.

In 1910 Scott sailed south again, with Wilson, H R Bowers, L E Oates and E Evans. This time, his main objective was to reach the South Pole. Shackleton, in 1908, had got within 97 miles (156 km) of the Pole, and Amundsen was known to be considering an attempt. Fate seemed to

Scott writing an entry in his diary at his Antarctic base. (Mary Evans Picture Library)

go against Scott from the start; there were numerous setbacks and delays, and when he did set out (October 1911) – with motor sledges, ponies and some dogs – there were further delays. The motor sledges very soon broke down, and all the horses had to be shot before the expedition reached 83°30′ S. They were ill-equipped to rely entirely on dog-drawn sledges, besides which Scott was reluctant to use the dogs, feeling that it was cruel to make them work in such extreme conditions. The small group continued towards the Pole, dragging their own provisions. When they got there, they had to face the awful disappointment that they had been beaten by Roald Amundsen, who had set off from a base 60 miles (97 km) closer than Scott's and had had an uneventful journey, his many dogs providing the best method of transporting supplies and equipment.

On their return from the Pole the five men experienced unseasonally bad weather – they were already weak from exhaustion, exposure and bitter depression. In his daily diaries Scott recorded their heroic struggle to reach the supply base. Evans died on 17 February. A month later, Oates, seriously weakened and suffering badly from frostbite, crawled out of the tent and staggered away in a raging blizzard to die. The remaining three, Scott, Bowers and Wilson, only managed to get a little further. Caught in a fierce and seemingly endless blizzard a mere 11 miles (17 km) from the safe refuge of their supply dump, they grew rapidly weaker. Scott's last entry in his diary ('For God's sake look after our people') was on 29 March.

The drama and tragedy of the expedition and the race for the Pole inevitably detracted from the vast amount of scientific observations made during the expedition, not only by the polar party, but from the *Terra Nova* and ashore by Raymond Priestley.

SHACKLETON, Ernest Henry. 1874–1922

Antarctic explorer who made his first expedition to the region with Scott in 1901–4. Shackleton returned in 1907 with Raymond Priestley, Douglas Mawson and Frank Wild and established a base at McMurdo Sound. Mawson led one scientific party in Victoria Land and located the South Magnetic Pole, while Priestley led another onto the plateau west of McMurdo Sound. Shackleton and Wild made a bid for the Pole but their progress was slower than expected, their use of horses to pull the sledges proving to be an unwise choice. With provisions running low, and in worsening weather conditions, Shackleton had to abandon his attempt with 97 miles (156 km) still to go.

In 1914 he returned to the continent with Wild, hoping to cross Antarctica from the Weddell Sea to the Ross Sea. Before they could reach the coast, however, the *Endurance* encountered thicker and thicker ice floes, and on 18 January 1915 it was finally locked in the ice in the middle of the Weddell Sea. The mass of ice gradually carried the *Endurance* north-west. On 27 October, having lasted through the winter, the ship began to break up and on 21 November, about 200 miles (320 km) east of Palmer Peninsula she sank, leaving the survivors with only a 22-foot (7 m) open boat, the *James Caird*. They drifted for another five months on ice floes, and eventually managed to reach Elephant Island, north of Palmer Peninsula. There a group of them prepared to cross the 1,000 miles (1,600 km) to South Georgia in their tiny vessel. They reached the island, and Shackleton made the first ever crossing of South Georgia to fetch help from the whaling station – and then led four relief expeditions to rescue all his men from Elephant Island. In 1921 Shackleton sailed once more for Antarctica, but he died in 1922 and was buried on South Georgia.

SHERLEY, Anthony. c 1565–1635

Travelled with his younger brother Robert Sherley and with John Mainwaring via Baghdad to Qazvin in Persia, where the Shah employed them to help train his army in readiness for attacks by the Turks. In 1599 Anthony Sherley was appointed an Ambassador of the Shah, and left for Europe with Mainwaring via Qazvin and the Caspian Sea. Robert Sherley later became Ambassador as well, but lost favour with the Shah in 1627 when he returned with Thomas Herbert after a visit to Europe.

SMITH, Jedediah. 1798–1831

Colourful and famous American explorer who was the first to reach California overland in 1826, after travelling to San Gabriel (Los Angeles) via Great Salt Lake. San Gabriel was then part of Mexico, and Smith was imprisoned for a while before he left through the Tehachapi Pass and north into the San Joaquin Valley. He went east across the Sierra Nevada and the formidable Great Basin back to Great Salt Lake. In 1827 Smith again entered Mexico to reach San Gabriel, travelled north to Monterey, and was again arrested. After his release he went by sea to San Francisco Bay, followed the Sacremento River and then the Willamette River to Fort Vancouver on the Columbia River, and then followed the Columbia to Flathead Post, before turning south through the Bitterroot Range and reaching more settled areas to the east in 1830. Smith's extensive explorations did much to open trading routes, and the old Spanish Trail in the south was rediscovered, although local Indians discouraged its frequent use.

SMITH, John. 1580–1631

Cartographer, writer and explorer who was the principal founder of the first permanent English settlement in North America at Jamestown, Virginia, opposite Williamsburg on the James River Estuary. Two previous expeditions at the start of the 17th century had opened the way for determined colonists. In 1602 Bartholomew Gosnold explored the area around present-day Boston and named Cape Cod, while a hopeful settler, George Waymouth, discovered and explored the Kennebec River and Penobscot Bay three years later. In 1606 James I of England gave patents to two companies to colonize North America – the London Company and the Plymouth Company, the latter being granted the more northerly regions.

Smith had for some time been advocating settlement in North America, and he was the London Company's immediate choice to head the first colony in 1606. At Chesapeake Bay Smith named the James River and on it founded the first settlement, which he also named after the King. Exploring inland the following year, he was captured by Indians and was saved from death only by the last minute intervention of the chief's daughter. Eventually Smith was initiated into the tribe. In 1609 he was injured by a fire in his gunpowder bag, and he had to return to England – but by then he had firmly established the settlement, and it was able to continue without his strong leadership. Five years later Smith went back to America, this time for the Plymouth Company on whose behalf he mapped the coast from Cape Cod to Penobscot River, naming the area New England. In 1615 Smith was captured at sea by pirates and only escaped, penniless, after three months. He tried to establish another colony in 1617, but his ships were windbound in harbour in England for three months and the attempt was abandoned. He never returned to North America.

SOTO, Hernando de. c 1499–1542

Spanish Conquistador who made a long journey in the south-eastern area

An eerie but romantic burial for de Soto, one of the less destructive Conquistadores. (Mary Evans Picture Library)

of North America. In 1516–20 de Soto was on an expedition which charted the coastal areas of Central America, and in 1523 he took part in the conquest of Nicaragua and, later, of Peru. For his efforts he was awarded governorship of Cuba and the right to conquer and occupy Florida, if he could. In May 1539 he landed at Tampa Bay on the west coast of Florida and went northwards into the mainland proper, approximately through present-day Atlanta. De Soto then headed north-east to cross the Savannah River, turned west over the Appalachian Mountains, followed the Tennessee River southwards, and crossed to the Alabama River.

He had seen nothing of interest to a Conquistador, and so travelled on in a long arc north-west to cross the Mississippi and meet up with the Arkansas River, downstream of its confluence with the Canadian River. The expedition followed the Arkansas down to the Mississippi. De Soto's travels had been in vain – he found no fortune, no riches at all, and map-makers received little new knowledge as a result of his journey. His disillusionment fatally aggravated an illness and he was buried in the Mississippi River.

SPEKE, John Hanning. 1827–1864

Discoverer of Lake Victoria, the source of the Nile (though he was unable to prove it conclusively) and, with Richard Burton, of Lake Tanganyika. Speke was with Burton on the aborted 1855 expedition, and on that of 1857 when they discovered Lake Tanganyika, known as the Sea of Ujiji (SEE BURTON). At Tabora in 1858, on their way back from the Lake, Burton and Speke disagreed vehemently about further possibilities for the Nile's source; Burton was very ill, so Speke headed due north without him to look for the great inland sea that was reported to lie north-east of Lake Tanganyika. So it was that Speke came to the huge lake, which he named after Queen Victoria. He returned hastily, without trying to determine the position or direction of its outflow, certain that it was the real source of the Nile. Burton, however, was not convinced and always remained antagonistic towards his companion. Speke lost no time in making elaborate claims and revelled in the tremendous publicity in England – which irked Burton even more.

Speke was given his own expedition in 1860, on which he was accompanied by James Grant. From Bagamoyo, on the east coast of Africa, they went inland to Tabora, then travelled up the western side of Lake Victoria, crossing the Kagera River (later proved to be the only river flowing into Lake Victoria). On the lake's northern shore they discovered the outflowing river (the Victoria Nile) with the Ripon Falls. However Speke and Grant did not follow the river to Lake Kyoga, but crossed it

270

Speke and Grant pay their respects to M'Tesa, King of Uganda. (Mary Evans Picture Library)

again (assuming it was the same river) between Karuma Rapids and Lake Albert. Again they did not follow it but met it once more (on the section later known as the Albert Nile) just before it is joined by the Aswa River and becomes the White Nile (Bahr-el Jebel). Further down river Speke and Grant met Mr and Mrs Baker, who were following the river upstream.

Mr and Mrs Baker and their expedition head up the Nile. (Mary Evans Picture Library)

Speke omitted to point out that he had not established the Nile's source beyond all doubt: he was to be continually attacked on this point by many detractors. Speke never knew whether his conviction was justified, for he accidentally shot himself while after partridges in England, just before a gathering at which he and Burton were to argue their respective theories, and long before the issue was properly resolved by Stanley in May 1875.

SPRUCE, Richard. 1817–1893

British botanist who accompanied the Wallace brothers on an Amazon expedition in 1849 (SEE ALFRED WALLACE). The three made numerous expeditions at Santarém, and Spruce remained there when the Wallaces went further up the Amazon to Manaus. Receiving an enthusiastic message about the abundance of interesting specimens to be found in the Negro River region, Spruce followed the Wallaces in 1851, and completed the work begun in that region and further up around the Uaupés River by Alfred Wallace. In 1854 Spruce returned to Manaus, and then went far west, taking the Marañon River tributary higher up into the Andes; he spent several years in the mountain range and on the western foothills between the equator and 6° S. Spruce was finally forced by ill health to return to England in 1861. Although he returned with some 30,000 rare plant specimens and did more than anyone to open the upper Amazon, he never received recognition on a scale befitting his achievements.

STADUKHIN, Mikhailo. (fl 1644)

Cossack explorer of eastern Siberia, 1641–4, who discovered the Kolyma River and followed it to its entrance into the East Siberian Sea (on 160° E), some 200 miles (320 km) north of the Arctic Circle. Stadukhin repeated the journey to the Kolyma in 1644 in an expedition led by Ivanov Deshnef, which continued around to the Bering Strait and the Bering Sea (SEE DESHNEF).

STANLEY, Henry Morton. 1841–1904

Welsh-born explorer (surname originally Rowlands) who went to America in 1859, and ten years later was sent by the *New York Herald* on a number of foreign assignments – among them the opening of the Suez Canal – which were to include an attempt to discover the whereabouts or fate of David Livingstone, whose precise actions had been unknown for some five years. On 10 May 1871, Stanley met Livingstone at Ujiji on Lake Tanganyika – just in time, for the missionary was ill and practically without food or any other provisions (SEE LIVINGSTONE). Stanley explored the northern part of the lake with Livingstone, and they went together to Tabora. The American was unable to persuade Livingstone to leave with him, so left him adequately supplied and returned to the coast and to acclaim in England.

Stanley's experiences with Livingstone had filled him with a zest for exploration, and he returned to East Africa in 1874 on the biggest expedition yet seen in Africa. On this journey he circumnavigated Lake Victoria and was therefore able to confirm Speke's assertion that the Rippon Falls was the only outlet; Stanley also established that the Kagera is the only inlet. He then went overland from the lake up the western shore to the equator, and then turned south for Ujiji. He explored the remainder of Lake Tanganyika (the part south of Ujiji) and in 1876 travelled from the western shore to Nyangwe on the Lualaba River to establish this river's course.

After re-assembling his 40-foot (12-m) portable boat, Stanley began his greatest adventure, sailing on a journey of extraordinary courage and endurance the full length of the Lualaba and the Congo to Boma, where he arrived in 1877, 999 days after leaving Zanzibar, and with only 114 left of the 356 followers who had set out from the east coast.

In 1879 Leopold II of Belgium sponsored Stanley on an expedition to prepare access to the Congo. He went up river from the Atlantic Ocean to beyond Stanley Falls and discovered Lake Tumba and Lake Leopold.

Stanley made his last expedition to the Congo in 1888, on a second rescue that was to take him across Central Africa once again, this time from west to east. Emin Pasha and the Equatoria garrison of 10,000 had been cut off from the outside world for six years by the Moslem revolt in northern Sudan. A Scottish shipowner, hopeful of establishing contracts in Africa, originated a relief fund to rescue him and asked Stanley to head it. Stanley insisted on taking a long roundabout route, transporting porters by ship from Zanzibar round the Cape of Good Hope to the mouth of the Congo, probably because he had contracted himself to various other commitments, some of which may well have involved the Belgian King's interests in the Congo.

In 1888 Stanley was at last ready to start the voyage up the Congo – an expedition of 700 people, including nine European assistants who had vied with hundreds of others for a place with the 'great Stanley'. By all accounts it was a terrifying, exhausting, miserable expedition that experienced almost every hardship and disaster that equatorial Africa could contrive. Pygmies took a horrible toll, often implanting poisoned arrow heads in the pathways – scores of bare-footed porters died this way.

Stanley, Emin Pasha and others at Emin's refuge. (Mary Evans Picture Library)

By the time Stanley himself reached Emin Pasha's camp at Lake Albert, almost half of the expedition had died, dozens had deserted, one European assistant had been murdered, and the survivors formed a bitter, disheartened and scattered line straggling some 700 miles (1,125 km) behind the leader. Stanley eventually had to go back along the trail, gathering his men together. He was a merciless leader, enforcing discipline and inflicting punishment with the ruthless severity of a slave trader, and achieving results by intimidation rather than by persuasion. So terrible were the hardships of the struggle through the hostile jungles, that eventually it was Emin who was Stanley's saviour, providing food, clothing and general provisions from his stronghold.

Initially there was considerable disagreement and conflict between Stanley and Emin Pasha, who had hoped for military aid against the Khalifa's Moslem rebels, rather than rescue. But eventually Stanley, Emin and their combined followers left Lake Albert, and between there and Lake Edward Stanley discovered the Semliki River and then the Ruwenzori Range (the Mountains of the Moon). Approaching the coastal area, they were met by a German search party, and received a triumphant welcome into Bagamoyo.

This had been Stanley's most unpleasant major expedition, and it finished on a sour note. Half of his expedition of 700 never reached home and fewer than 300 of Emin Pasha's Equatoria garrison of 10,000 men, women and children managed to get back to Cairo. A large haul of ivory that Stanley was meant to bring out of Africa was apparently removed by someone else, and written accounts by white officers who accompanied Stanley revealed the explorer's brutal singlemindedness. Even Emin Pasha was left rather worse for wear – during a dinner function in their honour in Bagamoyo's German garrison, Emin left the room after an emotional speech. His very poor eyesight misled him in the half-light and he fell over a balcony, landing 15 feet ($4\frac{1}{2}$ m) below and cracking his skull.

Whatever unpleasant memories Stanley may have had, they were easily forgotten amid the tremendous acclaim that awaited him on his return to Europe, and he was firmly established as one of the most remarkable and successful explorers in history.

STEFANSSON, Vilhjalmur. 1879–1962

Explorer of Icelandic descent who spent five consecutive years exploring vast areas of Canada's Arctic territory. Stefansson, for some time accompanied by Rudolph Anderson, a zoologist, adapted himself completely to an Eskimo way of life and, accompanied by his guide Natkusiak, lived with various Eskimo tribes. From 1906 to 1912 he travelled the length of the Mackenzie River, explored a large part of the Yukon River and covered most of the north coast from Mackenzie Bay to Victoria Island and the area north and north-east of Great Bear Lake. In 1913 Stefansson was appointed leader of the Canadian Arctic Expedition. Although its prime object was to chart the Beaufort Sea, it also revealed the potential resources in the northern regions of the continent.

STEIN, Aurel. 1862–1943

British archaeologist and geographer whose investigations in Central Asia gave a tantalizing glimpse of the archaeological richness of the area, before the Chinese once again closed the borders to Westerners. Stein's interest was aroused by Hedin's discovery of ancient ruins in the Taklamakan Desert in China's southern Sinkiang province. Between 1897 and 1927 Stein made six expeditions to Central Asia, accompanied by surveyors who at last enabled accurate maps of the territory to be made. The evidence he found revealed that the bleak desert was once fertile and well-inhabited. Stein uncovered the two cities found by Hedin – Miran, south-west of Lop Nor, and Loulan on its northern shores. Near Tunhwang a vast wealth of Chinese cultural artefacts was discovered at the 'Caves of 1,000 Buddhas'. He revisited the Lop Nor vicinity in 1913, with good results, and also explored the Nan Shan mountains. Stein later made short expeditions north from Peshawar, near the Khyber Pass on the Afghanistan border, and between Lahore and Quetta, further south. Not long afterwards, China put most of Central Asia out of bounds.

STUART, John McDouall. 1815–1866

One of the leading explorers of Australia, who accompanied Charles Sturt on his third expedition in 1844–5 (SEE STURT). In 1858 Stuart explored the area west of Lake Torrens, from the Stuart Range to Streaky Bay on the Great Australian Bight, and in the next year he discovered The Neales River west of Lake Eyre while making preparations for an attempt to cross Australia from south to north. Hoping for the substantial reward that awaited the first person to cross the continent, Stuart set out from Adelaide in 1860 (five months later than Burke, King and Wills) and followed a line practically bisecting the continent – the route subsequently taken by the Central Telegraph Line. Stuart planted the Union Jack on Mount Stuart, almost in the centre of Australia, but he was unable to go much further north before a shortage of food and water forced him to retrace his steps.

In 1861 Stuart tried the crossing again, and was very nearly successful. Only 60 miles (97 km) south of the Victoria River (which flows into Joseph Bonaparte Gulf), he met impenetrable thorny scrub and once again he had to turn back. Stuart was determined to succeed, and yet again he made preparations, though this time with the additional and practical objective of deciding the most suitable route for the Telegraph line. On 20 October 1861, Stuart's party left Adelaide and he again experienced the huge, empty space of central Australia. On this occasion he took a more easterly route north of $17°$ S, and this led him successfully to the Adelaide River. Thus on 21 January 1862, he saw the coast that had been his objective for so long. Stuart and his companions still had to return across the 1,800 miles (2,900 km), however, and he suffered very badly from scurvy, arriving in Adelaide ill, weak and thin. The explorers were well-rewarded by the Government, and Stuart received the Royal Geographical Society's gold medal.

STUART, Robert. 1785–1848

Went on an expedition from St Louis to North America's west coast to establish a base at the mouth of the Columbia River, on behalf of John Jacob Astor. (SEE WILSON HUNT.)

STURT, Charles. 1795–1869

One of Australia's foremost explorers, whose expedition down the Murrumbidgee and Murray rivers was one of the greatest in Australia's history, and potentially one of the most important. In 1828, accompanied by Hamilton Hume (SEE HUME for earlier explorations) and ten other men, with horses, bullocks and a boat on a wheeled carriage, Sturt crossed the Blue Mountains to look for grazing grounds and to explore the Macquarie River. This had been recorded by the Surveyor General as a wet morass clogged with reeds, and when Sturt reached it, it was during a

Charles Sturt at Depot Creek. (Mary Evans Picture Library)

worse than usual drought. Unchanged, however, was the impenetrable barrier put up by the reeds. The explorers tried in vain to reach the main course, but some distance further on discovered the Darling River which, although swiftly flowing, was salty and unfit to drink. They returned to the Macquarie, then headed north-east and again met the Darling in an enormous barren plain.

In the following year, 1829, Sturt decided to make a full exploration of the Darling River. This time the expedition followed Hume's route to the Murrumbidgee and carried a sectioned whale-boat. This river also flowed through uninspiring, featureless country, and once again seemed clogged by reeds. They built a second, smaller boat, struggled through the reeds, and at last came into open water. The river became narrower, the river grew more rapid, and the small boat sank. Sturt's discovery of the Murray was accidental and sudden when the Murrumbidgee swept them into its broad expanse. Large numbers of aborigines began to follow the expedition's progress from the banks, and some 600 gathered on a sandy spit that almost blocked the river shortly before its confluence with the Darling. It seemed as if all the members would be killed, but they were saved by the forceful intervention of a small group of natives from the opposite bank, who persuaded the crowd to leave the explorers in peace.

Sturt went some distance up the Darling to confirm which river it was, before following the Murray downstream to its large shallow lagoon (Lake Alexandrina) south-east of Adelaide, where it is almost cut off from the sea by the Younghusband Peninsula. Rough surf forced the group to return to their starting point by rowing upstream – a tremendously difficult task that took them over two months, and left Sturt thoroughly exhausted and temporarily almost blinded.

In 1844 Sturt, accompanied by John Stuart, left Adelaide in an attempt to reach the centre of the continent. Their route took them up the Darling River to Menindee, where they left it to travel northwards past Lake Frome and Lake Blanche, into the Sturt Desert. Sturt and Stuart discovered Cooper's Creek and The Warburton on their way towards Lake Eyre, but did not pass close enough to discover the lake itself. They eventually reached the Simpson Desert before returning – just short of their aim to reach the barren centre.

SVARSSON, Gardar. (fl AD 860)

The Viking who accidentally discovered Iceland (for the Vikings) in c AD 860. Svarsson's ships were blown off course in a storm, and he made a landfall on the south-east shore. Before returning to Norway he sailed close in-shore around the island. For the Irish monks who were already there, Svarsson's arrival was an ill omen, and within ten years they had all left. Within another 50 years, the Vikings had established a thriving, permanent colony.

SVERDRUP, Otto. 1855–1930

Nansen's assistant on all his explorations. SEE FRIDTJOF NANSEN.

SYKES, Percy. 1867–1945

The British explorer whose travels filled in the last unknowns on the map of Persia and her surrounds. Sykes began his extensive journeys in 1893 when he crossed the Caspian from Baku to the Atrak River in the south-east, and followed it to Mashhad. He carried out a number of crossings of Persia, repeatedly returning to Kermān and Isfahan, and made many voyages in the Persian Gulf, across the Arabian Gulf to Muscat, and to Karachi and Bombay. In 1896 Sykes served on the Perso–Baluch boundary commission, which entailed much travelling in south-east Persia and Baluchistan. He explored a route for the Central Persian Telegraph Line in 1898, investigating as well a large area between Kermān and Bandar Abbas. His final explorations, from 1906 to 1910, were in the area in which he began – between Mashhad and the Caspian Sea.

TASMAN, Abel. c 1603–1659

Dutch navigator and explorer who discovered Tasmania, New Zealand and the Fiji Islands. Tasman's principal voyage, during which he made these discoveries, took place in 1642–3 on the instructions of the governor-general of the Dutch East Indies, Anthony van Diemen. He had ordered that the southern Indian Ocean should be explored and the positions of New Guinea and the land that lay south of it be fixed. These instructions were demanding, as they covered a huge part of the area usually given over by mapmakers to 'Terra Incognita'. Tasman's route took him to Mauritius in the Indian Ocean, and from there he sailed slightly south of east, crossing the 40th parallel just before Australia and so coming to the middle of Tasmania's western shore. Tasman named the land (he did not know it was an island) after the voyage's sponsor, but it was changed from Van Diemen's Land to Tasmania in 1853. The explorer then sailed round the south of the island and, reaching his previous

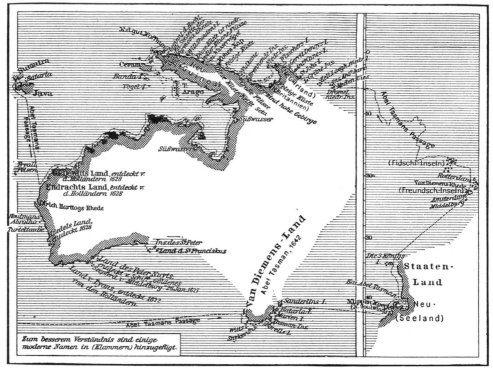

Tasman's map of 1642. (Mary Evans Picture Library)

latitude, continued east. That course brought his ship to an even bigger landmass, and as he sailed north along its coast, Tasman believed he had found part of the Southern Continent, and named the part he had seen Staaten Land.

Although he sailed into the gap between North Island and South Island, entering both Golden Bay and Tasman Bay, Tasman failed to notice the strait (later named Cook Strait) separating the two islands, and so assumed it was all one coastline. He followed it to the northern tip, Cape Maria van Diemen, and then sailed north-east to the Friendly (Tonga) Islands, after which he turned about to sail north-west, discovered the Fiji Islands, and continued across the western Pacific north of the Solomon Islands, heading for the roughly known position of New Guinea. Once again Tasman just missed an important discovery, for after he sighted the eastern shore of New Britain he unfortunately chose to sail north, and so travelled round the Bismarck Archipelago instead of discovering the strait between New Britain and New Guinea, which would have revealed the island's true northern shore. From the Bismarck Archipelago he sailed through the Moluccas and then returned to Holland.

Tasman's voyage had covered entirely new areas, and since he had for

280

much of the time been sailing over territory previously marked down as land, he had effectively pushed any possible 'southern continent' into a smaller area. But his discoveries also added to the uncertainty by appearing to be more comprehensive than they actually were – thus it was assumed by some that Staaten Island was the edge of a continent, and by others that New Holland (western Australia) filled a much larger area, including New Guinea and Tasmania. Apart from these considerations, Tasman had still not carried out all of his main tasks, and had yet to fix New Guinea's boundaries.

In 1644 he sailed again for the East Indies via the Cape of Good Hope and the Indian Ocean. Returning to his previous position in the Moluccas, he sailed through the Ceram Sea, then south-east past Kepulauan Aru, keeping a south-east bearing until he sighted the west coast of Australia's Cape York Peninsula. Thinking that this was an extension of New Guinea, Tasman turned south. This led him around the Gulf of Carpentaria and along Australia's coast until he came to the New Holland that had been made familiar by the landfalls of the early 17th-century Dutch merchant mariners.

Tasman's contribution to European knowledge of the Indian/Pacific belt was substantial, but by so narrowly missing Bass Strait, Cook Strait, and Torres Strait, he demonstrated the degree to which luck influenced major discoveries.

TELEKI, Samuel. 1845–1916

Discoverer of Lake Rudolf in East Africa. In 1887–8 Teleki travelled from Zanzibar with Ludwig van Höhnel, heading north-west from Pangani on the coast past Taveta to Mount Kilimanjaro, which he climbed. North of Nairobi, Teleki and van Höhnel passed Lake Naivasha and Lake Baringo before discovering Lake Rudolf (Lake Turkana), which is situated in a high semi desert, fed mainly by the Omo River (from the north and also discovered by Teleki), and has no outlet to the sea. East of the lake's northern tip Teleki discovered the marshy Lake Stefanie, and so added significantly to the map of eastern equatorial Africa.

THESIGER, Wilfred. 1910–

The last great explorer of Arabia. In 1945–6 Thesiger skirted the southern edge of the Empty Quarter (Rub'al Khālī) on a journey westwards from Salālah through the Hadramaut region, but soon afterwards he made his first crossing of that desolate desert from Salālah to the Liwa Oasis and then east into northern Oman, so gaining knowledge about the uncharted eastern region of the Empty Quarter. From Oman Thesiger returned to Salālah, and in 1947–8 he crossed the western region of the Empty Quarter from the Yemen (starting at Al Mukaliā) to the Tuwayq Mountains (at As Sulayyil), then making a west-to-east crossing of the northern region to the Trucial coast. Thesiger later made further explorations of the Oman 'bulge', but the discovery of vast amounts of oil brought mechanization and industrialization, changing the whole nature and threatening the romance of much of Arabia.

THOMAS, Bertram. 1892–1950

The first European to cross the vast and treacherous 'Empty Quarter' of Arabia (the Rub'al Khālī). Thomas worked for the Sultan of Muscat, and in 1926 travelled from Muscat to Ash Shāriqah, on the Trucial coast. From the following year until 1930 his travels took him to the Dhofar region of western Oman, and from Salālah Thomas made a number of expeditions, skirting the border of the Empty Quarter. In 1930 he began the first hazardous crossing, from Salālah almost through the centre of the desert, arriving eventually at Doha, on the Qatar Peninsula.

THOMPSON, David. 1770–1857

Explorer, fur trader and surveyor who was the first to explore the Columbia River from its source to its mouth. Between 1790 and 1811 Thompson made some of the most important journeys in North America, and his surveys of the western areas formed the foundation for all future maps. He covered a huge area from Lake Superior to the Pacific, and from Lake Athabasca in the north to the upper regions of the Columbia, Missouri and Mississippi rivers in the south. Thompson's expeditions, initially on behalf of the Hudson's Bay Company, included the Saskatchewan River, the Nelson River area and Lake Athabasca (by 1797), and Lake Winnipeg and Lake Superior in 1797–8, when he also reached the Missouri River. After other expeditions covering the North and South Saskatchewan Rivers, Peace River and Bow River, Thompson followed the Columbia to Fort Astoria in 1807–11. So thorough were Thompson's surveys, that he showed it was possible to travel from the Atlantic Ocean to the Pacific Ocean by river (via the St Lawrence), with only brief, occasional stretches overland.

THOMSON, Charles Wyville. 1830–1882

The principal instigator and leader of the scientific team aboard HMS *Challenger* which, commanded by George Nares, sailed on a $3\frac{1}{2}$-year, 69,000-mile-long (111,000 km) circumnavigation of the world, from December 1872 to May 1876. The combined Admiralty/Royal Society voyage was the first major expedition organized to explore and study the oceans below the surface.

Thomson's voyage in HMS *Challenger* was the birth of the new science of oceanography, impressing on many the fact that by far the greatest part of the world was still unknown. Apart from over 350 stops to take soundings to determine the ocean's depth, the expedition retrieved specimens of life from the ocean floor and from very deep regions, measured currents, salinity levels, temperature variations, and made many other observations that contributed to its 50-volume report.

THOMSON, Joseph. 1858–1895

Scottish geologist, naturalist, and explorer whose extensive explorations of East Africa, combined with those of Samuel Teleki, completed the map of that complex area. In 1878 Thomson took charge of a Royal Geographical Society expedition (after the death of its original leader) that was sent to find the most suitable route between Lake Nyasa (Malawi) and the east coast. Thomson travelled to the northern end of Lake Nyasa from Bagamoyo, but then continued to Lake Tanganyika and up its west shore to the Lukuga River. He established this as a likely tributary of the Lualaba/Congo, but was prevented from going further by hostile natives.

Returning to Lake Tanganyika, Thomson continued north to Ujiji before returning to the southern shore. To the east Thomson discovered Lake Rukwa, and he then travelled north to Tabora and east to Bagamoyo. In 1881 he explored the Rovuma Valley (between Lake Nyasa and the Indian Ocean) in a vain attempt to locate coal fields reported to be in the area, and the following year he was appointed to lead a Royal Geographical Society expedition to find the shortest distance between Zanzibar and Lake Tanganyika. Accompanied by James Martin, Thomson found and explored a new route, which involved travelling unarmed through frequently hostile Masai country east of Kilimanjaro to Lake Naivasha, beyond which Thomson discovered Lake Baringo. The expedition then crossed the Rift Valley to Port Victoria on the great lake; while returning to Baringo on a more northerly route, Thomson discovered Mount Elgon.

In 1885 Thomson travelled extensively in Nigeria, and three years later, in Morocco. He was in Southern Africa in 1890, and during his

283

A camp on the lower Congo River. (Mary Evans Picture Library)

employment with Cecil Rhodes' British South Africa Company he thoroughly explored the southern and western areas surrounding the southern half of Lake Nyasa, crossing the Muchinga Mountains to Lake Bangwelu. (The Thomson's gazelle is named after Joseph Thomson.)

THORWALD. (fl 1002)

Brother of Leif Ericsson, who was inspired by Ericsson's account of Vinland (north-east North America). Thorwald retraced his brother's steps in 1002, found Vinland as pleasant as he had imagined it, and decided to settle there. This was the best chance of a permanent Viking settlement, but local Indians determined the course of history, and during one of the frequent clashes Thorwald was killed.

THYSSEN, Francois. (fl 1627)

The first to sail into the Great Australian Bight. In 1627 Thyssen, in the

Gulden Zeepaard, sailed east on approximately 35° S. This course was further south than that taken by any of the other Dutch voyagers who had been blown towards New Holland (Western Australia). He passed the south-west cape and named it Point Nuyts (after a passenger on board) but turned back soon after entering the Bight.

TIMOFEYEV.
SEE YERMAK TIMOFEYEVICH.

TORRES, Luis Vaez de. ?–c 1613

Commanded a ship in the expedition led by Quiros, a pilot of Mendaña's, to search for the southern continent – an expedition that ended with general disenchantment at Espiritu Santo in the New Hebrides in 1606 (SEE PEDRO DE QUIROS). After the ships separated, Torres continued west and sailed along the southern coast of New Guinea, and, since he was the first to follow the coast from east to west, he duly discovered the strait between New Guinea and Australia, thereafter known as Torres Strait. Although this was an important discovery, proving that New Guinea was a large island and not part of a huge continent, some 200 years were to go by before the Strait's existence became widely known.

TURNER, Samuel. c 1749–1802

Leader of the second mission sent by Hastings, Governor General of India, to Tibet to establish a friendly alliance between that country, Britain and India. (SEE GEORGE BOGLE, for first mission.) Turner's journey took place at the time of the supposed reincarnation of the Tashi Lama, and when the Englishman arrived at Shigatse from Calcutta, the new Tashi Lama was only 18 months old. There was a further set-back to Hasting's plans in 1788 when Gurkhas from Nepal attacked Tibet. At first they were bought off, but they returned and captured Shigatse. The Chinese Army helped to get rid of the Gurkhas but then seized the mountain country for themselves.

URVILLE, Jules Dumont d'. 1790–1842

Explorer of the Antarctic who in 1837 sailed from South America towards the Weddell Sea, hoping to find it as free of ice as Weddell had 14 years before. D'Urville was unlucky, however, and only got as far as about 65° S before thick ice forced his retreat. Continuing west he sighted Graham Land and the nearby islands – not knowing they had already been discovered, he named the peninsula tip Louis Philippe Land and the islands Joinville Land (he also did not realize that they were ice-bound islands, and not continuous land). Subsequently, however, the two islands were named Joinville Island and D'Urville Island. The French explorer sailed on to Australia, and in 1840 sailed south from Tasmania to Antarctica, naming Adélie Land (on the Antarctic Circle, at 140° E), which he was the first to see.

VACA, Alvar Núñez Cabeza de. c 1490–1559

The treasurer on Narvaéz's ill-fated expedition in Florida and the Gulf of Mexico. Vaca was one of the few who survived the storm in 1528 that drowned Narvaéz and many others, and he was washed ashore near present-day Galveston, Texas. A group of nomadic Indians 'adopted' him and three companions and they spent the next eight years wandering over vast areas of the Gulf region of southern and south-western America, before they managed to escape from their persuasive hosts. In April 1536 they reached the boundaries of New Spain (Mexico). Vaca's allegations of rich Indian tribes in northern America, which he claimed to have heard about, were met with interest and a group were sent to gather more information, since no Conquistador worthy of the name would leave the rumour of gold uninvestigated. This group returned enthusiastic, even claiming that they had seen the treasure-filled Seven Cities of Cibola. What they had seen, and what Vaca had been told, were seemingly without substance, for Cibola turned out to be a poor Indian village, and neither Coronado nor de Soto found any riches among the Indians of North America.

VALDIVIA, Pedro de. c 1498–1554

Spanish Conquistador who defeated Chile and founded Santiago. After Diego de Almagro scorned Chile as a reward from the Spanish throne (while his partner, Pizarro, got the wealth of Peru), conflict broke out between the two Conquistadores and their followers, resulting in Almagro's capture and execution in 1538. Valdivia supported Pizarro against Almagro, and was subsequently allowed to lead an expedition into Chile in

1540; he was later to become governor of the country. Although his force only numbered 150 Spaniards and a small number of Indian allies, Valdivia defeated a large force of local Indians and in February 1541 founded Santiago. He continued his exploration and defeat of the country and by 1546 ruled the area south to the Bío Bío River; four years later he crossed the river and began conquests to the south of it, also founding Concepción at the mouth of the Bío Bío. Eventually, however, Valdivia was killed during an Indian revolt.

VANCOUVER, George. 1757–1798

Mariner and explorer who carried out one of the most difficult charting operations, and helped resolve the last myths about the Pacific. Vancouver gained a taste for exploration when he was a midshipman on Captain Cook's voyages of 1772–5 and 1776–80. In April 1791 he sailed with William Broughton to explore North America's north-west regions. They went the long way around, via Australia (New Holland, as the western part was then known) and on to Dusky Sound in New Zealand's South Island. Vancouver and Broughton took separate routes to Tahiti, Broughton discovering the Chatham Islands east of New Zealand on the way. In 1792 they left Tahiti and sailed north to the Sandwich Islands (Hawaii), then on to the North American coast.

While Broughton went on an inland expedition from the mouth of the Columbia, Vancouver began a precise and methodical survey of the coast from the Bay of San Francisco to Cook Inlet in Alaska. He made a thorough exploration of the numerous islands and inlets of Canada's west coast, and sailed around the large island that is named after him. With repeated returns to the Sandwich Islands, this survey took Vancouver more than three years, but eventually he sailed south along the west coast of the Americas and rounded Cape Horn to the Atlantic. Apart from supplying the first accurate details of a great length of North America's west coast, Vancouver's voyage was important in that it established that no easy route lay between the Atlantic and the Pacific, and confirmed Cook's conclusions that there was no vast, undiscovered southern continent.

VARTHEMA, Ludovico di. (fl 1502)

Venetian who left his native city in 1502, embarking on a six-year journey of distant travel and considerable adventure. In Arabia Varthema assumed the guise of a Moslem pilgrim, joined a caravan of pilgrims from

Damascus, and became the first European and Christian recorded to have entered (and left, alive) the holy Islamic city of Mecca. From Mecca he went to Jedda on the Arabian shore and sailed down the Red Sea to Aden – where he was arrested and accused of being a Christian spy. After two months in prison Varthema was sent to the Sultan's palace; by feigning madness he was acquitted and freed, after which he made a 600-mile (965-km) walking tour of Yemen and the south-west Arabian peninsula.

He then joined a ship at Aden and travelled to north-west India, but spent the major part of 1504 in southern Persia where he was joined by an old friend, with whom he attempted to go to Samarkand. That was unsuccessful, so Varthema returned to Hormuz, sailed south along India's west coast, exploring inland at Goa and visiting Calicut (Kozhikode) and Ceylon (Sri Lanka). He crossed from Madras to the Bay of Bengal and went to the Burmese capital of Pegu, and to Malacca. It is possible that the Venetian went as far as Celebes and the Spice Islands, but by 1505 he was back in India, and at Calicut he again posed as a Moslem until he was able to join the Portuguese garrison, with whom he fought on a number of occasions before beginning his return to Venice.

VESPUCCI, Amerigo. 1451–1512

The Florentine merchant after whom two continents were named – a distinction that surpasses any other memorial, though it is rather excessive in view of his achievements. On a Spanish-sponsored voyage with Juan de la Cosa in 1499–1500, Vespucci crossed the Atlantic to sight South America's north-west 'corner', Cape São Roque (approximately 5° S, 35° W) and sailed westwards along the coast, returning to Spain via the Caribbean Sea, Cuba and the Bahamas. Vespucci next led a Portuguese expedition (1501–2) sent to find the boundaries of 'Brazil' following Cabral's landing far south of Cape São Roque, at about 18° S.

Vespucci claimed that he sailed as far south as 50° on this voyage (which would have taken him almost to the Falkland Islands) but not everyone believed this, although his fame was quickly established. Vespucci did, however, sail as far as the Río de la Plata, and made the important – and then rather controversial – conclusion that the 'New World' was not part of Asia, but an entirely new continent (it was not yet clear that the islands and the landmass were only part of two huge continents joined by a narrow isthmus). It was mainly this assertion that engendered Waldseemüller's high regard for Vespucci, and in 1507 it was he who suggested that the continent should be named after Amerigo.

Amerigo Vespucci surrounded by various demons and damsels of the sea. The broken masts were a common artist's device to prevent the picture becoming simply a mass of sails and rigging. (The National Maritime Museum, London)

WALDSEEMÜLLER, Martin. c 1470–1520

Geographer and cartographer who published, in 1507, the first map on which the New World was named as America – Waldseemüller's tribute to Amerigo Vespucci, who was the first to insist that Columbus' and Cabral's discoveries indicated a new continent.

WALKER, Joseph Reddeford. 1798–1876

Explored North America's Sierra Nevada and coastal area after being commissioned in 1833 to explore the Great Salt Lake surroundings. Walker followed the Humboldt River to the Sierra Nevada, and gave his name to two discoveries, Walker River and Walker Lake. After crossing the range

289

he continued to San Francisco Bay and south to Monterey. The return journey took Walker round the southern end of the mountains, and about 120 miles (190 km) north of San Gabriel (Los Angeles), he named a previously unknown pass after himself.

WALLACE, Alfred. 1823–1913

Entomologist who took part in one of the earliest scientific expeditions in South America, and who arrived at much the same conclusions about the principles of natural selection as Darwin did, independently of him and mainly as a result of observations in South-east Asia's forest regions. Wallace made his first Amazon expedition in 1848, working in the Pará area (now Belém), and southwards along the Tocantins River with Henry Bates (SEE BATES). The next year Alfred Wallace was joined by his brother Herbert, and by Richard Spruce; they made their base at Santarém, at the Amazon's junction with the Tapajós River, and gathered thousands of specimens.

Eventually Alfred and Herbert Wallace went further up-river to Manaus, but Herbert Wallace soon decided to return to England; while waiting for a homeward-bound ship, he caught yellow fever and died at Pará in 1851. Alfred travelled up the Negro River in 1850–2, making observations as far north as the Orinoco River, and also followed the Uaupés River for a considerable distance. On his return to Manaus he heard of his brother's death, and since he too was suffering from a fever, he left the country. Wallace's theory on evolution was published simultaneously with Darwin's, in 1858.

WALLIS, Samuel. 1728–1795

English discoverer of Tahiti and the Society Islands in the Pacific (now forming French Polynesia). Wallis commanded the *Dolphin*, one of John Byron's ships which sailed in 1776 to search for 'Terra Australis'. Sailing with Wallis was Philip Carteret in the *Swallow*, but after entering the Pacific from the Strait of Magellan, the ships became separated in a storm. Unfavourable winds kept Wallis west of the conventional, well-sailed route to the Tropic of Capricorn, and by sailing north along the 100th meridian he cut away a large section of the Pacific that might have 'hidden' a new land. Later on in the voyage, sailing west, he discovered the exotic Tahiti and the Society Islands and, just west of Samoa, the Wallis Islands. Wallis called at the Marshall Islands, Guam, and Luzon on his way to the Moluccas and back to England.

WARBURTON, Peter. 1813–1889

The first to cross Australia from the south coast to central Australia, and on to the west coast. In 1858 Warburton disproved Eyre's impression of a horseshoe of salt lakes and marshes north of Spencer Gulf, when he crossed the land between Lake Torrens and Lake Eyre. Eight years later he gave his name to the river course across the Lake Eyre Basin between the lake and Goyder's Lagoon, north-east of the basin. Warburton's crossing took place in 1873, his route from Alice Springs taking him north of the Macdonnell Ranges, past Lake Mackay and across the Great Sandy Desert to Roebourne on the coast.

WEDDELL, James. 1787–1834

Mariner whose seal-hunting voyages took him to the southern Atlantic. On his third sealing trip Weddell was able to buy a share of the sealing brig he sailed in, and in 1821 he visited South Georgia and the South Shetland Islands. The following year he went further south trying to find richer sealing grounds, crossed the Antarctic Circle, and in a sea unusually free from ice floes, he sailed as far south as $74°15'$, between $20°$ and $40°$ W. Weddell made a number of scientific observations as well and named the sea after King George IV, though it was later renamed the Weddell Sea.

WELLS, Lawrence. 1860–1938

Led the first crossing of Western Australia's two deserts, leaving Perth in 1896 and travelling via Lake Barlee across Gibson Desert and then the Great Sandy Desert. The expedition crossed the Fitzroy River, which opens into King Sound.

WELLSTED, James. (fl 1834)

British naval officer who was the first European to venture inland on Arabia's southern coast, into the Hadramout region. In 1834 Wellsted sighted ruins on a cliff near Bi'r 'Alī while studying the shore from his survey ship, which was working in the area. He went ashore and copied down the ancient Himyaritic inscriptions, and also went ashore further east, at Al Mukaliā. In 1834–5 Wellsted made extensive inland explorations in the Oman 'bulge' of south-east Arabia; in spite of the dominance of the Wahhabis, fanatical followers of Islam, he was generously received. He went to the edge of the dreaded desert of Rub'al Khālī, the 'Empty Quarter', and remarked that even the Bedouin avoided it if possible. Later, Wellsted revisited the area of his first landing, and about 50 miles (80 km) inland of Belha he discovered the ruins of Nakab-al-Hayar.

WILD, Frank. 1873–1939

Seasoned Antarctic explorer – SEE ROBERT SCOTT, ERNEST SHACKLETON, DOUGLAS MAWSON.

WILKES, Charles. 1798–1877

US Naval officer and Antarctic explorer who commanded an exploring and surveying expedition to Antarctica in 1838–40. Wilkes sailed westwards off the Antarctic coast from 150° E to 97° E, near the Shackleton Ice Shelf, and though many discoveries claimed by him were disproved, he was undoubtedly one of the Antarctic pioneers – a large area falling between these meridians is named Wilkes Land. He later made another surveying voyage visiting many Pacific Islands, explored the west coast of North America, recrossed the Pacific, and eventually circumnavigated the world.

Charles Wilkes. (Mary Evans Picture Library)

WILKINS, Hubert. 1888–1958

Pioneered the use of aircraft and submarines in polar exploration. In 1913–16 Wilkins accompanied Stefansson in a Canadian Arctic expedition, and he was second-in-command of the British Antarctic expedition to Antarctica's Graham Land in 1920–1, subsequently joining Shackleton's 1921–2 expedition as a naturalist. Four years later Wilkins made trial polar flights over a remote Arctic region north of Point Barrow, and in

April 1928, accompanied by a co-pilot, he flew from Point Barrow to Spitzbergen, a 2,100-mile (3,400 km) journey over unknown territory that took 20½ hours. Later that year he went to Antarctica and made flights in the Palmer Peninsula region, during which a number of new islands off Graham Land were discovered. In 1931 Wilkins went to the other extreme, and captained the submarine *Nautilus* which travelled submerged below the Arctic ice to 82°15′ N.

WILLIAM of RUBROUCK. c 1215–1295

A French Franciscan friar who went on a missionary journey to Mongolia in 1252–5. While he met with no success in converting the Mongols, he was the first European to visit Karakoram, then the site of the Great Khan's principal Mongolian court. William was received with friendliness, but was eventually ordered back; on his return he wrote an acclaimed and accurate account for Louis IX.

WILLIAMS, William. (fl 1839)

The first European to cross New Zealand's North Island from south to north, in 1839. Williams started at Port Nicholson (east of Wellington) and travelled via the Rangitiki River, Lake Taupo and Lake Rotorua to the Bay of Plenty.

WILLOUGHBY, Hugh. ?–1554

Sailed with three ships from Deptford in 1553, with Richard Chancellor on another ship as pilot-major, on an expedition to find a North-west Passage to the Orient. The ships were separated in a storm north of the Lofoten Islands and Willoughby went to the agreed rendezvous near Vardø, then beyond it, perhaps as far as Novaya Zemlya. Returning to Vardø, the ship was wrecked and sank with all hands. Chancellor, however, eventually arrived in Moscow. (SEE RICHARD CHANCELLOR)

WILLS, William. 1834–1861

The second-in-command on the ill-fated south-to-north crossing of Australia led by Burke, in which Wills lost his life. (SEE ROBERT BURKE.)

WILSON, Edward. 1872–1912

Antarctic explorer, who died on Scott's expedition. (SEE ROBERT SCOTT)

XAVIER, Saint Francis. 1506–1552

The Roman Catholic missionary who took Christianity into India, the East Indies, and Japan. He met Ignatius Loyola in Paris in 1525 and became one of the first seven Jesuit missionaries. In 1540 Xavier left Rome for the East, arrived in Goa in May 1542 and after three years of very successful preaching travelled on to Malaya and the Spice Islands. After a brief return to India, he went to Japan, the second European to visit the islands (after Pinto). He was again able to convert many to Christianity and returned to India in 1551, to prepare for his long cherished ambition to go to China. However Xavier died of fever before he could leave for China.

YERMAK TIMOFEYEVICH. ?–1584

A Cossack leader who became a folklore hero in Russia after successfully defending Siberian homes and commercial trading interests against the Mongol marauders. In 1581 he captured the Mongol capital of Sibir, near Tobolsk, and presented the territory to Czar Ivan. Under his protection, Russian knowledge and influence in Siberia expanded, but during a revolt Yermak Timofeyevich was drowned in the Irtysk River, probably dragged under by the weight of his chain-mail armour.

YOUNGHUSBAND, Francis Edward. 1863–1942

British Army officer and explorer who explored extensively in the Far East, visiting Burma, Manchuria, Peking, the Gobi and Taklamakan Deserts, and who discovered the Mustagh Pass through the Karakoram mountains. From 1889 to 1895 Younghusband made a number of surveying and exploration journeys among the Karakoram, Pamir and Hindu Kush mountains. Early in the 20th century the British tried to counter the growing Russian influence in Tibet, and the Viceroy of India, Lord Curzon, sent Younghusband at the head of a 'mission' of 3,000 Indian soldiers and 10,000 survey team members, porters, etc, to persuade the Dahlai Lama to come to an agreement with Britain.

It was always Younghusband's desire to visit Tibet, and after a clash (in 1903) with 2,000 Tibetan soldiers at Guru – in which the Tibetans were overrun and several hundreds killed – Younghusband arrived at Lhasa in August 1904, the first European to enter it since Huc and Gabet over 50 years previously. The Dahlai Lama had fled to China, however, and though an agreement was eventually signed, the physical barriers between Tibet and India made the association impractical, and the country fell under Chinese dominance. Younghusband's surveyors were able to carry out valuable work on this rare opportunity, among which was the exploration of the Tsangpo–Brahmaputra River from Shigatse to near its source.

Science and Technology
in Exploration

The history of exploration and discovery clearly demonstrates the degree to which one science, art or technology relies on developments in another. The introspective, turbulent Dark Ages avoided exploration, and there was little enough skill in boatyards to enable voyages to be made in safety, even had the will been there. When people again began to look beyond their horizons with curiosity instead of fear, they were at first bound to short coastal trips by insecure boats and the inability to navigate with accuracy. More or less simultaneously, however, shipbuilding skills gave the newly curious and confident Europeans the ability to sail into unknown seas, while navigation and cartography developed to enable these voyages to be made with some safety and recorded with new accuracy. Such developments do not, of course, always take place simultaneously; some power other than wind-blown sails was required on Arctic voyages long before steam-driven engines were invented, and recently the implementation of theoretical space and aeronautical designs has had to wait until, for instance, new metal alloys have been developed.

That greatly uneven progress was avoided in the early years of exploration by European countries was largely due to the Renaissance, the sudden revival of art, literature and science that originated in Italy in the 14th century, and influenced Europe so greatly for the next two hundred years. These were the centuries that saw the world expand beyond unimagined horizons. Routes to the East were found, continents discovered and explored and their boundaries noted, the world circumnavigated and eventually depicted on charts and maps whose artistry is still impressive. The Great Age of Exploration was also the Great Age of Cartography, of Navigation and of Shipbuilding.

Cartography

Believing correctly that one picture is worth a thousand words, there can be few people who have not themselves practised cartography in its simplest form – a map on the back of an envelope showing the way to shops or a house, a plan of an intended garden layout. In fact it seems so logical to sketch plans of maps instead of resorting to lengthy verbal descriptions that it is surprising that cartography made such a late start in history.

In the sense that cartography is the art and science of graphically representing earth's physical features, it was not even used, for example, in Marco Polo's account of his travels in Cathay and other parts of Asia, as recorded by his cell mate Rusticello in 1298. All that that widely popular work contained was one map, a totally unusable representation of the earth – worth a good deal less than a thousand words, for it was no more than a circle of sea containing two blobs of land, the word *oriens* appearing at the top, and *occidens* at the bottom. Fortunately not all historians, travellers or thinkers were as sparing as Marco Polo and Rusticello, who were even then still under the influence of the starkly representational religious cartography initiated by Beatus in 776 AD, which was to dominate geography for over 400 years.

In all likelihood, maps represented one of the earliest forms of written communication, and primitive man is thought to have portrayed rich hunting areas through rudimentary maps. As early as c 2300 BC, Babylonians represented earth on clay maps as a flat disk with the known land – Babylonia and little else – surrounded by water. (One consistency in the widely different maps of flat earths before the Renaissance was that no land ever went right to the edge; instead, earth's end invariably lay beyond the sea's horizon.)

Apart from the transition from clay to more refined surfaces, nothing much happened until the time of the Greek philosophers and geographers (the two pursuits were closely related in that scholars of both disciplines argued the state of man and earth, and the nature of the heavens and stars). By 600 BC the centre of this new scientific–philosophic enquiry had become established at Miletus, on the Aegean Sea. About one hundred years later the first significant book on geography was written by Hecataeus, and it was on this that the historian Herodotus based much of his own work and his surprisingly well informed world map.

It was about this time, too, that the concept of the earth as a sphere, not flat and disk-shaped, was first mooted – perhaps by Pythagoras. By 350 BC this concept was widely accepted and it received the stamp of authority when Aristotle argued conclusively in its favour. Aristotle stimulated scholastic thinking on all the subjects that he turned his mind to, and it was one of his disciples, Dicaerchus, who introduced the first line of orientation on a map representing the earth, an east–west line that ran through Rhodes and Gibraltar. This led rapidly to a comprehensive system of parallel and intersecting lines.

Ptolemy marked the next major stage in the understanding of the earth, and while his world map contained a number of basic inaccuracies that Herodotus had not made centuries earlier, his eight-volume *Geography* became the standard work throughout the Middle Ages. The volume dealing with the drawing of his world maps and with mathematical geography represented the accumulation of all skills and knowledge of the subject.

The Romans had an entirely different approach. Where Greeks envisioned the whole world and tried to discover its form and the meaning of life, the Romans looked at small parts of lands and put a premium on clarity and ease of reading and interpretation. They even resumed the disk shape for their infrequent world maps, the Roman general Agrippa taking a patriotic view and basing his 'world map' on the vast network of Roman roads.

The Christian era, paradoxically, suppressed and reversed a great deal of mankind's knowledge in many fields – including geography and cartography. The Roman flat circle theory persisted, and Beatus of Valcavado produced a typical map of the time which put Jerusalem and the Orient near the top while Europe, Asia and Africa were represented only by obscure shapes. 'Beatus' maps were also known as 'T' maps or 'O' maps: the Mediterranean Sea and the massively out-of-proportion Nile River bisected the landmasses to form a rough T, while the oceans completely encircled the land, hence the O. (Placing the east, or *oriens*, at the top led to the use and meaning of the word orientation. By this stage it could be seen that every country that produced a map automatically put itself at the centre of the world; this was as true for early European maps as it was for Babylonian maps or even early Chinese maps.)

The insularity of thinking in early Christian Europe fortunately did not prevent other countries from forging ahead, and when Marco Polo's travels began to unveil the rest of the world to an awakening Europe, it was not necessary to start all over again from the beginning. The Arabs had translated Ptolemy, and the great Arab geographer of that time, Idrīsī, wrote another one of the most important early books on geography as the accompanying text to his silver planisphere, having also devised a map that divided the world into climatic zones.

In Baghdad astronomers were experimenting with compasses, and developed the sexagesimal system which gave a circle 360 equal divisions, or degrees, and dominated cartography from that day on. As always, China pursued her independent course. Although the oldest known Chinese map dates back only to about AD 1137, most of the country was represented on maps before Europeans became involved, although the later Jesuit missionaries had some influence on Chinese presentation.

Marco Polo's journey broadened Europe's horizons, but it was the mathematician Sacrobosco (originally John Holywood) whose *Treatise of the Sphere* in 1230 was the first definitive and enduring work to oppose Christian dogma in the Middle Ages. Not only that, but it became a source of learning and a starting point for related arts and sciences of the Renaissance.

Increasingly sophisticated theorizing about the shape of the world did nothing for the practical usefulness of maps, however, and it was not until the compass became quite widely used in the 14th century that maps began to bear some semblance of reality, and for the first time could be used effectively in navigation at sea. These early maps, distinguished by the numerous compass roses marked upon them, with dozens of intersecting lines and lines of shortest navigation, were known as seamen's, or portolan maps. They derived their name from the *portolanos*, which were Mediaeval sailing handbooks with pilot's instructions, details and depths of harbours and anchorages, sailing courses, etc, on whose compilation and

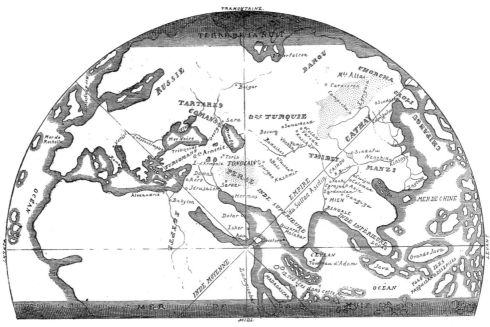

The travels of Marco Polo in the East. (Mary Evans Picture Library)

revision the pilots and captains of many ports and ships would co-operate.

Another landmark in the growth of cartography was the Catalan Atlas of Abraham Cresques, depicted on eight panels in about 1375. This was the first to include an interpretation of the information brought back by Marco Polo and by Odoric. With the collapse of Byzantium after the Turks captured Constantinople in 1453, the Great Age received an added bonus, for among the refugees seeking security in Italy and other European countries were scholars with carefully salvaged manuscripts, among them those of Ptolemy. This led to the 'rediscovery' of his works at an ideal time, for the printing industry was just finding its feet and scholars were among the first to benefit. Ptolemy still provided the foundation for most geography, but the scholarship derived from his theories, with the considerable help of printing developments that took place in the Great Age of Exploration, led to a Great Age of Cartography as well (by 1600, there were over 30 Latin and Italian editions of Ptolemy).

Geographic knowledge expanded with exploration, which became more and more far-ranging as navigation improved and as new shipbuilding techniques permitted longer voyages. Cartographers were frequently explorers as well – Martin Behaim possibly travelled along Africa's west

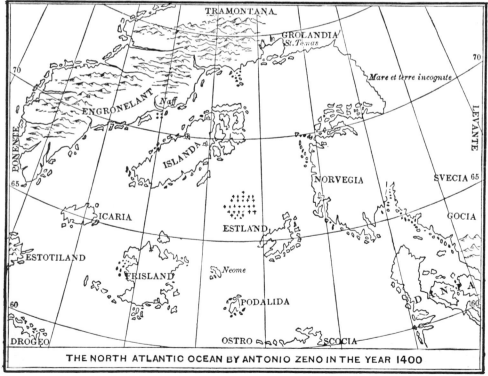

A map of the North Atlantic Ocean by Antonio Zeno in 1400. (Mary Evans Picture Library)

coast as navigator to Portugal's King John II, and in 1490 he began constructing the earliest surviving globe, the Nürnberg Terrestrial Globe.

Navigational needs demanded larger scales, and it was not long before cartographers concentrated on surveys of specific, restricted areas as well as on more grandiose global views – Waldseemüller, for instance, issued an edition of Ptolemy in which he included 20 maps. It was Waldseemüller who in 1507 drew the first map that showed the 'New World' as a distinctly different part of the world from Asia, and who put on that map the name America, after Amerigo Vespucci.

The rapid spread of exploration and the steady stream of discoveries, conjecture, denial or proof, kept 16th-century cartographers constantly busy. The American eastern coastlines were established, then the west coast was roughly depicted. Rivers rose and changed their courses (Gutiérrez drew one of the first maps of South America to show the Amazon, after Orellana had completed his journey down the river, but much of its course was the result of conjecture – and a lot of that originally came from Sebastian Cabot).

Another characteristic of the Renaissance also had a bearing on cartography: the surge of enthusiasm for art, from illuminated manuscripts to frescoes, manifested itself in maps, and seas and lands were filled with more and more elaborate symbols and representations of animals, fishes, winds and sea monsters. Title blocks grew extraordinarily elaborate and inevitably this became the special preserve of copper engraving which took over from woodcuts. Gastaldi of Venice made good use of new printing techniques as his maps developed from his first (Spain in 1544) to a great map of Asia, printed on six sheets.

Waldseemüller had shown the Americas distinct from Asia in his huge world map of 1507, but he still had little idea of the American west coast, and Magellan had yet to sail into the Pacific. The Spanish king's cosmographer, Diego Ribero, managed to interview survivors of Magellan's voyage, and in 1529 he was able to show Magellan Strait and give an indication of the Pacific Ocean's extent, though he joined Tierra del Fuego to Terra Australis Incognito.

In the early part of the 16th century, the centres of cartography were principally in Spain or Portugal, in Venice or the Netherlands, but the maritime power and colonial expansion of England and France forced their ascendancy in cartography. An atlas of 16 charts of sea routes to the East by Martin Llewellyn, dating back to about 1598, lay unknown in Oxford for over 350 years before its discovery elevated Llewellyn to the upper ranks of cartographers.

No cartographer made such a lasting impact as Gerardus Mercator,

A selection of marine instruments from a 1715 volume published in Venice. (The National Maritime Museum, London)

however, a distinction earned by the straightforward and versatile solution to the problem of map projection that he devised in 1569. The practical use of maps had evolved to the stage where they had become essential navigational aids, and the need to display entire oceans and continents brought to the fore the difficulties of projecting a curved surface onto a flat plane. There is, of course, no way in which this can be done without distortion, and the bigger the area depicted, the greater the distortion. This is immediately apparent if one tries to arrange a whole orange peel on a flat surface, and then flattens a small square cut from it.

Initially cartographers had had few problems – maps of the earth were representational, and even if some detail was required, with a flat earth there was little to worry about. Even after it was accepted that the earth was a sphere, the shape of continents was not properly known and vast areas were simply guesswork. Polar regions and most of the Pacific could be taken up with imaginative artwork and an elaborate titleblock or cartouche. This all had to change when navigators made direct use of maps and charts to aid them in reaching their destinations.

Mercator's solution was to convert the earth's sphere into a cylinder open at each end (the North and South Pole), and then unroll the cylinder to form a flat rectangle. Obviously the distortion increases towards the Poles, reaching the stage where the point of a Pole becomes a line as long as the equator. Areas in high latitudes become vast, which explains why Greenland on a globe is far, far smaller than Greenland on a Mercator projection world map. The advantage of the Mercator (and other cylindrical projections), however, is that lines of latitude and longitude are all at right angles. Courses can therefore be plotted on these maps and a steady compass reading can be represented as a straight line. Except for 'great circle' charts, and charts of polar regions, all navigational charts are still based directly on Mercator's deduction of more than two hundred years ago. (The shortest distance between two points on a map is only a straight line if both points are on the same line of longitude or on the equator. In other cases, the shortest distance is along the imaginary line that would join the two points if a circumference of the earth was drawn passing through those points; this line is a 'great circle' connecting the points.)

In the 18th century emphasis was increasingly laid on accurate detail as a result of the rapid application and growing importance of science, and the expectations that arose from improved telescopes for astronomy, accurate chronometers and other instruments. Britain's escalating maritime strength and her growing colonial obligations led directly to her supremacy in mapping and charting vast areas of the world and the major sea routes. But even with all that activity, there were still enormous areas which were not at all well mapped even as late as World War II – in 1940 less than 10 per cent of the world was mapped in sufficient detail to fulfil the basic requirements of aircraft pilot charts.

The enormous progress made since 1945 in mapping and surveying, through aerial photography (which inspired photogrammetry principles for translating aerial photographs into maps), the development of computer technology and satellite mapping has meant that maps have grown more and more detailed and accurate. The cartographer's art and science today is a far cry from that of cartographers of the 15th century, who drew their maps after hours of talking to seamen and travellers, attempting to depict those memories with only rudimentary measurements to guide them. But with what they had at their disposal, the cartographers of old were no less skilled than those of today; and they have also taken many secrets with them to the grave. How, for instance, did Mercator, Ortelius and Wytfliet

in the 16th century know that New Guinea was not joined to Terra
Australis, when Torres was apparently the first to find the Strait in 1606 –
and when even that discovery was not generally known for so long that
some maps as late as 1763 still showed the island as being joined to
Carpentaria? And why did Ortelius depict in 1570 something remarkably
like Hudson Bay in North America, when the Bay was not discovered until
1610?

Navigation

'Navigation' is derived from two Latin words meaning 'ship driver', which
closely defines the English word's original meaning. Navigation
encompassed all the skills and aptitudes of seamanship – steering skills
required to prevent damage or foundering in storms and to negotiate
narrow channels, and the experience and knack for correct sail setting.
Navigation was 'the art of conducting a vessel on its ways'. Experienced
seamen of old were therefore widely referred to as navigators, though at sea
today that title is reserved for the officer who has the special duty of
plotting the vessel's intended course and recording its actual course –
which he hopes will be the same. Navigators were soon needed in aircraft
as well, and with that the word stepped into its new, wider context.
(Navigation skills as we now understand the term, are just as necessary for
crossing a desert or penetrating a jungle as they are for crossing a sea – or
the vast emptiness of space.)

In this context navigation has begun to employ increasingly
sophisticated methods, and thanks to the inventions of radio-wave
transmission, of satellites and of computers, the automatic and accurate
pinpointing of the position of a ship, aircraft or spacecraft is now possible
in seconds – or less. For space journeys navigation has reached the stage
where an uncorrected error of even the smallest part of a degree could
result in a deviation from the planned path by thousands of miles – a far
cry from the early days of seafaring when continents and islands were
discovered by chance, sometimes only to be 'lost' again.

The early sea voyages were cautious journeys, during which land was kept in
sight as much as possible, and doubtless many ambitious adventurers who
did sail into the unknown were not seen again. Most of the voyages made
would have been trading journeys, along familiar shorelines with many
landmarks being used as steering points. To identify concealed entrances to
ports, or ports on featureless coasts, beacons were built, and at night fires
were lit at harbour entrances, at least if ships were expected. The same

happened during storms to guide any ship needing to run for shelter. This practice was exploited by wreckers, the callous murderers and plunderers rife on the coasts of many lands. In a storm at night, wreckers would light beacons on the tops of cliffs or on rocky shores, hoping to entice passing ships into taking 'shelter'. The wreckers would wait for the ship to sail in and be dashed on the rocks – and would then help themselves to the cargo washed ashore and any other valuables they could retrieve. Some wreckers went so far as to tie lights to cattle, whose gradual movements could resemble those of ships' lights, giving a look-out at sea the impression that a safe anchorage was within reach.

In some respects – fortunately excluding the wreckers – coastal navigation practice has not really changed all that much. Lighthouses and light-ships mark dangerous areas, and beacons and buoys indicate deep-channel routes, entrances, shallows and a great deal more information through combinations of colours, bells, lights and sirens. With the aid of navigation charts for a particular coastline, a sailor can work out his exact position and the correct harbour approach by counting the phases of light-flashes, identifying bell-buoys and picking out the colours and shapes of buoys – something that can also be done at night. All this information is available from Admiralty charts, and no ship or boat now cruising coastal waters would sensibly be without such a guide, or without the guidance of an experienced port pilot. Mariners of long ago were no different. The *portolano*, a book of information for pilots and captains compiled by navigators from numerous ports, gave its name to the portolan maps which were the next great aid to navigation after the compass.

Out in the open sea accurate sailing used to be almost impossible, especially in overcast weather and at the hours around midday, while at night it took years of experience to remember which stars were where at different times of the year, and at different hours of the night. Clearly, the discovery of the earth's magnetic field and of magnetism, even if it was some time before it was understood, was the most important single technological development in the history of exploration. Not only did it allow mariners to venture out of sight of land, and land explorers to go further afield, but it allowed realistic maps to be made and courses to be followed.

The Chinese were probably the first to use the lodestone compass, but it is possible that the Vikings also made use of it in about AD 868 on their journeys to Iceland. By AD 1000 compasses were definitely being used by many of Europe's mariners. Initially, the needle was fashioned from lodestone – the naturally magnetic iron ore known as magnetite – which was then laid on straw floating on water in a wooden bowl. (Scandinavian navigators used wood to float the lodestone in the bowl – the effect of iron on a compass was obviously one of the first drawbacks to be discovered.)

Mariner's pivot compass, gimbal-mounted, c 1600. (The National Maritime Museum, London)

The limitations of these early compasses were many; in rough seas and overcast weather, just when they were needed most, they were almost impossible to use. The first important development came in the 13th century, again in China, when the first pivot compass, also called the dry compass, was used. The first models were certainly an improvement on the floating compass, but they made only a slow impact in the West and were not widely used in Europe until they were introduced, or re-introduced, in the 16th century by the Portuguese and the Dutch.

Charts were first used as a direct navigation aid on board ship in the 13th century – the first recorded usage is dated 1270 – but they only became really widespread in Europe with the Portuguese exploration of Africa's west coast and with frequent use of compasses. It was discovered soon enough that the direction of true north was at variance with the compass' pointing, though it was many years before it was understood why there was a variation, and hundreds of years before the Magnetic North Pole was located. In the 19th century tables were drawn up indicating the variation of the compass point from true North in different parts of the world.

By mounting the compass card and pointer inside a gimbal, most of the rough-sea disadvantages were overcome, but any quantity of iron aboard ship continued to cause problems until the invention of the gyro-compass, which soon succeeded the dry compass on all ships on the high seas. (This invention acts on the principle that a perfectly balanced wheel mounted rotatably at its centre of gravity will rotate with its axis of rotation parallel to the earth's axis of rotation. The gyrocompass therefore points to true north, and is not affected by steel or magnetism. Since gyrocompasses require power for their operation, magnetic compasses are always kept as a standby.)

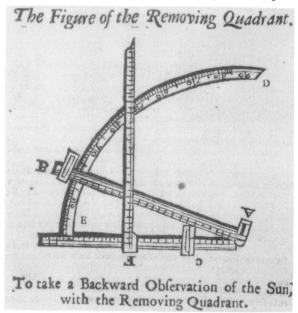

The Figure of the Removing Quadrant.

To take a Backward Obfervation of the Sun, with the Removing Quadrant.

The quadrant – from a 1672 book on navigation. (The National Maritime Museum, London)

Far older than the first compass, however, were instruments for measuring the angle of declination of the sun or a star. Simple wooden disks with pointers to align with the celestial body – forerunners of the astrolabe – were in use as early as the 3rd century BC. The most suitable stars for determining latitude in the Northern Hemisphere are the sun – which is known to be at its highest point at noon, and the pole star – which not only has a very slight variation in position, but is practically over the North Pole, so that its angle of declination virtually corresponds with the latitude of the observer. The observer who finds that the pole star's angle of declination is 50° (i.e. that a line from him to the star would

A brass quadrant fitted with sights and a plumb bob, c 1600. (The National Maritime Museum, London)

308

An astrolabe of c 1585. (The National Maritime Museum, London)

be 50° above the horizontal) then knows that he is practically on latitude 50° N. At the equator (latitude 0°), the pole star becomes invisible. If other stars are to be used, however, or if an extremely accurate position has to be established, very exact measuring devices have to be applied to the position of at least two stars. The natural outcome of the cross-staff and the astrolabe, long after metal had been substituted for wood, was the sextant, so called because the first model utilized a 60° arc.

Determining the longitude was not nearly so easy, although how it could be done in theory was known for some time. By taking the angle of declination of the sun at a known latitude and at a time when its declination at another specific meridian would be known for the same hour, it could be calculated how far east or west of that known longitude the observer was. The normal method was to take 12 noon, GMT (Greenwich Mean Time), which is on longitude 0°, but the essential information – knowing precisely when it was 12 noon GMT – was dependent on having an accurate timepiece, which technology had not yet produced. The pendulum clock was obviously totally unsuitable for travel, and in the middle of the 17th century a substantial prize was offered to whoever could devise an accurate method of calculating degrees of

309

longitude. This amounted to inventing a clock which would operate accurately in a ship at sea, and led to the invention of the balance wheel and hairspring, and eventually to the ship's chronometer, an extremely accurate timepiece.

Radio was as revolutionary a boon to navigation as was the compass – not only did it permit total accuracy of clocks, but it led to the method of navigation by radio direction signals; the point of interception of direction lines from two or more radio signal sources can be plotted on a map to give the precise position of the receiver.

In early times fixing a ship's position was a laborious procedure, but there was little risk of collision at sea and speeds were slow enough to allow any necessary avoiding action. Besides, charts were frequently rudimentary and there was little point in knowing an exact position every hour or so if it meant plotting the position on a map which may have missed out a group of islands, a reef, or displaced a cape by a dozen miles – unless the ship itself, like Cook's or Flinders', was surveying a coast. 'Dead reckoning' (from 'deduced reckoning') therefore played a substantial role in navigating during ordinary voyages. By this method, the only information needed was the time elapsed since the last recording, the speed maintained over that time (or time spent at various known speeds), and the compass bearing steered. Time and compass bearing were easily obtainable, and speed was originally measured by throwing a small log overboard, to which was attached a line knotted at regular intervals. The amount of rope uncoiled by the log left floating behind the ship was measured by the number of knots, and represented the distance the ship travelled during a specific time, measured by a timeglass. The speed was simply expressed as 'knots', which is still the term used to represent one nautical mile per hour (a nautical mile being 6,076.12 feet, or 1,852 metres), and speed measuring devices at sea are still called logs. The distance covered for dead reckoning navigation was then simply the speed in knots multiplied by the hours travelled at that speed, and the course could be drawn as straight lines on a chart using lines of longitude and latitude which intersect at right angles (making some allowance for currents, and drifting).

Another nautical term which has come from the earliest seafaring days via the pages of seamen's *portolanos* is 'fathom', the nautical measure of depth, equivalent to 6 feet, or 1.8 metres. Norse mariners took depth soundings with a lead weight on a line, which they hauled in as it became slack, counting out the amount of line retrieved by measuring it with an arm's span. To watching fellow sailors the action resembled wide embraces, the Norse for which was *fathmr*.

Considering the instruments they worked with, ancient navigators were often startlingly accurate, and it has certainly not been necessary to re-survey the whole world – even if there were errors, such as Mendaña losing the Solomon Islands. A South American navy survey recently determined that Cape Horn was really 3 miles (5 km) further north than maps had been showing it for some 200 years, and began to redraw charts. Later, however, a pinpoint fix by satellite confirmed that the original survey had been correct all along.

As important as charts and navigation were, nothing mattered so much to early explorers as the performance of the vessels that took them on their journeys, and the development of the early sailing ships played a major role in the discovery of the world.

Shipbuilding

Whether it was by accident or the result of agonized deliberation, the first man who floated down a river, balanced precariously on a fallen tree, gave mankind a new dimension of freedom through which he eventually discovered the world beyond his horizons. Men and women who braved rivers became the survivors of catastrophes or of stagnation, and their descendants became the people who braved seas and oceans to discover new lands, new trade, wealth and power; only in the most recent years has it been possible for a country to be powerful without also being a dominant seafaring nation.

The value of boats and ships was appreciated early, and it is not surprising that the first recorded resettlement of people from an overpopulated village took place with the help of boats, down the Euphrates from Jarmo, sometime about 7000 BC. The eastern Mediterranean has many islands and is scarcely the 'high seas' – but it can produce violent storms in a very short time; excavations on Crete, however, reveal that the oldest known sea-going craft were found in that vicinity, and were built by 5000 BC. A thousand years later Eridu boatyards in the Tigris–Euphrates valley, a little north of the Persian Gulf, were building vessels large and strong enough to carry up to 10 oxen. The people of Mesopotamia would not have taken long to move to the protected waters of the Persian Gulf and discover the advantages of fishing in new and deeper waters. Curiosity, the need for bigger catches and the simple enjoyment of sailing took these early sea-farers into the Gulf of Oman, along the Hadramaut coast and eventually to the first meeting of two great civilizations, when Mesopotamian met Egyptian.

The Egyptians were somewhat slower to develop sailing vessels. The Nile dominated Egypt and affected the life-style of Egyptians as the sea influenced Polynesians, or mountains ruled the Tibetans. There was no need to construct sea-going ships when the large and placid Nile carried all the necessary traffic so leisurely downstream, and when prevailing winds assisted the upstream passage. Engravings on rocks in the Nile Valley and paintings on vases show ancient Egypt's traders using rudimentary rafts of planks and logs, which by 3300 BC were carrying simple sails. The Egyptians evolved the basic principles of boat construction over the next 500 years, the provision of sides being the first progression from a straight-forward raft.

The materials that are available obviously influence boat construction. The Egyptians soon substituted bundles of reeds for planks and logs, as the rate of water absorption was quite slow enough for the voyages these craft were called on to make. The first sails to be fitted were simple square sails made from papyrus, which acted on the boat through a 'bipod' mast – two spars joined at the top, forming a triangle across the middle of the boat. The sail (which was later more likely to be made of cotton) was laced onto a heavy horizontal spar bound to the top of the mast. Egyptian nautical designs were considerably influenced by the boats of the adventurers from Mesopotamia, and by 2000 BC a single pole mast was universal, though as a source of power the sail was still secondary to the strong rowers. Steering was by one or two oars at the stern.

The Arabian mariners were later to make a significant contribution to shipping, though it was the Roman and Mediterranean world which gave its name to its development. Early Roman ships had also relied heavily on rowers, and the first sails were primitive, rectangular and rather ineffectual. Throughout the Mediterranean, wooden hulled boats had carvel construction – closely joined planks laid flush and nailed onto numerous ribs, the joins caulked with pitch – and this method of shaping the hull onto the ribs remained typical of all Mediterranean boats. It was the Romans who then adopted the triangular sail, hung from a long slantwise yard, which was commonly seen on Arab dhows in the Red Sea and the Indian Ocean, and which is still widely employed. Their use soon became widespread in Latin and other Mediterranean countries, and that type of sail became known as the lateen sail.

Beyond the Mediterranean, the first major sea-faring countries to make their mark in shipbuilding were the Scandinavians with their extraordinary Viking ships. Characterized by upswept and sharply pointed double ends, and by the low freeboard in the centre, these boats also differed in that their hulls were clinker built – a method that overlapped the planks on the ribs, instead of flush fitting as on the carvel, and which was still very much in use well after 1066. The Viking ships carried one mast and a substantial

A Phoenician galley. (Mary Evans Picture Library)

square sail, but primary power was still obtained by oars, while a side-mounted oar near the stern took care of the steering.

Mediterranean nations were involved in fairly complex trading from very early times, and either developed their own merchant fleets or relied heavily on seafaring peoples, such as the Phoenicians or the Carthaginians, to be their carriers. North European boats tended to be used mainly for aggressive reasons, and therefore placed emphasis on speed, but in the Mediterranean a wide variety of boats and ships developed, many with the emphasis on strength and cargo capacity. A great difference soon arose between warships and cargo ships. The former remained largely dependent on oars for speed and manoeuvrability, while trading vessels developed greater freeboard and gained extra stowage space by having fewer rowers and relying more on sails. With a higher freeboard, cargoes could be piled one on top of the other, and it was then logical to separate and protect the bottom cargoes by covering them with a base for the top cargoes to rest upon. So decks were 'invented', and a gradual development took place naturally. By the mid-12th century, Genoese ships had two decks, and there were three-deckers, with two masts, sailing the Mediterranean by the late 13th century.

A major advance in ship design was the invention of the stern rudder. The earliest illustration of a ship fitted with one is on an English civic seal dated 1200, and these rudders originally followed the curve of the sternpost. When flat sterns became widespread, however, the stern rudder could be larger, stronger and far more effective. This was one development

313

Ships of ancient Greece. (Mary Evans Picture Library)

that the Mediterranean boatyards were slow to pick up, and their side rudders did not lose popularity until the 14th century; possibly the early designs gave less effective steering on the larger vessels – often of well over 100 feet (30 m) – than did two lateral rudders.

The variety of shapes and styles of boats that could be seen from the Gulf of Aden to the Gulf of Bothnia proved that there was no universal law of boat design, and in China considerably different responses had been made to the same basic problems. Europe knew nothing about China or her ships until Marco Polo returned in the late 13th century, and told of his admiration for the Chinese junks. But the Chinese junk was perhaps the most efficient sailing vessel in the world for a long period, and, unlike European designs, changed only very slightly in more than 1,000 years. Even contemporary Chinese junks are little different from those that made the first long voyages to India, that dominated the Indian Ocean in the 9th century, and that travelled regularly in the Middle Ages to Indonesia, Ceylon, India, Yemen and the ports of East Africa. Had China been driven by the same zeal to conquer, change and possess the world which obsessed the nations of Europe, there is no doubt that their sea-going vessels would have reached distant lands long before Columbus or da Gama. And, while it is quite possible that Phoenicians crossed the Atlantic to Central America well over 2,000 years ago, it is almost certain that the Chinese knew of Australia and many Pacific islands long before Europe's expansion at the end of the 14th century.

The extraordinary sea-worthiness of the junks was well demonstrated in 1848 when a traditionally built vessel sailed from China to Boston, New York and to London; yet junks are very simple boats whose design was quite probably suggested by the structure of that ubiquitous Chinese plant, the bamboo. The plan of a junk is not dissimilar to the section of a length of bamboo – a blunt bow and stern, and in between usually about four watertight compartments whose walls also act as strengthening bulkheads. Within that broad similarity of design, up to 70 different types of junks have been recognized, all specifically adapted for use as a small river boat, deep-sea fishing craft, house-boat-cum-fishing-boat, high-seas trader, and so on. Commonly they had no keel, but often massive rudders also acted as centreboards preventing leeward drifting, and anything from one to five masts would carry the sails whose series of longitudinal panels could be close-hauled individually, giving great flexibility of sail settings.

Apart from the Chinese, however, it was the Mediterraneans who held the lead in ship design – though the Polynesians, regularly undertaking voyages of up to 300 miles (480 km) between groups of islands, had great mastery of the sea and of stellar navigation, with a flair for designing fast,

Portuguese ships of the 13th century. (The National Maritime Museum, London)

narrow-hulled boats whose principles were only recently appreciated in the evolution of catamarans and trimarans.

At the start of the 15th century, three-masted ships were common in the Mediterranean, while Northern Europe did not advance beyond the single mast until later in that century. Three-masted ships had a short foremast, a tall main-mast, and a stern mast known as the mizzenmast; initially, lateen sails were carried on all masts. The growing importance of commerce had made the carrack the most popular design. The carrack was a deep, broad ship typically used by Venetian, Genoese and Spanish mariners. They were characterized by their very high 'poop' sterns and

A model of a Portuguese caravel of 1450, with lateen rigging. (The National Maritime Museum, London)

prominent forecastles – the tower-like structure at the bow that was an off-shoot of the fighting 'castles' on warships, and that has given bow deck sections the nautical term foc's'le. Castle structures were also put on the sterns, but these high, dumpy ships, while carrying a good deal of cargo in their deep hulls, were unwieldy, and unsuited to travelling the unknown seas beyond Gibraltar where explorers might make frequent landings in shallow, often turbulent water.

Henry the Navigator's maritime school at Sagres encouraged experimentation in all things connected with the sea and exploration, and trial and error eventually produced the vessel which was to take the Portuguese to the East, and the Spanish to America. This was the Portuguese caravel, a vessel adapted from the carvel-built, narrow-hulled fishing boats. With its slender shape and shallow draught, a caravel was a good deal faster than a carrack, and could sail in far shallower waters. At this time navigation instruments, such as the compass and the astrolabe, were becoming more familiar. All at once it seemed that the chief maritime countries, Spain and Portugal, could realize the expansionist zeal that made them look beyond the horizon through a simultaneous advance in ship design that began to make long sea journeys possible and in navigation techniques that made them both safer and more effective.

Each voyage down the coast of Africa was an opportunity to experiment with sails and rigging, and the caravels became ever more versatile, with navigators capable of altering features to adapt to different priorities of speed, weight carrying, manoeuvrability, or to eking movement from unfavourable winds. Columbus, for instance, completely re-rigged the *Niña*, one of his caravels, at the Azores, from three lateen sails to two square sails with a lateen mizzensail. Later, as trade once again began to build up

Columbus' Niña – a picture of a 19th-century reconstruction, which explains the US flag. (Mary Evans Picture Library)

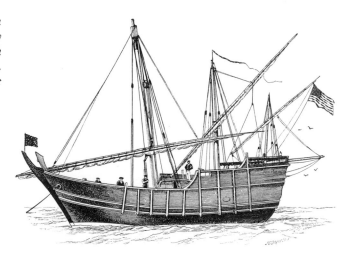

A Flemish ship of 1560. (The National Maritime Museum, London)

— this time to distant lands — equipment, rigging and experience had progressed sufficiently to bring back ships that more closely resembled the carrack.

The trade in the East, and later across the Atlantic, brought competition between the merchantmen of England, Holland, France and Portugal, and in the 17th and 18th centuries shipbuilders had to satisfy numerous and conflicting requirements. There had to be maximum space for cargoes — anything from slaves to peppercorn — but also enough room for guns and for the sailors to man them, while speed could not be ignored. Ship development had largely switched to refining the man-o'-war as co-existence between nations became more transient, and the merchantmen for the British and Dutch East India Companies were little more than fuller men-o'-war, which, from their round, 'galleon' appearance, gave rise to the inevitable phrase 'fat East Indiamen'. Some of the English ships in this category carried over 20 guns, but there was little speed to be wrung from such cumbersome vessels. The Spanish frigate was quickly copied and refined, first by the French, and then by the English, for not only did speed give commercial advantages, but a ship which could bring its guns to bear rapidly, and which could outmanoeuvre another, would be more than

318

Ship-building in the New World. Plans were rarely used and great ingenuity had to be displayed to make extensive repairs — or even complete ships — in the remotest parts of the world. (Mary Evans Picture Library)

Dutch merchantmen under construction in 1640. (The National Maritime Museum, London)

a match for a slow, heavy vessel, even if the latter bristled with guns.

New materials and engineering techniques brought a steady refinement to the rigging of sailing ships; more sails could be set, and settings could be altered more quickly than ever. The availability of copper brought greater waterline protection from shot, and it was soon found that this was an ideal way of retarding marine growth – especially in tropical waters, giving ships longer lives and faster voyages without the drag of underwater barnacles. In the 19th century, however, the square rigged sailing ship reached its maturity. Fully rigged three-masted ships were carrying at least 26 sails, calling for constant vigilance by the officer on watch and considerable skill and exertion from the crew. The only way to increase sail, since masts could go no higher, was to make the spars wider, and indeed this was done by the addition of studding spars and sails which overhung the sides of the ship (in suitable weather). This practice eventually reached the absurd extravagance of the East Indiaman *Essex* which was able to set no fewer than 63 sails.

The New World showed the way to fast ships when America refined Dutch designs to build the very fast schooners, which were in turn modified to become the famous Baltimore clippers. British shipyards soon adopted this design, and the British tea-clippers became the fastest ships afloat, bringing the age of sail to a gloriously exciting and heroic end. Practically every voyage was a 'race', for the first cargo landed in London brought better payment, and an earlier second voyage. In 1866 a race from Foochow to London was completed by the first three clippers in 98 days. All three reached the Thames on the same ingoing tide and sailed up the river at some 13 knots.

These were trading vessels, however. Explorers' ships were generally far less dashing, and had to sacrifice speed for strength and reliability. On a voyage which could easily last four years, a captain had no use for a delicate, temperamental ship, but needed one which could be man-hauled onto tropical beaches or half turned-over to be scraped, which could have a new mast fitted from a tree cut in some distant jungle, and which could be persuaded to finish a journey with rotting timbers and disintegrating sails.

Sail and wood discovered the world, but steam and steel were needed at last to take man, twisting and turning, through the floating ice packs to the Antarctic shores, the last unexplored continent. It seems incongruous that furnaces, fire, steam and the acrid smoke of black coal would finally enable man to reach the remote, untouched, white world of Antarctica. In a generation, sailmakers and ship's carpenters lost their exalted posts, and cartographers were able to finish their maps.

Bibliography

Very few explorers resisted the temptation to write a paper or a book about their adventures when they returned to civilization. While a large number of these never saw a wider readership than the members of the Royal Geographical Society, there are still a great many books in print, or in reference libraries, written by a number of the explorers mentioned in this book. In addition, almost all who accomplished anything significant have been the subject of at least one biography.

Readers wishing to pursue an explorer or his discoveries more closely should first look in the appropriate shelves of biographies and countries, and under the explorer's name in booklists and library indexes.

The selection of books below omits biographies, autobiographies, and accounts written by individual explorers, for these are easy to find, and their inclusion would take up many pages. Instead, a number of books on different facets of exploration or covering a fairly narrow field are suggested.

Africa and Asia: Mapping Two Continents (1973: Jupiter Books, Ldn; Aldus Books, NY)

The Age of Reconnaissance: discovery, exploration and settlement 1450–1650, John H Parry (1963: Weidenfeld & Nicolson, Ldn; New American Library, NY)

Antique Maps for the Collector, R Van De Gohm (1973: Macmillan, NY)

The Conquistadores, Hammond Innes (1972: Fontana, Ldn)

The Discovery of Australia, Andrew Sharp (1963: Oxford UP; Oxford Clarendon Press, NY)

The Discovery of the Pacific Islands, Andrew Sharp (1976: Oxford UP; Oxford Clarendon Press, NY)

Earth's Last Frontiers (1973: Jupiter Books, Ldn; Aldus Books, NY)

Eastern Islands, Southern Seas (1973: Jupiter Books, Ldn; Aldus Books, NY)

Discovery and Exploration

The European Discovery of America: the Northern Voyages AD 500–1600, Rear Adm Samuel E Morison (1974: Oxford UP; Oxford Clarendon Press, NY)

The Exploration of the Pacific, J Beaglehole (1966: Black, Ldn; Stanford UP)

Explorers' Maps, R A Skelton (1958: Routledge, Ldn: Praeger, NY)

Explorers of the World, William R Clark (1964: Aldus, Ldn; Doubleday, NY)

From Lodestone to Gyro Compass, H L Hitchins & W E May (1952: Hutchinson, Ldn)

The Great Age of Sail, B W Bathe *et al* (1971: Patrick Stephens, Camb; Viking Press, NY)

The Great Travellers (2 vols), ed Milton A Rugoff (1960: Simon & Schuster, NY)

History of Cartography, Leo Bagrow, rev R A Skelton (1964: Harvard UP)

A History of Marine Navigation, P A Collinder (1954: Batsford, Ldn)

A History of Polar Exploration, David Mountfield (1974: Dial, NY)

History of the World's Shipping, Adm Barjot & Jean Savant (1965: Sportshelf, NY)

The Last Secrets: the final mysteries of exploration, John Buchan (1927: Nelson, Ldn)

Maps and Map-makers, R V Tooley (1970: Batsford, Ldn)

The New World (1973: Jupiter Books, Ldn; Aldus Books, NY)

The Opening of the World, David Divine (1973: Collins, Ldn)

The Portuguese Pioneers, E Prestage (1933: Black, Ldn; 1967: Barnes & Noble, NY)

The Quest for Africa, Heinrich Schiffers (1957: Odhams, Ldn)

The Search Begins (1973: Jupiter Books, Ldn; Aldus Books, NY)

Sea Road to the Indies, Henry Hersch Hart (1950: Macmillan, Ldn; Greenwood Press, Conn)

The Ship, Bjorn Landström (1961: Allen & Unwin, Ldn)

Ships and Seamanship in the Ancient World, Lionel Casson (1971: Princeton UP)

Silks, Spices and Empire: Asia seen through the eyes of its discoverers, ed Owen Lattimore (1968: Delacorte Press, NY)

South from the Spanish Main, Earl P Hanson (1967: Delacorte Press, NY)

Sovereign of the Seas, David Howarth (1974: Collins, Ldn; Atheneum, NY)

To the Arctic by Canoe 1819–1821, Robert Hood, ed C Stuart (1974: McGill UP)

The Ulysses Factor—the exploring instinct in man, J R L Anderson (1970: Hodder & Stoughton, Ldn; Harcourt Brace Jovanovich, NY)

Voyagers to the New World: fact and fantasy, Nigel Davies (1979: Macmillan, Ldn)

Westviking: the ancient Norse in Greenland and North America, Farley M Mowat (1966: Secker & Warburg, Ldn; Little, Brown, Boston)

The White Nile, Alan Moorehead (1970: Penguin, Ldn; 1964: Dell, NY)

Index

Smith, Jedediah 54, **268**
Smith, John 38, **268**
Snake River 224
Society Islands 290
Socotra 109
Sofala 22, 166
Sokoto 150
Solis, Juan Diaz de 249
Solomon Islands 32, 50, 131, 145, 177, 234, 247
Soto, Hernando de 32, **269–70**
South Georgia Island 48, 160
South Pole 67, 68, 69, 115, 138, 180, 189, 265
South Saskatchewan River 50, 202
space – also see moon 190, 223
Spanberg, Martin 127
Speke, John Hanning 59, 60, 118, 136, 137, **270–2**
Spencer Gulf 183
Spice Islands – see Moluccas
Spitzbergen 37, 55, 64, 116, 121, 134, 238, 293
Spruce, Richard **272**, 290
Staaten Land – see New Zealand 48
Stadukhin, Mikhailo 43, 169, **272**
Stanley, Henry Morton 61, 62, **272–5**
Stefanie, Lake 64, 281
Stefansson, Vilhjmur 69, **275**, 292
Stein, Aurel **275–6**
Storms, Cape of 171
Stuart, John McDouall 62, **276**, 278
Stuart, Mount 276
Stuart, Robert 212, **277**
Sturt, Charles 58, 212, **277–8**
Sturt Creek 144
Sturt Desert 135, 196, 278
Sumatra 159
Superior, Lake 39, 50, 133, 198
Svarsson, Gardar 17, **278–9**
Sverdrup, Otto 64, 238, **279**
Swallow 145
Swan River 182
Sydney – see Port Jackson
Sykes, Percy **279**
Syra Orda 145

Tahiti 158–161, 290
Taklamakan Desert 66, 194, 201–2, 218, 255, 275, 294
Tampa Bay 31, 239, 254, 270
Tana, Lake 40, 48, 132, 228, 244
Tanganyika, Lake 59, 61, 62, 64, 136, 137, 143, 223, 227, 270, 273, 283
Tapajós River 124, 290
Tashkent 148
Tasman, Abel 41, 42, 123, **279**
Tasmania 41, 51, 123, 161, 182, 279
Teleki, Samuel 64, **281**, 283

Tenochtitlan – see Mexico City
Tensing Norgay 205, 212
Terra Australis 32, 35, 40, 46, 131, 138, 145, 161, 174, 234
Terra Incognita – see Terra Australis
Terror 184, 262
Texcoco, Lake 114, 164
Thesiger, Wilfred **281**
Thomas, Bertram 68, **282**
Thompson, David 50, 213, **282**
Thomson, Charles Wyville **283**
Thomson, Joseph **283–4**
Thorwald **284**
Thule (see also Iceland) 13, 17
Thyssen, Francois 41, **284–5**
Tibet 42, 49, 50, 65, 66, 116, 130, 140, 141, 170, 201, 202, 208, 217, 232, 236, 237, 256, 295
Tien Shan Mts 201, 255
Tierra del Fuego 29, 33, 128, 167, 174, 222, 231
Tigris River 111, 130
Timbuktu 52, 56, 64, 123, 141, 213, 219–20, 222
Tisisat Falls 40, 228
Tocantins River 123, 180
Tonga Islands – see Friendly Islands
Tordesillas, Treaty of 25, 141
Torrens, Lake 62, 178, 194, 276, 291
Torres, Luis Vaez de 40, 285
Torres Strait 40, 42, 159, 285
Toscanelli 22, 151
Trans-Americas Expedition 129
Trans-Antarctic Expedition 190, 205
Transglobe Expedition 70, 180
Trinidad 157, 259
Tsangpo River 65, 238, 295
Tsaparang 42, 116, 117, 141
Tuamotu Islands 40
Tumbes 112, 250
Turner, Samuel 285

Ubangi River 184
Uele River 61, 265
Ujiji 136, 143, 227, 273, 283
Ujiji, Lake – see Lake Tanganyika
Ur (see Eridu) 11
Urville, Jules Dumont d' 56, **285–6**

Vaca, Alvar Nuñez Cabeza de 31, 32, 161, 240, **286**
Valdivia, Pedro de **286–7**
Vancouver, George 51, **287**
Vancouver Island 175
Van Diemen's Land – see Tasmania
Varthema, Ludovico di 27, **287–8**
Velasquez, Diego 162–4

Veracruz 31
Verde, Cape 204
Vespucci, Amerigo 26, 27, 166, 198, **288**
Victoria 29, 144, 232
Victoria Falls 60, 61, 226
Victoria, Lake 59, 60, 61, 62, 137, 270–1, 273
Vigneau, Nicolas 147
Vikings 17, 71
Vinland 17, 178, 204, 216, 284
Viscount Melville Sound 55
Vostok I 190
Vrangelya Island 169

Waikaremoana, Lake 150–1
Waldseemüller, Martin 27, 288, **289**, 302
Walker, Joseph Reddeford **289–90**
Wallace, Alfred 123–4, **290**
Wallis Islands 46
Wallis, Samuel 46, 145, **290**
Walvis Bay 143, 171
Watling Island – see Guanahani
Warburton, Peter 62, **291**
Weddell, James 56, **291**
Weddell Sea 291
Wells, Lawrence 63, 144, **291**
Wellsted, James 57, **291**
Western Australia 182, 183, 194, 196–7
Whales, Bay of 115, 138
Waymouth, George 38, 268
White Nile River 49, 64, 118, 132, 237
Wild, Frank 67, 232, 265, 267, **292**
Wilkes, Charles 69, **292**
Wilkes Land 292
Wilkins, Hubert 69, **292**
William of Rubrouck 19, **293**
Williams, William **293**
Willoughby, Hugh 36, 148, **293**
Wills, William 63, 135–6, **293**
Wilson, Edward 265, 267, 294
Winnipeg, Lake 217
Wisconsin River 39, 43

Xavier, Saint Francis 34, **294**
Xingu River 180

Yangtse River 208
Yarkand 40
Yermak, Timofeyevich **294**
York, Cape 40, 42, 159, 182, 215
Yorke Peninsula 63
Younghusband, Francis Edward 66, 294
Yucatan 27, 30, 114, 197

Zaïre River – see Congo River
Zaïre River Expedition 129
Zambezi River 52, 143, 226–7
Zimbabwe Ruins 127

328